Cooking

Healthy

with a

Food Processor

Also by JoAnna M. Lund

The Healthy Exchanges Cookbook
HELP: The Healthy Exchanges Lifetime Plan
Cooking Healthy with a Man in Mind
Cooking Healthy with the Kids in Mind
Diabetic Desserts
Make a Joyful Table
Cooking Healthy Across America
A Potful of Recipes
Another Potful of Recipes
The Open Road Cookbook
Sensational Smoothies
Hot Off the Grill: The Healthy Exchanges Electric Grilling Cookbook
Cooking Healthy with Splenda®
Cooking Healthy with a Microwave
The Diabetic's Healthy Exchanges Cookbook
The Strong Bones Healthy Exchanges Cookbook
The Arthritis Healthy Exchanges Cookbook
The Heart Smart Healthy Exchanges Cookbook
The Cancer Recovery Healthy Exchanges Cookbook
String of Pearls
Family and Friends Cookbook
JoAnna's Kitchen Miracles
When Life Hands You Lemons, Make Lemon Meringue Pie
Cooking Healthy with Soy
Baking with Splenda®
Cooking for Two

Cooking

Healthy

with a

Food Processor

A HEALTHY EXCHANGES® COOKBOOK

JoAnna M. Lund

with
Barbara Alpert

A Perigee Book

A PERIGEE BOOK
Published by the Penguin Group
Penguin Group (USA) Inc.
375 Hudson Street, New York, New York 10014, USA

Penguin Group (Canada), 90 Eglinton Avenue East, Suite 700, Toronto, Ontario M4P 2Y3, Canada
(a division of Pearson Penguin Canada Inc.)
Penguin Books Ltd., 80 Strand, London WC2R 0RL, England
Penguin Group Ireland, 25 St. Stephen's Green, Dublin 2, Ireland (a division of Penguin Books Ltd.)
Penguin Group (Australia), 250 Camberwell Road, Camberwell, Victoria 3124, Australia
(a division of Pearson Australia Group Pty. Ltd.)
Penguin Books India Pvt. Ltd., 11 Community Centre, Panchsheel Park, New Delhi—110 017, India
Penguin Group (NZ), Cnr. Airborne and Rosedale Roads, Albany, Auckland 1310, New Zealand
(a division of Pearson New Zealand Ltd.)
Penguin Books (South Africa) (Pty.) Ltd., 24 Sturdee Avenue, Rosebank, Johannesburg 2196,
South Africa

Penguin Books Ltd., Registered Offices: 80 Strand, London WC2R 0RL, England

While the author has made every effort to provide accurate telephone numbers and Internet addresses at
the time of publication, neither the publisher nor the author assumes any responsibility for errors, or for
changes that occur after publication. Further, publisher does not have any control over and does not as-
sume any responsibility for author or third-party websites or their content.

First edition: September 2006

For more information about Healthy Exchanges products, contact:
Healthy Exchanges, Inc.
P.O. Box 80
DeWitt, IA 52742-0080
(563) 659-8234
www.HealthyExchanges.com

Library of Congress Cataloging-in-Publication Information

Lund, JoAnna M.
    Cooking healthy with a food processor : a Healthy exchanges cookbook / by JoAnna
  M. Lund, with Barbara Alpert.
      p.   cm.
    Includes index.
    ISBN 0-399-53281-1
    1. Food processor cookery.   I. Alpert, Barbara.   II. Healthy Exchanges, Inc.   III. Title.

TX840.F6L96   2006
641.5'892—dc22

                                                                        2005056495

PRINTED IN THE UNITED STATES OF AMERICA

10   9   8   7   6   5   4   3   2   1

PUBLISHER'S NOTE: The recipes contained in this book are to be followed exactly as written. The
publisher is not responsible for your specific health or allergy needs that may require medical supervi-
sion. The publisher is not responsible for any adverse reactions to the recipes contained in this book.

Dedication

This cookbook is dedicated in loving memory to my parents, Jerome and Agnes McAndrews. While food processors were not yet invented when Mom was cooking for her family, I know she would have especially loved this kitchen appliance! She was an avid gardener and was always stirring up something tasty for us with her homegrown vegetables and fruits. And, of course, my father greatly enjoyed everything she placed on the table.

Mom also loved writing poetry. She wrote this lovely poem in her later years, when her hands were weakened by arthritis and her gardening days were well behind her. My hope is that both my mother's words and my food processor recipes will bring you years of enjoyment!

Town Gardens

The vegetable gardens of yesterday
* are disappearing into the past.*
They used to be so plentiful that I thought
* they would always last.*
Like many others, my backyard is now
* mowed where I used to hoe—*
No more corn, peas, squash, and cabbages
* that once grew row after row.*
It isn't just that I'm too old to plant and
* pull the weeds anymore.*
But fresh and frozen produce now can easily
* be purchased at the store.*
I used to enjoy my big garden—watching
* little shoots sprout and grow.*
I also miss the pleasant backyard chats
* with my neighbors of long ago.*
We visited while we planted seeds or
* exchanged our choicest plants,*
And shared friendly advice on how to rid
* our gardens of pests and ants.*
I remember watching the garden plow turn
* furrows of fresh black sod.*
And when I planted the rows of seeds
* I felt like a coworker with God.*
Those old gardens are now lush emerald carpets
* and are truly beautiful scenes.*
But somehow the ones that I still like best
* grow old-fashioned spuds and beans.*

—Agnes Carrington McAndrews

Acknowledgments

As I am truly mechanically challenged, I was a bit hesitant to create an entire book of recipes for the food processor. I still remember what happened about twenty years ago, when I decided that I just *had* to have a food processor for Christmas. Well, I got the food processor all right, but I found it so tricky and complicated that I used it once and then stuck the whole thing in the back of the pantry, never to be used again.

However, this past year, when I decided to once again give food processors a try, I was pleasantly surprised to discover that today's versions are so much easier to use and to clean! Now I wonder why I waited so long to let this "wonder machine" do the work instead of me!

For helping me "process" another book filled with "common folk" healthy recipes, I want to thank:

Cliff Lund, my husband and truck-drivin' man. He gladly tasted just about everything I put in front of him—except, of course, the broccoli and cauliflower recipes. I chose other tasters for those dishes!

Shirley Morrow, Gina Griep, Jean Martens, Rita Ahlers, Phyllis Bickford, and Cheryl Hageman, my trusted employees. Each did her part to help me meet my deadline, be it washing and chopping veggies, typing and retyping recipes, or tasting and retasting the many, many dishes every day at lunchtime until everything was deemed just right. All agreed that these healthy recipes were indeed tasty!

Barbara Alpert, my writing partner. While her hectic teaching schedule meant that she had to devote many a late evening and weekend to this project, she did it with a smile and still made sure I spelled my words correctly. Truly, this book would not have been "processed" without her help!

Coleen O'Shea, my agent. She's been helping me expand my

culinary expertise and Grandma Moses style of writing ever since I first met her more than a decade ago. Best of all, she never tires of hearing of the new ideas I've "cooked" up for future books!

John Duff, my publisher. It was his idea for me to write this book in the first place. While I was reluctant in the beginning, he has been so supportive of all my other cookbook projects that I dearly wanted to create the best possible healthy food processor book just for him. Of course, he's pleased to share these recipes with you, too!

God, my creator and savior. As with every cookbook project I've ever done, I first prayed to Him for the guidance to do the best I could . . . the best I could, and then trusted that He would show me the way. And He didn't let me down!

Contents

Are You Stuck in a Belief Rut? I Was . . .

Did you know that the original food processor, the very first one, was invented back in 1971, the same year as the VCR (videocassette recorder, in case you've forgotten what those initials stand for!)? Then a man named Carl Sontheimer (whose previous job involved inventing a microwave direction finder used by NASA on a mission to the moon) launched the Cuisinart—and the cooking world as we knew it changed forever!

It's true: Once the food processor became widely available, recipes and cooking were never the same. Today, many recipes include steps that say "With the metal blade inserted in the work bowl . . ." or "Pulse until coarsely chopped but do not puree." And food processors didn't just speed up things in home kitchens— restaurants began using industrial-strength food processors to produce chopped or pureed everything in seconds.

So of course, I *had* to have one. Cliff got me one for Christmas back in 1979. I unpacked all the pieces, tried it a few times, then decided it was too complicated, too confusing, and not worth it. I put it back in the box, put it away in the back of a closet, and never used it again.

I guess I should have expected to have problems using the food processor. After all, I'm one of the VCR-challenged, and even after years of using my computer, I'm not sure how it works, or why!

And I wasn't the only one among my friends who didn't join the ranks of the food processor fans. Shirley, who types my recipes, wasn't even interested in getting one. She told me that she wasn't going to make space on her counter for a machine she didn't want or need.

So life went on. I stirred up thousands upon thousands of recipes over the years. I learned to use an assortment of kitchen appliances, from slow cookers to pressure cookers, from electric grills to ice cream makers and bread machines. But I still never went back to the food processor I'd barely given a chance all those years ago.

Until now.

A combination of factors helped me see that I was stuck in a belief rut—and it was way past time to give food processors another chance. Every time I went to QVC, I would watch demonstrations of the latest models from KitchenAid and other manufacturers. I had to admit that they looked easy to use, and they were able to do so much to speed up food preparation. They came in every color, and the prices were excellent. But all that didn't change my mind . . . not yet.

Then my publisher called and asked, "Would you write a Healthy Exchanges book using the food processor?"

Was it a sign? Maybe.

I didn't hesitate for very long. I was curious to find out just what this miracle machine could do for me—and I was finally ready to take the plunge.

I didn't want to tackle this alone, however. I called on my friend Phyllis, a food processor whiz, with whom I'd worked during my years at Iowa Mutual. Shirley, Phyllis, and I had taken many a lunch break together back then, and I considered her a great resource in this latest adventure.

I asked Phyllis to sit Shirley and me down and give us a hands-on food processor demonstration. "I want the kindergarten course, not the one for graduate students," I told her. "Start with the basics and go slowly."

She laughed, and then that's exactly what she did. She taught us about how the different blades worked, how to put it together and take it apart easily, and how to get good results from each food we processed in the machine. Once she did that, it all "fell into place." I could not get over how easy it was to use. Now I think I'll be using my food processor daily for the rest of my life. It's going to sit on my counter where it's accessible and I can use it on a regular basis.

I had to get past my resistance before I could add this culinary miracle worker to my cook's "bag of tricks." And it got me thinking about other kinds of ruts we get into, other beliefs that hold us back or keep us from living fully.

My friend Barbara, for example, was too nervous to pass her driving test when she was a teenager, and so she went off to college without getting a license, lived on campus, and didn't think much about it. (She told me, "I never really needed an ID to get into a bar—I guess I looked old enough to be there, and I don't drink, anyway.") After she finished school, she moved to New York City, where most residents don't own a car. Years passed, and except for the occasional inconvenience of not being able to cash a check using her library card or video store photo ID, she never thought much about not having a license, until she reached her mid-thirties—and decided it was time she faced her fears about driving.

"I'd had nearly twenty years to grow really afraid about getting behind the wheel of a car, and the idea of learning to drive in New York City was more than a little frightening," she said. "But I loved to travel, and not being able to rent a car limited where I could go and what I could see and do. I couldn't let my fear control me any longer."

So she found a driving school, started all over from the beginning, learned how to survive on the city streets in a sea of taxis—and finally got her precious license. Soon after that, she went on a road trip alone to Montana (!), visited a dinosaur dig, pumped gas on an Indian reservation, and started making up for lost time!

Let's take a look at some of the ways people get stuck and need a push to escape a belief rut.

Food

Think of the last few grocery store trips you've made. Did you race through the produce section, pick up a head of iceberg lettuce, a tomato or two, and maybe one cucumber, because that's how you've always made a salad? Don't worry, you're not alone—but you also don't have to stick with old habits. Next time, be daring, and opt for romaine or red leaf instead. Buy some red cabbage as well as green cabbage; if your store carries purple cauliflower in addition to plain old white (beige?), try it!

We all get into these ruts, and they produce a dangerous kind of boredom that can lead us to overeat. It's even possible to do so with healthy products. Ever looked in your Jell-O drawer (okay, maybe I'm the only person out there with a Jell-O drawer) or wherever you keep yours and noticed that you had three boxes of strawberry and nothing else? Be brave, be adventurous—buy the lime, the lemon, the orange, or even the strawberry-kiwi for a change. I had a friend at work who always (always!) bought the same flavor of yogurt—mixed berry. I said to her, "What do you do if the store runs out of your flavor?" She looked worried but told me it had never happened . . . yet. Don't be like that—act now, and vary your choices. Go for the peach, the mango, the key lime pie! They say variety is the spice of life, after all, so spice up your food choices wherever you can.

It's a good test of whether you're really living in the present, alive in the moment. Catch yourself reaching for the same box of cereal and *choose* something else—it's bound to be a better morning wake-up call than eating the same thing for *years*!

Exercise

When you walk, do you always take the same route and walk for approximately the same time?

When you go to the gym, do you tend to choose the same machine in the same spot over and over again?

We may be creatures of habit, but our bodies get b-o-r-e-d! The only way to prevent a slowdown and loss of commitment is to push yourself in a different direction *on purpose*.

Decide today, then, that instead of walking thirty minutes on the third treadmill from the end at a 3.5 mph pace, you're going to try a totally different machine, and instead of walking on the flat surface, you're going to increase the incline and walk uphill for twenty minutes at a slower pace, say, 3.3.

Or if you're feeling really courageous, skip the treadmill, take a Pilates class, spend ten minutes each on an elliptical trainer and a rowing machine, and see how it feels. You'll meet some new people (since most people do stick with the same equipment at the health club) and you'll get a new view of things—and maybe of yourself and your fitness goals.

Work

We all get into ruts at work, even in volunteer work. We might call it "settling in" or "getting comfortable" but many people grow resistant to change. And yet change is constant in most workplaces, and our ability to be flexible and react to these changes is vital to building a career and growing in our work.

Can you think of the last time you were challenged to do something out of your comfort zone? Maybe you were sent to a training in a nearby city and had to mingle with strangers during a day of workshops and lectures. You may have been nervous about how the day would unfold but ultimately were surprised by how stimulating and even fun it was to visit with people who work in your field.

Sometimes you have to find your own challenges, new ways to make an old assignment more satisfying. You might volunteer to organize a canned food drive to benefit a local food pantry or join the leadership team at your child's school in order to influence how the school's budget is allocated. Or you might simply decide to take a new staffer or volunteer under your wing and share your valuable knowledge with someone else.

I guess what I'm saying is, don't settle for comfortable. You're capable of so much more—and the world needs your active participation.

Family and Love

So many things hold us back when it comes to relationships. We develop beliefs about ourselves, about spouses and children and parents that can really limit our lives in powerful ways.

Maybe you were the baby of the family growing up, and even now, when you're in your fifties, your parents still treat you that way when it comes to making important family decisions. It's going to take some assertiveness from you to help them see you as you are now—but the effort will be worth it.

Or if you're a woman who's raised her kids and is now contemplating revitalizing an old career or launching a new one in midlife, it's going to require a giant emotional push to make the leap. You may feel that the odds are stacked against you, and they may be—at some level. But women have always reinvented themselves throughout their lives, and you'll find plenty of inspiration out there to give you hope.

If you feel that you're stuck listening to old "tapes" that make you feel unworthy, unable to change, or afraid to risk doing something new, please let me encourage you to turn off that internal voice and do it anyway. Your life is precious, every moment of it, and it's meant to be used and filled with what truly matters to you.

But it won't necessarily be easy. Belief ruts are *deep* and they take work to escape. Even something as minor as my resistance to using a food processor took years to change. It also took a willingness to practice, to feel a little clumsy at first with the machine. Expect that any changes you make will take practice and more than a little faith. Anything worthwhile does!

A few last words about this book and the marvelous machine that inspired it. I wrote this book for people like me—cooks interested in common folk healthy cooking, not fancy food that requires elaborate cooking techniques. The food processor was originally conceived to provide shortcuts for cooks to prepare complicated meals quickly, but it's also a great assistant for stirring up family-friendly comfort food.

If you're an experienced food processor user, you probably won't learn anything new from this book but I hope you'll enjoy the tasty, healthy recipes that I created for the rest of us!

Jo Anna

Please note:

In many of my cookbooks, I've included my Healthy Exchanges eating plan, which explains how to use my version of the "exchange" system for planning what to eat and how much to eat for optimum health and weight loss (or maintenance). Because this is a "special-interest" cookbook, I've chosen to focus just on the recipes in this volume. If this is your first Healthy Exchanges cookbook, please check one of my other books for an explanation of the exchange system and an abundance of healthy cooking tips! Good recent choices include *The Open Road Cookbook* or *Cooking Healthy with a Man in Mind*.

A Peek Into My Healthy Exchanges Pantry

I do almost all of my shopping at a supermarket in my small town of DeWitt, Iowa. If I can't find it there, I don't use it in my recipes. I want you to be able to make any and all of these dishes without struggling to locate a particular ingredient. That's what it means to cook *The Healthy Exchanges Way.*

That said, I have tested brands from many different manufacturers, looking for the healthiest, tastiest, and easiest-to-get items that deliver the most flavor for the least amount of fat, sugar, or calories. I update this list for every cookbook and for my newsletter readers every year in the March issue. If you find others you like as well *or better*, please use them. This is only a guide to make shopping and cooking easier for you.

Here are my preferred brands, as of this time:

Egg substitute—*Egg Beaters*
Fat-free plain yogurt—*Dannon*
Nonfat dry milk powder—*Carnation*
Evaporated fat-free milk—*Carnation*
Fat-free milk
Fat-free cottage cheese
Fat-free cream cheese—*Philadelphia*
Fat-free half & half—*Land O Lakes*
Fat-free mayonnaise—*Kraft*

Fat-free dressings—*Kraft*

No-fat sour cream—*Land O Lakes*

"Diet" margarine—*I Can't Believe It's Not Butter! Light*

Cooking sprays

    Olive oil–and Butter-flavored—*Pam*

    Butter-flavored—for spritzing *after* cooking—*I Can't Believe It's Not Butter!*

Cooking oil—*Puritan Canola Oil*

Reduced-calorie whipped topping—*Cool Whip Lite* or *Free*

White sugar substitute—*Splenda*

Baking mix—*Bisquick Heart Smart*

Quick oats—*Quaker*

Graham cracker crumbs—*Nabisco Honey Maid*

Sugar-free pancake syrup—*Log Cabin* or *Cary's*

Parmesan cheese—*Kraft Reduced Fat Parmesan Style Grated*

Reduced-fat cheese (shredded and sliced)—*Kraft 2% Reduced Fat*

Processed cheese—*Velveeta Light*

Shredded frozen potatoes—*Mr. Dell's* or *Ore Ida*

Reduced-fat peanut butter—*Peter Pan, Skippy,* or *Jif*

Spreadable fruit spread—*Welch's* or *Smuckers*

Chicken and Beef broth—*Swanson*

Dry beef or chicken bouillon—*Wyler's Granules Instant Bouillon*

Tomato sauce—*Hunt's*

Canned soups—*Healthy Request*

Tomato juice—*Healthy Request*

Ketchup—*Heinz No Salt Added*

Pastrami and corned beef—*Carl Buddig Lean*

Luncheon meats—*Healthy Choice* or *Oscar Mayer*

Ham—*Dubuque 97% Fat Free* or *Healthy Choice*

Bacon bits—*Oscar Mayer* or *Hormel*

Kielbasa sausage and frankfurters—*Healthy Choice* or *Oscar Mayer Light*

Canned white chicken, packed in water—*Swanson*

Canned tuna, packed in water—*Starkist*

Canned salmon, packed in water—*Starkist*

95% to 97% lean ground sirloin beef or turkey breast

Crackers—*Nabisco Soda Fat Free* and *Ritz Reduced Fat*
Reduced-calorie bread (40 calories per slice)
Small hamburger buns (80 calories per bun)
Rice—instant, regular, and wild—*Minute Rice*
Instant potato flakes
Noodles, spaghetti, macaroni, and rotini pasta
Salsa
Pickle relish—dill, sweet, and hotdog
Mustard—Dijon, prepared yellow, and spicy
Unsweetened apple juice—*Musselman's*
Reduced-calorie cranberry juice cocktail—*Ocean Spray*
Unsweetened orange juice—*Simply Orange*
Unsweetened applesauce—*Musselman's*
Fruit—fresh, frozen, and canned in fruit juice
Vinegar—cider and distilled white
Lemon and lime juice (in small plastic fruit-shaped bottles,
    found in produce section)
Diet lemon-lime soda pop—*Diet Mountain Dew Caffeine Free*
Instant fruit beverage mixes—*Crystal Light*
Reduced calorie chocolate syrup—*Hershey's Lite Syrup*
Sugar-free and fat-free ice cream—*Wells' Blue Bunny*

Remember, these are my suggestions. You are always free to
use other national or local brands. Just keep in mind that if your
choice is higher in fats and carbs, then you must adjust the recipe
nutritional data accordingly.

If you keep your pantry stocked with these products, you can
whip up any recipe in this cookbook. I suggest you start a running
list, and whenever you use up anything (or start to run low),
remember to make a note of it. Your shopping trips will become
quicker and thriftier!

A Note of Thanks

I especially want to thank KitchenAid for providing me with a food
processor for testing these recipes. I also purchased a standard food
processor at a local discount store and tested all the recipes in both.

While the standard version worked fine, using the KitchenAid made the work go quickly and smoothly. It truly was the difference between driving a Chevy and a Caddie when it came to chopping, grating, and slicing fruits and veggies!

JoAnna's Top Food Processor Tips

Your food processor is a modern marvel, capable of many amazing and useful feats in the kitchen, but it's worth knowing a few important things about how to make the most of this magnificent machine. The first is basic but worth repeating: Read the directions that came with your machine very carefully. Every brand and model has its pluses and minuses, but you're more likely to be happy with the results if you do what the manufacturer recommends.

Now, here are some of the helpful things I've learned from testing a lot of recipes on two different food processors—one a moderate-priced discount-store purchase, and the other provided by KitchenAid for this book.

1. Different foods require different pressure for shredding and slicing. Usually a light pressure works best for soft foods like tomatoes, while a firmer pressure is necessary for harder foods such as carrots, apples, and potatoes.

2. Your food processor will *not* crush ice or grind grains, coffee beans, and hard spices. It also won't grind bones and other inedible foods, liquefy vegetables or fruits, slice hard-boiled eggs, or chop up solidly frozen meats. Foods that are too hard can damage the processor motor or blade. Others, like the eggs, just fall apart.

3. Hard or firmly frozen meat should not be processed. Let it thaw on a plate in the refrigerator until it can be pierced with the tip of a fork.

4. Do not process soft cheeses. You'll end up with mush. Instead, process only well-chilled, firm cheeses. It's actually best to set most cheeses in the freezer for 10 to 20 minutes or so before processing.

5. To slice cooked meat or poultry, including salami, cut pieces to fit the feed tube—and make sure your meat is very cold.

6. A few large pieces of food may remain on the top of the slicing/shredding disc after processing. You can discard or cut by hand.

7. Certain foods will stain your food processor's plastic parts. These include carrots, tomatoes, and some berries. I've found that cleaning the processor parts with lemon juice can help.

8. Always pack the food tube lightly. Stuffing it snugly will not produce a good result, and it can damage the machine.

9. Trim leaves or other unwanted parts from the food you wish to chop—the processor won't discard those the way a juicer does.

10. Fill your food processor bowl only up to the recommended level (this is usually marked directly on the bowl), or it will leak.

11. Don't try to whip cream with your food processor. Instead, use a hand mixer. Most food processors don't have the speed to make good peaks.

12. Before chopping nuts in a food processor, dust them with a little flour. This keeps the nuts from sticking to the processor.

13. Avoid blending very hot liquids or foods, as that could harm the processor.

14. Use the right blade at the correct intensity for the job! I've given you specific directions in the recipes, but when you're preparing your own, here are a few guidelines:

- Use the Slicer disc on Low for cucumbers, apples, and mushrooms, and on High to julienne vegetables.

- Use the S-Blade on Low to chop nuts and mince vegetables, and on High to chop meat and purée cooked foods.

- Use the Shredder disc on Low to chop cabbage, and on High to process firm cheeses.

15. Your processor needs to rest for a minute for every minute of operating. Most foods take eleven to thirty seconds to be processed, though this also depends on the quantity you're working with.

16. For best results, slow down the speed for juicy foods. Set the speed first, and then feed the food into the filling tube while the motor is switched off.

17. It's not a good idea to sharpen the blades for your food processor. If they become dull or damaged, it's best to replace them.

18. Some parts of your food processor can go into the dishwasher, though I usually do them in the sink. If you wash your dishes by hand, clean the blades with a brush immediately after use and keep them apart from the rest of the dishes.

19. For shredding and slicing, remember to position items in the food tube according to size. Carrots, for example, should usually be stacked side by side.

20. To keep the lid of your food processor work bowl clean while it's in use, cover the bowl with plastic wrap before fitting the lid, making sure the bowl is completely covered. Process as directed. When you're done, lift off the clean lid and discard the splattered plastic wrap. Obviously this won't work if you are using the feeder tube. You can also use this trick with the blender.

21. Invest in a disc storage holder that hangs on your kitchen wall. I've got a six-disc one that has worked really well for

me. I know KitchenAid makes one, and I bet other manufacturers do, too.

22. Once you start making a lot of recipes from this book, you may want to pick up a couple of extra work bowls so you're not constantly washing yours out. Remember, each food processor has a different feel to it, and it takes using it a few times to get really comfortable. But once you get the knack of how your bowl goes on and off, you'll be fine.

Yes, But How Much Should It Be? A Healthy Exchanges Chopping Chart

E ver since I began sharing recipes all those years ago, readers have asked me to clarify what I mean by a particular size vegetable. They've also wanted to know if it was okay to use a little bit more of this or that in a specific recipe, rather than throw it away or freeze it.

I decided this was the perfect book to provide you with a chart based on my experience preparing thousands of recipes over the years. I hope this will make it even easier to stir up Healthy Exchanges recipes each and every day. Now, everyone's idea of what a medium onion is might be slightly different. Some may think that it should chop up to ½ cup; others may believe that it produces at least a cup or even more. So to help you get a sense of a realistic "output" for my recipes, I've compiled the following Chopping Chart.

Just remember that in most cases we're talking about veggies with very minimal calorie counts. If your "medium" onion chops up to more than I suggest it should, you have my blessing to use it all. However, that does *not* mean that you can replace a small head of cabbage with a large one and expect the final quantity of the recipe to be the same!

Fruits

Apple:
  Medium = 1 cup chopped
Peaches:
  Medium = ¾ cup chopped
Pear:
  Medium = 1 cup chopped

Vegetables

Broccoli:
  Small = 3 cups chopped
  Medium = 5 cups chopped
  Large = 7 cups chopped
Cabbage:
  Small = 4 cups chopped
  Medium = 6 cups chopped
  Large = 8 cups chopped
Carrots:
  Medium = ⅓ cup chopped
  Large = ⅔ cup chopped
Cauliflower:
  Small = 3 cups chopped
  Medium = 5 cups chopped
  Large = 7 cups chopped
Celery:
  Medium stalk = ⅓ cup chopped
Cucumber:
  Small = 1 cup chopped
  Medium = 2 cups chopped
Green or Red Bell Pepper:
  Small = ⅓ cup chopped

Medium = ½ cup chopped

Large = ¾ cup chopped

Lettuce:

Small = 4 cups shredded

Medium = 6 cups shredded

Onion:

Small = ½ cup chopped

Medium = ¾ cup chopped

Large = 1 cup chopped

Potato:

5-ounce raw = ¾ cup chopped

Tomato:

Medium = ¾ cup chopped

Large = 1 cup chopped

Turnips:

Medium = ¾ cup chopped

Zucchini:

Small = 1 cup chopped

Medium = 2 cups chopped

JoAnna's Ten Commandments of Successful Cooking

A very important part of any journey is knowing where you are going and the best way to get there. If you plan and prepare before you start to cook, you should reach mealtime with foods to write home about!

1. **Read the entire recipe from start to finish** and be sure you understand the process involved. Check that you have all the equipment you will need *before* you begin.

2. **Check the ingredient list** and be sure you have *everything* and in the amounts required. Keep cooking sprays handy—while they're not listed as ingredients, I use them all the time (just a quick squirt!).

3. **Set out *all* the ingredients and equipment needed** to prepare the recipe on the counter near you *before* you start. Remember that old saying, *A stitch in time saves nine?* It applies in the kitchen, too.

4. **Do as much advance preparation as possible** before actually cooking. Chop, cut, grate, or do whatever is

needed to prepare the ingredients and have them ready before you start to mix. Turn the oven on at least ten minutes before putting food in to bake, to allow the oven to preheat to the proper temperature.

5. **Use a kitchen timer** to tell you when the cooking or baking time is up. Because stove temperatures vary slightly by manufacturer, you may want to set your timer for five minutes less than the suggested time just to prevent overcooking. Check the progress of your dish at that time, then decide if you need the additional minutes or not.

6. **Measure carefully.** Use glass measures for liquids and metal or plastic cups for dry ingredients. My recipes are based on standard measurements. Unless I tell you it's a scant or full cup, measure the cup level.

7. **For best results, follow the recipe instructions exactly.** Feel free to substitute ingredients that *don't tamper* with the basic chemistry of the recipe, but be sure to leave key ingredients alone. For example, you could substitute sugar-free instant chocolate pudding for sugar-free instant butterscotch pudding, but if you used a six-serving package when a four-serving package was listed in the ingredients, or you used instant when cook-and-serve is required, you won't get the right result.

8. **Clean up as you go.** It is much easier to wash a few items at a time than to face a whole counter of dirty dishes later. The same is true for spills on the counter or floor.

9. **Be careful about doubling or halving a recipe.** Though many recipes can be altered successfully to serve more or fewer people, *many cannot*. This is especially true when it comes to spices and liquids. If you try to double a recipe that calls for 1 teaspoon pumpkin-pie spice, for example, and you double the spice, you may end up with a too-spicy taste. I usually suggest increasing spices or liquid by 1½ times when doubling a recipe. If it tastes a little bland to you, you can increase the spice to 1¾ times the original

amount the next time you prepare the dish. Remember: You can always add more, but you can't take it out after it's stirred in.

The same is true with liquid ingredients. If you wanted to **triple** a main dish recipe because you were planning to serve a crowd, you might think you should use three times as much of every ingredient. Don't, or you could end up with soup instead! If the original recipe calls for 1¾ cups tomato sauce, I'd suggest using 3½ cups when you **triple** the recipe (or 2¾ cups if you **double** it). You'll still have a good-tasting dish that won't run all over the plate.

10. **Write your reactions next to each recipe once you've served it.**

Yes, that's right, I'm giving you permission to write in this book. It's yours, after all. Ask yourself: Did everyone like it? Did you have to add another half teaspoon of chili seasoning to please your family, who like to live on the spicier side of the street? You may even want to rate the recipe on a scale of 1 ☆ to 4 ☆, depending on what you thought of it. (Four stars would be the top rating—and I hope you'll feel that way about many of my recipes.) Jotting down your comments while they are fresh in your mind will help you personalize the recipe to your own taste the next time you prepare it.

The Recipes

How to Read a Healthy Exchanges Recipe

The Healthy Exchanges Nutritional Analysis

Before using these recipes, you may wish to consult your physician or health-care provider to be sure they are appropriate for you. The information in this book is not intended to take the place of any medical advice. It reflects my experiences, studies, research, and opinions regarding healthy eating.

Each recipe includes nutritional information calculated in three ways:

> Healthy Exchanges Weight Loss Choices or Exchanges
> Calories; Fat, Protein, Carbohydrates, and Fiber in grams;
>   Sodium and Calcium in milligrams
> Diabetic Exchanges
> Carb Choices for those who prefer to count their carbs

In every Healthy Exchanges recipe, the Diabetic Exchanges have been calculated by a registered dietitian. All the other calculations were done by computer, using the Food Processor II software.

When the ingredient listing gives more than one choice, the first ingredient listed is the one used in the recipe analysis. Due to inevitable variations in the ingredients you choose to use, the nutritional values should be considered approximate.

The annotation "(limited)" following Protein counts in some recipes indicates that consumption of whole eggs should be limited to four per week.

Please note the following symbols:

☆ This star means read the recipe's directions carefully for special instructions about **division** of ingredients.

✳ This symbol indicates **FREEZES WELL.**

Bountiful Soups

With the food processor at your side, you're ready to become a soup-making magician! You'll be slicing and dicing every vegetable under the sun (if you want to) and stirring up pots of delicious, nutritious, and utterly satisfying homemade soups and stews, steamy chilis, and soothing broths. My soups have always been pretty simple to stir up, but even I have been inspired to use more raw, fresh vegetables because of the increased ease of preparation.

So what will you put on the menu from this irresistible chapter of recipes? For a glorious taste of the ocean, try *Deep-Sea Tuna Pasta Chowder*. For a thick and rich and oh-so-creamy treat, *Zucchini Tomato-Rice Bisque* is a luscious choice. If your mouth waters at the promise of a cheese soup, *Cheesy Cream of Cauliflower* will delight you to the bottom of the bowl. And to satisfy the nearest hungry man or teen, I'd recommend *Mighty Filling Minestrone*!

Anytime Vegetable Soup

The title says it all—all year long, day or night, this veggie-rich combo is delicious, nutritious, and easy to fix. I think it makes a tasty snack, especially when combined with some baked chips.

○ Serves 6 (1½ cups)

1 medium onion, peeled and cut into 6 wedges
2 medium carrots, scraped and each cut into 2-inch pieces
2 medium stalks celery, cut into 2-inch pieces
3 cups reduced-sodium tomato juice
½ small head cabbage, cut into 6 wedges
1 (15-ounce) can diced tomatoes, undrained
1 tablespoon Splenda Granular
2 teaspoons Italian seasoning
¼ teaspoon black pepper

Lock food processor bowl in position. Insert the steel knife blade. Drop onion wedges, carrot pieces, and celery pieces into the food processor bowl. Attach food chute cover and lock in place. Turn on processor and pulse 6 to 12 times or until vegetables are finely chopped. Transfer chopped vegetables to a medium saucepan sprayed with butter-flavored cooking spray. Repeat process with cabbage wedges. Stir chopped cabbage into vegetable mixture. Add tomato juice, undrained tomatoes, Splenda, Italian seasoning, and black pepper. Mix well to combine. Place saucepan over medium heat and bring mixture to a boil, stirring occasionally. Lower heat, cover, and simmer for 30 minutes, stirring occasionally.

Each serving equals:

HE: 2½ Vegetable • 1 Optional Calorie

80 Calories • 0 gm Fat • 3 gm Protein • 17 gm Carbohydrate • 213 mg Sodium • 72 mg Calcium • 3 gm Fiber

DIABETIC EXCHANGES: 3 Vegetable

CARB CHOICES: 1

Chunky Gazpacho Soup

One of my favorite warm-weather sippers is this Spanish-inspired "salad in a glass"! You get so much fresh vegetable flavor in every mouthful, you'll feel healthier in minutes—and you can enjoy seconds, since it's so low in calories!   ❍   Serves 4 (1 cup)

2 cups reduced-sodium tomato juice
2 teaspoons olive oil
1 tablespoon white distilled vinegar
1 tablespoon Splenda Granular
½ teaspoon chili seasoning
1 small red onion, peeled and quartered
1 small red bell pepper, stem and seeds removed and cut into 6 strips

1 small green bell pepper, stem and seeds removed and cut into 6 strips
2 medium tomatoes, peeled and each cut into 6 wedges
1 medium unpeeled cucumber, halved lengthwise and cut into 1-inch pieces
1 medium stalk celery, trimmed and cut into 2-inch pieces
1 sprig parsley, stem removed

In a large bowl, combine tomato juice, olive oil, vinegar, Splenda, and chili seasoning. Lock food processor bowl in position. Insert the steel knife blade. Drop onion, red pepper, and green pepper into the food processor bowl. Attach food chute cover and lock in place. Turn on processor and pulse 3 or 4 times or until vegetables are finely chopped. Transfer chopped vegetables into bowl with tomato juice mixture. Repeat process with tomatoes, cucumber, celery, and parsley. Stir chopped vegetables into soup mixture. Cover and refrigerate for at least 1 hour. Gently stir again just before serving.

Each serving equals:

HE: 2½ Vegetable • ½ Fat • 2 Optional Calories

87 Calories • 3 gm Fat • 2 gm Protein • 13 gm Carbohydrate •
106 mg Sodium • 37 mg Calcium • 2 gm Fiber

DIABETIC EXCHANGES: 2½ Vegetable • ½ Fat

CARB CHOICES: 1

Cold Borscht

I love making soups in the food processor because it blends and chops so beautifully. This Eastern European chilled soup is a favorite worldwide—refreshing and oh-so-creamy. And it's pink!

● Serves 4 (¾ cup)

> 1 (15-ounce) can sliced beets, drained and ½ cup liquid
>   reserved
> 1 (14-ounce) can Swanson Lower Sodium Fat Free Beef
>   Broth
> 2 tablespoons lemon juice
> 1 teaspoon lemon pepper
> ½ cup Land O Lakes no-fat sour cream

Lock food processor bowl in position. Insert the steel knife blade. Drop beets into the food processor bowl. Attach food chute cover and lock in place. Turn on processor and pulse 2 or 3 times or until beets are coarsely chopped. Transfer chopped beets to a medium saucepan. Add reserved beet liquid and beef broth. Mix well to combine. Bring mixture to a boil, stirring occasionally. Lower heat and simmer for 10 minutes, stirring occasionally. Transfer soup to a medium bowl. Cover and refrigerate for at least 1 hour. Just before serving, stir in lemon juice and lemon pepper. When serving, top each bowl with 2 tablespoons sour cream.

Each serving equals:

HE: 1 Vegetable • ¼ Slider • 18 Optional Calories

52 Calories • 0 gm Fat • 3 gm Protein • 10 gm Carbohydrate •
304 mg Sodium • 54 mg Calcium • 1 gm Fiber

DIABETIC EXCHANGES: 1 Vegetable

CARB CHOICES: ½

Creamy Cabbage Soup

Most cabbage soups are clear and chock-full of vegetables, not creamy-smooth and rich. But I thought it would be fun to see what the result would be of blending in a transforming touch of dairy . . . and we all loved it! ◗ Serves 4 (1½ cups)

> 1 small head cabbage, quartered
> 2 medium stalks celery, trimmed and each cut into 2-inch pieces
> 1 medium carrot, scraped and cut into 2-inch pieces
> 2 cups water
> 1 (10¾-ounce) can Healthy Request Cream of Mushroom Soup
> ⅓ cup Carnation Nonfat Dry Milk Powder
> ½ cup Land O Lakes Fat Free Half & Half
> ½ teaspoon dried dill weed
> ⅛ teaspoon black pepper
> ¼ cup Land O Lakes no-fat sour cream

Lock food processor bowl in position. Insert the slicer disc. Attach food chute cover and lock in place. Drop cabbage wedges into the food chute. Position food pusher over cabbage. Turn on processor and use medium pressure to push cabbage through. Transfer sliced cabbage to a large saucepan when full level is reached. Repeat process as necessary. Remove slicer disc from food processor and insert the steel knife blade. Drop celery and carrot pieces into the food processor bowl. Attach food chute cover and lock in place. Turn on processor and pulse 3 or 4 times or until vegetables are finely chopped. Transfer chopped vegetables to saucepan. Add water. Mix well to combine. Bring mixture to a boil. Lower heat, cover, and simmer for 15 minutes or just until vegetables are tender, stirring occasionally. Do not drain. Stir in mushroom soup, dry milk powder, half & half, dill weed, and black pepper. Continue cooking for 5 to 6 minutes or until mixture is heated through, stirring often. When serving, top each bowl with 1 tablespoon sour cream.

Each serving equals:

HE: 1½ Vegetable • ¼ Fat Free Milk • ¾ Slider • 14 Optional Calories

150 Calories • 2 gm Fat • 7 gm Protein • 26 gm Carbohydrate •
448 mg Sodium • 284 mg Calcium • 3 gm Fiber

DIABETIC EXCHANGES: 2 Vegetable • 1 Other Carbohydrate

CARB CHOICES: 2

Cheesy Cream of Cauliflower Soup

Cheese soups taste decadent, and in many restaurants, they are full of high-fat ingredients like heavy cream and butter. I'm inspired by culinary challenges like that one, so I created this luscious soup so good, you won't believe it's good for you, too!

○ Serves 4 (1½ cups)

> 1 small onion, peeled and cut into 4 wedges
> 2 medium stalks celery, trimmed and each cut into 2-inch pieces
> 2 cups frozen chopped cauliflower, thawed
> ½ cup hot water
> 1 (12-fluid-ounce) can Carnation Evaporated Fat Free Milk
> 3 tablespoons all-purpose flour
> ½ cup Land O Lakes Fat Free Half & Half
> 1 (2-ounce) jar chopped pimiento, drained
> 1 cup diced Velveeta Light processed cheese
> ⅛ teaspoon black pepper

Lock food processor bowl in position. Insert the steel knife blade. Drop onion wedges and celery pieces into the food processor bowl. Attach food chute cover and lock in place. Turn on processor and pulse 3 or 4 times or until vegetables are finely chopped. Transfer chopped vegetables to a medium saucepan. Repeat process with cauliflower pieces. Stir hot water into chopped vegetables. Cook over medium heat for 10 minutes or just until vegetables are tender, stirring occasionally. Pour evaporated milk and flour into food processor bowl. Re-cover and pulse 3 times or until mixture is blended. Pour milk mixture into undrained vegetables. Add half & half, pimiento, Velveeta cheese, and black pepper. Mix well to combine. Lower heat and simmer for 5 minutes or until mixture thickens and cheese melts, stirring often.

Each serving equals:

HE: 1½ Vegetable • 1 Protein • ¾ Fat Free Milk • ¼ Bread •
18 Optional Calories

200 Calories • 4 gm Fat • 14 gm Protein • 27 gm Carbohydrate •
638 mg Sodium • 452 mg Calcium • 2 gm Fiber

DIABETIC EXCHANGES: 1½ Vegetable • 1 Meat • 1 Fat Free Milk

CARB CHOICES: 2

Chunky Cream of Carrot Soup

One of the tricks of making soup is deciding how smooth or chunky the soup should be. I did a lot of experimenting on this book, and my recipes show the results of all that testing. Some soups are all silken flow down your throat, while others, like this one, arrive with savory chunks of veggie, which retain a bit of crunch. ❂ Serves 4 (1 cup)

> 1 (12-fluid-ounce) can Carnation Evaporated Fat Free Milk
> 3 tablespoons all-purpose flour
> 2 tablespoons I Can't Believe It's Not Butter! Light
>   Margarine
> 3 sprigs parsley, stems removed
> 1 cup fat-free milk
> ½ cup Land O Lakes Fat Free Half & Half
> ½ teaspoon lemon pepper
> 3 medium carrots, scraped and each cut into 2-inch pieces
> 1 small onion, peeled and cut into 4 wedges

Lock food processor bowl in position. Insert the steel knife blade. Place evaporated milk, flour, margarine, and parsley in food processor bowl. Attach food chute cover and lock in place. Turn on processor and pulse 2 or 3 times or until mixture is blended. Transfer mixture into a large saucepan sprayed with butter-flavored cooking spray. Stir in milk, half & half, and lemon pepper. Cook over medium heat while processing carrots, stirring occasionally. Remove steel knife blade from food processor and insert the shredder disc. Attach food chute cover and lock in place. Drop carrot pieces and onion wedges into the food chute. Position food pusher over vegetables. Turn on processor and use medium pressure to push vegetables through. Transfer shredded vegetables to a large bowl when full level is reached. Repeat process as necessary. Stir carrots and onions into milk mixture. Continue cooking for 10 minutes or until vegetables are tender, stirring occasionally.

Each serving equals:

HE: 1 Fat Free Milk • 1 Vegetable • ¾ Fat • ¼ Bread • 4 Optional Calories

175 Calories • 3 gm Fat • 10 gm Protein • 27 gm Carbohydrate • 329 mg Sodium • 365 mg Calcium • 2 gm Fiber

DIABETIC EXCHANGES: 1 Fat Free Milk • 1 Vegetable • 1 Fat

CARB CHOICES: 2

Broccoli Soup Almondine

I cook a lot with fresh broccoli, especially when my husband, Cliff, the truck drivin' man, is on the road in his rig. But sometimes I've only got the frozen kind on hand—and I'm in the mood for an elegant soup. The almonds give this a unique flavor and texture that I think you'll adore. ☻ Serves 4 (1¼ cups)

> 3 cups frozen cut broccoli, thawed
> 1 medium onion, peeled and cut into 6 wedges
> ¼ cup almonds ☆
> 3 tablespoons all-purpose flour
> ¼ cup Land O Lakes no-fat sour cream
> ½ cup Land O Lakes Fat Free Half & Half
> 1 teaspoon lemon pepper
> 1 (14-ounce) can Swanson Lower Sodium Fat Free Chicken
>   Broth ☆

Lock food processor bowl in position. Insert the steel knife blade. Place broccoli, onion, and 2 tablespoons almonds in food processor bowl. Attach food chute cover and lock in place. Turn on processor and pulse 3 times or until mixture is coarsely chopped. Uncover and add flour, sour cream, half & half, lemon pepper, and ½ cup chicken broth. Re-cover and continue pulsing 5 times or until mixture is smooth. Transfer mixture to a medium saucepan sprayed with butter-flavored cooking spray. Stir in remaining chicken broth. Cook over medium heat for 12 minutes or until broccoli and onion are tender, stirring often. Remove steel knife blade and wipe food processor bowl with a clean cloth. Insert the slicer disc. Attach food chute cover and lock in place. Drop remaining 2 tablespoons almonds into the food chute. Position food pusher over almonds. Turn on processor and use medium pressure to push almonds through. When serving, top each bowl with 1½ teaspoons sliced almonds.

HINTS: 1. Thaw broccoli by rinsing in a colander under hot water
        for 1 minute.

2. If desired, toast sliced almonds in a small skillet sprayed with butter-flavored cooking spray for 2 to 3 minutes.

Each serving equals:

HE: 2 Vegetable • ½ Fat • ¼ Bread • ¼ Protein • ¼ Slider • 19 Optional Calories

153 Calories • 5 gm Fat • 8 gm Protein • 19 gm Carbohydrate • 329 mg Sodium • 147 mg Calcium • 4 gm Fiber

DIABETIC EXCHANGES: 2 Vegetable • ½ Fat • ½ Starch/Carbohydrate

CARB CHOICES: 1

Three-Cheese Veggie Soup

I'm fond of saying that if one appetizing ingredient is good, two are better, and three—yes, three!—are even more appealing! That's the cheese story in this rich vegetable soup that simply "sings" with the addition of Cheddar, mozzarella, and Parmesan cheese.

◐ Serves 4 (1½ cups)

> 4 medium stalks celery, trimmed and each cut into 2-inch pieces
> 3 medium carrots, scraped and each cut into 2-inch pieces
> 1 medium onion, peeled and cut into 6 wedges
> 1 (14-ounce) can Swanson Lower Sodium Fat Free Chicken Broth
> 1 (12-fluid-ounce) can Carnation Evaporated Fat Free Milk
> 3 tablespoons all-purpose flour
> ½ cup Land O Lakes Fat Free Half & Half
> ¾ cup shredded Kraft reduced-fat Cheddar cheese
> ¾ cup shredded Kraft reduced-fat mozzarella cheese
> ¼ cup Kraft Reduced Fat Parmesan Style Grated Topping
> ⅛ teaspoon black pepper

Lock food processor bowl in position. Insert the steel knife blade. Drop celery pieces into the food processor bowl. Attach food chute cover and lock in place. Turn on processor and pulse 3 or 4 times or until celery is finely chopped. Transfer chopped celery to a medium saucepan. Repeat process with carrots and onion. Add chicken broth to saucepan. Mix well to combine. Cook over medium heat for 8 to 10 minutes or just until vegetables are tender. In a covered jar, combine evaporated milk and flour. Shake well to blend. Stir milk mixture into saucepan. Add half & half, Cheddar cheese, mozzarella cheese, Parmesan cheese, and black pepper. Mix well to combine. Continue cooking for 8 to 10 minutes or just until mixture thickens and cheeses melt.

Each serving equals:

HE: 1¾ Protein • 1½ Vegetable • ¾ Fat Free Milk • ¼ Bread

293 Calories • 9 gm Fat • 23 gm Protein • 30 gm Carbohydrate •
801 mg Sodium • 661 mg Calcium • 3 gm Fiber

DIABETIC EXCHANGES: 2 Meat • 1½ Vegetable • 1 Fat Free Milk

CARB CHOICES: 2

Tex-Mex Fresh Tomato Soup

Some people are surprised by how many vegetables are used in southwestern-style cooking, since they envision a dry, desert environment that shouldn't be good for growing tomatoes and other fresh veggies. But there are green patches almost everywhere, and they produce the ingredients that make this dish sizzle!

☻ Serves 4 (1 cup)

> 2 medium stalks celery, trimmed and each cut into 2-inch
>   pieces
> 1 medium onion, peeled and cut into 6 wedges
> 1 medium carrot, scraped and cut into 2-inch pieces
> 3 medium tomatoes, peeled and each cut into 6 wedges
> 1½ cups reduced-sodium tomato juice
> 3 tablespoons all-purpose flour
> 1 cup fresh or frozen whole-kernel corn, thawed
> 2 tablespoons Splenda Granular
> 2 teaspoons chili seasoning
> ⅛ teaspoon black pepper

Lock food processor bowl in position. Insert the steel knife blade. Drop celery pieces into the food processor bowl. Attach food chute cover and lock in place. Turn on processor and pulse 3 or 4 times or until celery is finely chopped. Transfer chopped celery to a medium saucepan. Repeat process with onion, carrot, and tomatoes. Stir ½ cup tomato juice into saucepan with vegetable mixture. Cook over medium heat for 12 to 15 minutes or just until mixture starts to boil. Meanwhile, place remaining 1 cup tomato juice and flour into food processor bowl. Attach food chute cover and lock in place. Position food pusher in chute to prevent mixture from splashing out of bowl. Turn on processor and pulse 2 or 3 times or until mixture is blended. Add juice mixture to vegetable mixture. Mix well to combine. Stir in corn, Splenda, chili seasoning, and black pepper. Lower heat and simmer for 15 to 20 minutes, stirring occasionally.

HINT: Thaw corn by rinsing in a colander under hot water for 1
   minute.

Each serving equals:

HE: 2¼ Vegetable • ¾ Bread • 3 Optional Calories

120 Calories • 0 gm Fat • 4 gm Protein • 26 gm Carbohydrate •
146 mg Sodium • 41 mg Calcium • 3 gm Fiber

DIABETIC EXCHANGES: 2 Vegetable • 1 Starch

CARB CHOICES: 2

Zucchini Tomato Rice Bisque

If you've never prepared a bisque-style soup, let me share with you that the name usually refers to a thick, creamy soup, sometimes based on seafood. In this case, I've created a splendidly flavorful blend of scrumptious veggies that will roll across your taste buds like a velvety river. ❂ Serves 4 (1 cup)

> 1 medium unpeeled zucchini, cut in half lengthwise and
>   crosswise
> 1 small onion, peeled and cut into 4 wedges
> 1 medium tomato, peeled and cut into 6 wedges
> 1 (10¾-ounce) can Healthy Request Tomato Soup
> 1 cup fat-free milk
> ¼ cup Land O Lakes Fat Free Half & Half
> 1 teaspoon Italian seasoning
> 1 cup cooked rice

Lock food processor bowl in position. Insert the steel knife blade. Drop zucchini into the food processor bowl. Attach food chute cover and lock in place. Turn on processor and pulse 3 or 4 times or until zucchini is finely chopped. Transfer chopped zucchini to a medium saucepan sprayed with olive oil–flavored cooking spray. Repeat process with onion and tomato. Sauté vegetable mixture for 6 to 8 minutes. Stir in tomato soup, milk, half & half, and Italian seasoning. Add rice. Mix well to combine. Lower heat and simmer for 6 to 8 minutes or until mixture is heated through, stirring occasionally.

HINTS: 1. Usually ⅔ cup uncooked instant or ½ cup regular rice cooks to about 1 cup.
2. Also good with 1 tablespoon reduced-fat Parmesan cheese sprinkled over top of each bowl. If using, don't forget to count the additional calories.

Each serving equals:

HE: 1 Vegetable • ½ Bread • ¼ Fat Free Milk • ½ Slider •
14 Optional Calories

141 Calories • 1 gm Fat • 5 gm Protein • 28 gm Carbohydrate •
340 mg Sodium • 108 mg Calcium • 2 gm Fiber

DIABETIC EXCHANGES: 1½ Starch/Carbohydrate • 1 Vegetable

CARB CHOICES: 2

Cheesy Potato Noodle Soup

Soups made with potatoes often taste as if they've got to be made with butter and cream, and that's because of their natural starch, which enriches any long-cooking dish made with them. Mixed here with some cheese and tender noodles, the humble potato delivers a delectable starter.   ○   Serves 4 (1⅓ cups)

> *2 (5-ounce) raw, unpeeled potatoes, each cut into 4 wedges*
> *1 small onion, peeled and cut into 4 wedges*
> *3 medium stalks celery, trimmed and each cut into 2-inch*
>   *pieces*
> *1¼ cups hot water*
> *¾ cup uncooked noodles*
> *1 (12-fluid-ounce) can Carnation Evaporated Fat Free*
>   *Milk*
> *1½ tablespoons all-purpose flour*
> *2 sprigs parsley, stems removed*
> *¾ cup diced Velveeta Light processed cheese*
> *⅛ teaspoon black pepper*

Lock food processor bowl in position. Insert the steel knife blade. Drop potato wedges into the food processor bowl. Attach food chute cover and lock in place. Turn on processor and pulse 2 or 3 times or until potatoes are coarsely chopped. Transfer chopped potatoes to a medium saucepan. Repeat process with onion and then with celery. Add water to vegetables in saucepan. Mix well to combine. Stir in uncooked noodles. Bring mixture to a boil. Lower heat, cover, and simmer for 10 to 15 minutes or until vegetables are tender. Do not drain. Remove food chute cover from processor. Place evaporated milk, flour, and parsley in food processor bowl. Re-cover and pulse 3 or 4 times or until mixture is blended. Pour milk mixture into soup mixture. Add Velveeta cheese and black pepper. Mix well to combine. Continue simmering for 8 to 10 minutes or until mixture thickens and cheese melts, stirring often.

Each serving equals:

HE: 1 Bread • ¾ Fat Free Milk • ¾ Protein • ½ Vegetable

235 Calories • 3 gm Fat • 14 gm Protein • 38 gm Carbohydrate • 486 mg Sodium • 386 mg Calcium • 2 gm Fiber

DIABETIC EXCHANGES: 1 Starch • 1 Fat Free Milk • 1 Meat • ½ Vegetable

CARB CHOICES: 2½

Easy French Onion Soup

Even if the real thing—*Soupe a la oignon*—takes hours to stew on the stove, you can get a remarkably good version of this French classic in minutes instead! I usually make this with the onions I have on hand, but if you want to experiment, you can pick up several different kinds of onions and see how they transform the taste.

♥ Serves 4 (1 cup)

> 3 medium onions, peeled and each cut into 6 wedges
> 1 (14-ounce) can Swanson Lower Sodium Fat Free Beef Broth
> 2½ cups water
> 1 tablespoon reduced-sodium ketchup
> 1½ teaspoons Worcestershire sauce
> ⅛ teaspoon black pepper
> 1 cup seasoned fat-free croutons
> ¼ cup Kraft Reduced Fat Parmesan Style Grated Topping

Lock food processor bowl in position. Insert the slicer disc. Attach food chute cover and lock in place. Drop onion wedges into the food chute. Position food pusher over onions. Turn on processor and use medium pressure to push onion wedges through. Transfer sliced onions to a medium saucepan sprayed with butter-flavored cooking spray. Place saucepan over medium heat and sauté onions for 6 to 8 minutes or just until soft. Add beef broth, water, ketchup, Worcestershire sauce, and black pepper. Mix well to combine. Bring mixture to a boil, stirring occasionally. Lower heat, cover, and simmer for 15 minutes, stirring occasionally. For each serving, spoon 1 cup soup into a soup bowl, sprinkle ¼ cup croutons over soup, and sprinkle 1 tablespoon Parmesan cheese over top. Serve at once.

Each serving equals:

HE: 1½ Vegetable • ½ Bread • ¼ Protein • 19 Optional Calories

139 Calories • 3 gm Fat • 5 gm Protein • 23 gm Carbohydrate • 285 mg Sodium • 88 mg Calcium • 2 gm Fiber

DIABETIC EXCHANGES: 1½ Vegetable • 1 Starch

CARB CHOICES: 1½

Potato-Onion Bisque

Did you know that research suggests that people who start their meals with soup generally eat fewer calories overall and are satisfied with smaller portions of other foods? It's true, and it's another great reason for adding soups like this luscious one to your daily menus.

♥ Serves 4 (1¼ cups)

> 1 medium onion, peeled and cut into 6 wedges
> 2 medium stalks celery, trimmed and each cut into 2-inch
>   pieces
> 2 sprigs parsley, stems removed
> 1 tablespoon + 1 teaspoon I Can't Believe It's Not Butter!
>   Light Margarine
> 3 (5-ounce) raw potatoes, peeled and each cut into 4 wedges
> 1 (10¾-ounce) can Healthy Request Cream of Mushroom
>   Soup
> ½ cup water
> 1 (12-fluid-ounce) can Carnation Evaporated Fat Free Milk
> ⅛ teaspoon black pepper

Lock food processor bowl in position. Insert the steel knife blade. Drop onion wedges, celery, and parsley into the food processor bowl. Attach food chute cover and lock in place. Turn on processor and pulse 3 or 4 times or until vegetables are finely chopped. Transfer vegetables to a slow cooker container sprayed with butter-flavored cooking spray. Add margarine. Mix well to combine. Repeat process of chopping potatoes in food processor. Add chopped potatoes, mushroom soup, water, evaporated milk, and black pepper to onion mixture. Mix well to combine. Cover and cook on LOW for 6 hours. Mix well before serving.

Each serving equals:

HE: ¾ Fat Free Milk • ¾ Bread • ¾ Vegetable • ½ Fat • ½ Slider • 1 Optional Calorie

211 Calories • 3 gm Fat • 10 gm Protein • 36 gm Carbohydrate • 489 mg Sodium • 322 mg Calcium • 2 gm Fiber

DIABETIC EXCHANGES: 1 Fat Free Milk • 1 Starch • ½ Vegetable • ½ Fat

CARB CHOICES: 2

Mexicali Corn Chowder

Corn is such a staple of Mexican cooking, in many different forms, which certainly makes this Iowa-born cook happy! For anyone who's ever felt that corn chowder was just a little bit "bland," here's a spicier version that celebrates the abundant pleasures of those golden ears.　　**❂**　Serves 6 (1⅓ cups)

> 1 clove garlic, peeled
> 1 medium onion, peeled and cut into 6 wedges
> 1 medium red bell pepper, stem and seeds removed and cut into 6 strips
> 1 (14-ounce) can Swanson Lower Sodium Fat Free Chicken Broth
> 1 (12-fluid-ounce) can Carnation Evaporated Fat Free Milk
> 1 (15-ounce) can cream-style corn
> 1 cup frozen whole-kernel corn, thawed
> 2 medium tomatoes, peeled and each cut into 6 wedges
> ½ teaspoon chili seasoning
> ¾ cup shredded Kraft reduced-fat Cheddar cheese
> 1 small bunch fresh cilantro or parsley

Lock food processor bowl in position. Insert the steel knife blade. Drop garlic, onion wedges, and red pepper into the food processor bowl. Attach food chute cover and lock in place. Turn on processor and pulse 4 or 5 times or until vegetables are finely chopped. Transfer chopped vegetables to a large saucepan sprayed with butter-flavored cooking spray. Sauté chopped vegetables for 5 to 6 minutes. Stir in chicken broth, evaporated milk, and cream-style corn. Add whole-kernel corn. Mix well to combine. Cook over medium heat for 5 minutes or just until vegetables are tender, stirring occasionally. Meanwhile, drop tomato wedges into the food processor bowl. Attach food chute cover and lock in place. Turn on processor and pulse 2 or 3 times or until tomatoes are coarsely chopped. Stir chopped tomatoes into soup mixture. Add chili seasoning. Mix well to combine. Lower heat and simmer for 10 to 15 minutes or until tomatoes soften, stirring often. Stir in Cheddar cheese. Continue simmering for 2 to 3 minutes or until cheese melts. Meanwhile, remove steel blade and wipe food processor bowl with a clean cloth. Reinsert steel blade. Drop cilantro or parsley into food processor bowl. Attach food chute cover and lock in place. Turn on processor and pulse 3 or 4 times or until cilantro is minced. When serving, evenly sprinkle cilantro over top of each bowl.

HINT: Thaw corn by rinsing in a colander under hot water for 1 minute.

Each serving equals:

HE: 1 Bread • 1 Vegetable • ½ Fat Free Milk • ½ Protein • 5 Optional Calories

199 Calories • 3 gm Fat • 11 gm Protein • 32 gm Carbohydrate • 522 mg Sodium • 262 mg Calcium • 3 gm Fiber

DIABETIC EXCHANGES: 1 Starch • 1 Vegetable • ½ Fat Free Milk • ½ Meat

CARB CHOICES: 2

Spring Pea Soup

When freshly harvested peas are removed from their pods, they're quickly flash-frozen, their rich nutrition preserved for us to relish during all those months when fresh peas are unavailable. Thawed, they taste as irresistibly good as they do eaten right after picking.

⦿ Serves 4 (1¼ cups)

> 1 small head iceberg lettuce, cut into 8 wedges
> 2 green onions, trimmed and each cut into 1-inch pieces
> 2 tablespoons I Can't Believe It's Not Butter! Light Margarine
> 2 cups frozen peas, thawed
> 1 (14-ounce) can Swanson Lower Sodium Fat Free Chicken Broth
> 1 (12-fluid-ounce) can Carnation Evaporated Fat Free Milk
> 1 tablespoon Splenda Granular
> ⅛ teaspoon black pepper

Lock food processor bowl in position. Insert the slicer disc. Attach food chute cover and lock in place. Drop lettuce wedges and green onion pieces into the food chute. Position food pusher over vegetables. Turn on processor and use light pressure to push vegetables through. In a medium saucepan sprayed with butter-flavored cooking spray, melt margarine. Transfer sliced vegetables to saucepan and sauté for 2 minutes. Stir in peas and continue to sauté for 2 minutes. Add chicken broth. Mix well to combine. Bring mixture to a boil. Lower heat, cover, and simmer for 15 minutes. Remove slicer disc from food processor and insert the steel knife blade. Place soup in food processor bowl. Attach food chute cover and lock in place. Position food pusher in chute to prevent mixture from splashing out of bowl. Turn on processor and pulse 25 or 30 times. Pour blended part back into saucepan. Repeat process with remaining soup. Return saucepan to heat. Stir in evaporated milk, Splenda, and black pepper. Continue cooking for 5 minutes or until mixture is heated through, stirring often.

HINT: Soup will not be smooth. It should have some texture.

Each serving equals:

Mighty Filling Minestrone

This "kitchen-sink" soup that is one of Italy's most beloved dishes is also a favorite here in the Midwest. It's protein-rich and still vegetarian, because of those beans, and it's a great way to use up the contents of your vegetable bin. ☻ Serves 6 (1½ cups)

1 medium onion, peeled and cut into 6 wedges
3 sprigs parsley, stems removed
1 tablespoon olive oil
1 (14-ounce) can Swanson Lower Sodium Fat Free Beef
    Broth
3 cups water
1 (5-ounce) raw unpeeled potato, cut into 4 wedges
2 cups frozen cut green beans, thawed
3 medium tomatoes, peeled and each cut into 6 wedges
2 medium stalks celery, trimmed and each cut into 2-inch
    pieces
2 medium carrots, scraped and each cut into 2-inch pieces
1 (15-ounce) can red kidney beans, rinsed and drained
3 tablespoons reduced-sodium ketchup
2 teaspoons Italian seasoning
⅛ teaspoon black pepper
⅓ cup uncooked elbow macaroni

Lock food processor bowl in position. Insert the steel knife blade. Drop onion wedges and parsley sprigs into the food processor bowl. Attach food chute cover and lock in place. Turn on processor and pulse 3 or 4 times or until finely chopped. Transfer chopped vegetables to a large saucepan sprayed with olive oil–flavored cooking spray. Add olive oil. Mix well to combine. Cook over medium heat for 5 minutes, stirring occasionally. Stir in beef broth and water. Drop potato pieces into the food processor bowl. Attach food chute cover and lock in place. Turn on processor and pulse 3 or 4 times or until potatoes are coarsely chopped. Stir into soup mixture. Repeat process with green beans, then with tomatoes. Stir each into soup mixture. Remove steel knife blade from food processor and insert the slicer disc. Attach food chute cover and lock in place. Drop celery and carrots into the food chute. Position food pusher over vegetables. Turn on processor and use medium pressure to push vegetables through. Transfer sliced vegetables to soup mixture. Add kidney beans, ketchup, Italian seasoning, black pepper, and uncooked macaroni. Mix well to combine. Bring soup to a boil, stirring often. Lower heat and simmer for 45 to 50 minutes or until vegetables are tender, stirring occasionally.

Each serving equals:

HE: 2 Vegetable • ¾ Protein • ½ Bread • ½ Fat • 13 Optional Calories

171 Calories • 3 gm Fat • 7 gm Protein • 29 gm Carbohydrate • 143 mg Sodium • 52 mg Calcium • 7 gm Fiber

DIABETIC EXCHANGES: 2 Vegetable • 1 Starch • ½ Meat • ½ Fat

CARB CHOICES: 2

Deep-Sea Tuna Pasta Chowder

Now here's a soup that "eats like a meal," to quote a popular expression for those hearty stews and chowders that have so much in them, you could almost eat them with a fork instead of a spoon. I'm proud to offer this one to join the group.

○ Serves 4 (1¼ cups)

> 1 cup fresh whole mushrooms, each cut in half
> 1 small onion, peeled and cut into 4 wedges
> 1 medium carrot, scraped and cut into 2-inch pieces
> 1 tablespoon + 1 teaspoon I Can't Believe It's Not Butter!
>   Light Margarine
> 1 (10¾-ounce) can Healthy Request Cream of Mushroom
>   Soup
> 1 cup fat-free milk
> ½ cup Land O Lakes Fat Free Half & Half
> 2 sprigs parsley, stems removed
> 1 (6-ounce) can white tuna, packed in water, drained and
>   flaked
> 1 cup cooked tiny shell macaroni, rinsed and drained

Lock food processor bowl in position. Insert the slicer disc. Attach food chute cover and lock in place. Drop mushroom pieces into the food chute. Position food pusher over mushrooms. Turn on processor and use light pressure to push mushrooms through. Transfer sliced mushrooms to a medium saucepan sprayed with butter-flavored cooking spray. Remove slicer disc from the food processor and insert the shredder disc. Attach food chute cover and lock in place. Drop onion wedges and carrot pieces into the food chute. Position food pusher over vegetables. Turn on processor and use medium pressure to push vegetables through. Transfer shredded vegetables to saucepan with mushrooms. Stir in margarine. Sauté for 6 to 8 minutes, stirring constantly. Remove shredder disc from food processor and insert the steel knife blade. Place mushroom soup, milk, half & half, and parsley in food processor bowl. Re-cover and pulse 2 or 3 times or until smooth. Pour soup mixture into mushroom mixture. Add tuna and macaroni. Mix well to combine. Lower heat and simmer for 10 to 12 minutes or until vegetables are tender and mixture is heated through, stirring often.

HINT: Usually ⅔ cup uncooked shell macaroni cooks to about 1 cup.

Each serving equals:

HE: 1 Protein • ¾ Vegetable • ½ Bread • ½ Fat • ¼ Fat Free Milk • ¾ Slider • 1 Optional Calorie

201 Calories • 5 gm Fat • 14 gm Protein • 25 gm Carbohydrate • 519 mg Sodium • 200 mg Calcium • 1 gm Fiber

DIABETIC EXCHANGES: 1½ Meat • 1½ Starch/Carbohydrate • 1 Vegetable • ½ Fat

CARB CHOICES: 1½

Creamy Chicken-Vegetable Soup

If you've rarely used evaporated milk to make soups, it may surprise you to find that there is an amazingly good fat-free product that turns every dish prepared with it into a lusciously creamy sensation! Blended with a little Bisquick, it will thicken your soup into an impressive and satisfying meal. ☻ Serves 4 (1 cup)

> 8 ounces skinned and boned uncooked chicken breast, cut into bite-size pieces
> 1 (14-ounce) can Swanson Lower Sodium Fat Free Chicken Broth
> ⅛ teaspoon black pepper
> 1 small onion, peeled and cut into 4 wedges
> 1 medium carrot, scraped and cut into 2-inch pieces
> 2 medium stalks celery, trimmed and each cut into 2-inch pieces
> 1 (12-fluid-ounce) can Carnation Evaporated Fat Free Milk
> 3 tablespoons Bisquick Heart Smart Baking Mix

In a medium saucepan, combine chicken pieces, chicken broth, and black pepper. Cook over medium heat, stirring occasionally. Meanwhile, lock food processor bowl in position. Insert the steel knife blade. Drop onion, carrot pieces, and celery pieces into the food processor bowl. Attach food chute cover and lock in place. Turn on processor and pulse 3 or 4 times or until vegetables are finely chopped. Transfer chopped vegetables into saucepan with soup mixture. Bring mixture to a boil, stirring occasionally. Lower heat and simmer for 10 to 15 minutes or until chicken and vegetables are tender, stirring occasionally. In a covered jar, combine milk and baking mix. Shake well to blend. Pour milk mixture into soup mixture. Continue to simmer for 8 to 10 minutes or until mixture thickens, stirring often.

Each serving equals:

HE: 1½ Protein • ¾ Fat Free Milk • ¾ Vegetable • ¼ Bread •
16 Optional Calories

178 Calories • 2 gm Fat • 20 gm Protein • 20 gm Carbohydrate •
261 mg Sodium • 267 mg Calcium • 1 gm Fiber

DIABETIC EXCHANGES: 1½ Meat • 1 Fat Free Milk • 1 Vegetable

CARB CHOICES: 1

Midwest Chicken Gumbo

I've always loved the word "gumbo," even when I was a little girl growing up in an Iowa small town. Maybe it's because it sounded exotic and as if any dish with that name must contain tons of appealing ingredients. It's still a synonym for a glorious mélange of goodness!   ☻   Serves 4 (1½ cups)

> 2 medium stalks celery, trimmed and each cut into 2-inch pieces
> 1 small green bell pepper, stem and seeds removed and cut into 6 strips
> 1 small red bell pepper, stem and seeds removed and cut into 6 strips
> 1 small onion, peeled and cut into 4 wedges
> 1 medium tomato, peeled and cut into 6 wedges
> 2 sprigs parsley, stems removed
> 1 (14-ounce) can Swanson Lower Sodium Fat Free Chicken Broth
> 1 cup water
> 8 ounces cooked chicken breast, cut into strips
> 1 cup frozen cut green beans, thawed
> ½ cup frozen whole-kernel corn, thawed
> ⅛ teaspoon black pepper

Lock food processor bowl in position. Insert the steel knife blade. Drop celery pieces into the food processor bowl. Attach food chute cover and lock in place. Turn on processor and pulse 2 or 3 times or until celery is coarsely chopped. Transfer chopped celery to a medium saucepan. Repeat process with green pepper, red pepper, and onion; then with tomato wedges and parsley. Transfer chopped tomato to saucepan with other vegetables. Stir in chicken broth and water. Drop chicken strips into food processor bowl. Attach food chute cover and lock in place. Turn on processor and pulse 3 or 4 times or until chicken is coarsely chopped. Add chicken and green beans to soup mixture. Mix well to combine. Bring mixture to a boil, stirring occasionally. Stir in corn and black pepper. Lower heat, cover, and simmer for 15 minutes, stirring occasionally.

HINTS: 1. If you don't have leftovers, purchase a chunk of cooked chicken from your local deli. Chicken can be chopped by hand or in the food processor.

2. Thaw vegetables by rinsing in a colander under hot water for 1 minute.

Each serving equals:

HE: 1¾ Vegetable • 1½ Protein • ¼ Bread • 8 Optional Calories

122 Calories • 2 gm Fat • 14 gm Protein • 12 gm Carbohydrate • 228 mg Sodium • 43 mg Calcium • 3 gm Fiber

DIABETIC EXCHANGES: 2 Vegetable • 1½ Meat

CARB CHOICES: 1

Florentine Chicken Rice Soup

Students of culinary chitchat know that "Florentine" always means that a dish is prepared with spinach. This delightful soup calls for fresh leaves, not frozen, which makes all the difference in flavor, texture, and appearance.   ☻   Serves 4 (full 1 cup)

> 2 medium carrots, scraped and each cut into 2-inch pieces
> 1 medium onion, peeled and cut into 6 wedges
> 1 (14-ounce) can Swanson Lower Sodium Fat Free Chicken Broth
> ¼ cup water
> 1 cup diced cooked chicken breast
> 1 (10¾-ounce) can Healthy Request Cream of Chicken Soup
> ½ cup Land O Lakes Fat Free Half & Half
> ⅓ cup uncooked Minute Rice
> 1 teaspoon Italian seasoning
> 1 cup fresh spinach leaves, washed and stems removed and discarded
> ¼ cup Kraft Reduced Fat Parmesan Style Grated Topping

Lock food processor bowl in position. Insert the shredder disc. Attach food chute cover and lock in place. Drop carrot pieces and onion wedges into the food chute. Position food pusher over vegetables. Turn on processor and use medium pressure to push vegetables through. Transfer shredded vegetables to a medium saucepan. Stir in chicken broth, water, and chicken. Bring mixture to a boil. Add chicken soup, half & half, uncooked instant rice, and Italian seasoning. Mix well to combine. Lower heat and simmer for 5 minutes, stirring occasionally. Meanwhile, remove shredder disc from food processor and insert the steel knife blade. Place spinach leaves in food processor bowl. Re-cover and pulse 2 or 3 times or until leaves are coarsely chopped. Stir chopped spinach leaves into soup mixture. Continue simmering for 3 to 4 minutes, stirring occasionally. When serving, top each bowl with 1 tablespoon Parmesan cheese.

Each serving equals:

HE: 1¼ Protein • ¾ Vegetable • ¼ Bread • ¾ Slider • 7 Optional Calories

196 Calories • 4 gm Fat • 16 gm Protein • 24 gm Carbohydrate •
594 mg Sodium • 112 mg Calcium • 2 gm Fiber

DIABETIC EXCHANGES: 1½ Meat • 1 Vegetable • 1 Starch/Carbohydrate

CARB CHOICES: 1½

Pizza Pronto Soup

For all the pizza lovers at your house (or in your extended family of friends), this soup comes to the table fast, seducing anyone nearby with the scrumptious aroma of PIZZA! This dish is splendidly savory and thick with fantastic flavor. ☻ Serves 4 (1 cup)

> 1 medium onion, peeled and cut into 6 wedges
> 1 cup fresh whole mushrooms, each cut in half
> 8 ounces extra-lean ground sirloin beef or turkey breast
> 2 medium tomatoes, peeled and each cut into 6 wedges
> 1 (10¾-ounce) can Healthy Request Tomato Soup
> 1 cup water
> 1½ teaspoons pizza or Italian seasoning
> 4 slices reduced-calorie white bread, toasted and each cut
>   into 4 strips
> ¼ cup Kraft Reduced Fat Parmesan Style Grated Topping

Lock food processor bowl in position. Insert the steel knife blade. Drop onion wedges and mushroom pieces into the food processor bowl. Attach food chute cover and lock in place. Turn on processor and pulse 2 or 3 times or until coarsely chopped. Transfer vegetables to a large saucepan sprayed with olive oil–flavored cooking spray. Stir in meat. Brown mixture for 5 to 6 minutes. Meanwhile, drop tomato wedges into the food processor bowl. Attach food chute cover and lock in place. Turn on processor and pulse 3 or 4 times or until tomatoes are finely chopped. Stir chopped tomatoes into meat mixture. Add tomato soup, water, and pizza seasoning. Mix well to combine. Bring mixture to a boil. Lower heat and simmer for 10 minutes, stirring occasionally. Wipe food processor bowl and blade with a clean cloth. Drop in bread strips. Attach food chute cover and lock in place. Turn on processor and pulse 2 or 3 times or until bread is coarsely chopped. When serving, evenly spoon ¼ of the bread crumbs into soup bowl, spoon about 1 cup soup over bread crumbs, and sprinkle 1 tablespoon Parmesan cheese over top.

Each serving equals:

HE: 1¾ Protein • 1 Vegetable • ½ Bread • ½ Slider • 5 Optional Calories

209 Calories • 5 gm Fat • 14 gm Protein • 27 gm Carbohydrate •
698 mg Sodium • 79 mg Calcium • 3 gm Fiber

DIABETIC EXCHANGES: 2 Meat • 1 Vegetable • 1 Starch/Carbohydrate

CARB CHOICES: 2

Chunky Pea Soup with Bacon

We're so lucky to have delectable chicken broth available now in versions with less sodium than the traditional kind. It's downright easy to make homemade soups when you use it!

○ Serves 4 (1 cup)

1 small onion, peeled and cut into 4 wedges
2 medium stalks celery, trimmed and each cut into 2-inch pieces
1 medium carrot, scraped and cut into 2-inch pieces
1½ cups frozen peas, thawed

1 cup Land O Lakes Fat Free Half & Half
1 (14-ounce) can Swanson Lower Sodium Fat Free Chicken Broth
3 tablespoons all-purpose flour
¼ cup Oscar Mayer or Hormel Real Bacon Bits

Lock food processor bowl in position. Insert the steel knife blade. Drop onion wedges, celery pieces, and carrot pieces into the food processor bowl. Attach food chute cover and lock in place. Turn on processor and pulse 3 or 4 times or until vegetables are finely chopped. Transfer chopped vegetables to a medium saucepan sprayed with butter-flavored cooking spray. Sauté over medium heat for 10 minutes or just until vegetables are tender. Place peas, half & half, chicken broth, and flour in food processor bowl. Attach food chute cover and lock in place. Position food pusher in chute to prevent mixture from splashing out of bowl. Turn on processor and pulse 25 times or until mixture is well blended and smooth. Transfer mixture to saucepan with vegetables. Mix well to combine. Continue cooking for 6 to 8 minutes or until mixture is heated through, stirring often. When serving, top each bowl with 1 tablespoon bacon bits.

Each serving equals:

HE: 1 Bread • ¾ Vegetable • ½ Protein • ½ Slider • 3 Optional Calories

142 Calories • 2 gm Fat • 9 gm Protein • 22 gm Carbohydrate •
441 mg Sodium • 94 mg Calcium • 4 gm Fiber

DIABETIC EXCHANGES: 1 Starch • 1 Vegetable • ½ Meat

CARB CHOICES: 1½

Meat Lover's Veggie Chili

Some chili recipes require an iron pot and a campfire, while others rely on exotic ingredients like ostrich or hot peppers you've never heard of! Here's a yummy dish for the rest of us, who like our chili quick to the table and lip-smacking good!

○ Serves 6 (1 cup)

> 2 medium onions, peeled and each cut into 6 wedges
> 2 medium stalks celery, trimmed and each cut into 2-inch
>   pieces
> 1 medium carrot, scraped and cut into 2-inch pieces
> 16 ounces extra-lean ground sirloin beef or turkey breast
> 1 (10¾-ounce) can Healthy Request Tomato Soup
> 1 (15-ounce) can diced tomatoes, undrained
> ½ cup water
> 2 teaspoons chili seasoning

Lock food processor bowl in position. Insert the steel knife blade. Drop onions into the food processor bowl. Attach food chute cover and lock in place. Turn on processor and pulse 3 or 4 times or until onions are coarsely chopped. Transfer onions to a medium bowl. Repeat process with celery pieces and carrot pieces. In a large saucepan sprayed with butter-flavored cooking spray, brown meat and chopped vegetables for 10 minutes. Stir in tomato soup, undrained tomatoes, water, and chili seasoning. Lower heat and simmer for 30 minutes or until vegetables are tender, stirring occasionally.

Each serving equals:

HE: 2 Protein • 1½ Vegetable • ¼ Slider • 17 Optional Calories

164 Calories • 4 gm Fat • 16 gm Protein • 16 gm Carbohydrate • 370 mg Sodium • 26 mg Calcium • 2 gm Fiber

DIABETIC EXCHANGES: 2 Meat • 1½ Vegetable

CARB CHOICES: 1

San Antonio
Vegetable Beef Soup

It's the home of the Alamo and some of the tastiest food in Texas! San Antonio spells spicy satisfaction for fans of Tex-Mex cooking, so I decided to honor that tradition with this original and aromatic veggie soup that has plenty of beef, too.

○ Serves 4 (1½ cups)

> 1 medium unpeeled zucchini, cut in half lengthwise and
>   crosswise
> 1 medium onion, peeled and cut into 6 wedges
> 2 medium carrots, scraped and each cut into 2-inch pieces
> 2 medium stalks celery, trimmed and each cut into 2-inch
>   pieces
> 1 small green bell pepper, stem and seeds removed and cut
>   into 6 strips
> 1 small red bell pepper, stem and seeds removed and cut into
>   6 strips
> 8 ounces extra-lean ground sirloin beef or turkey breast
> 1 (15-ounce) can diced tomatoes, undrained
> 1 (14-ounce) can Swanson Lower Sodium Fat Free Beef
>   Broth
> 1 teaspoon chili seasoning mix
> 1 tablespoon Splenda Granular
> ⅛ teaspoon black pepper
> 1 cup frozen whole-kernel corn, thawed
> 4 sprigs parsley, stems removed

Lock food processor bowl in position. Insert the shredder disc. Attach food chute cover and lock in place. Drop zucchini pieces into the food chute. Position food pusher over vegetables. Turn on processor and use medium pressure to push zucchini through. Transfer shredded zucchini to a large bowl. Repeat process with onion, carrots, celery, and bell peppers. In a large saucepan sprayed with butter-flavored cooking spray, brown meat for 6 to 8 minutes. Stir in undrained tomatoes, beef broth, chili seasoning, Splenda, and black pepper. Add shredded vegetables and corn. Mix well to combine. Meanwhile, remove shredder disc from food processor and insert the steel knife blade. Drop parsley into the food processor bowl. Attach food chute cover and lock in place. Turn on processor and pulse 2 or 3 times or until parsley is finely chopped. Stir parsley into soup. Bring soup to a boil, stirring often. Lower heat and simmer for 30 to 35 minutes or just until vegetables are tender.

HINTS: 1. This is a thick, hearty soup.
2. Those who like spicier foods, add another ½ teaspoon to 1 teaspoon chili seasoning.

Each serving equals:

HE: 2½ Vegetable • 1½ Protein • ½ Bread • 8 Optional Calories

175 Calories • 3 gm Fat • 15 gm Protein • 22 gm Carbohydrate • 383 mg Sodium • 52 mg Calcium • 5 gm Fiber

DIABETIC EXCHANGES: 2½ Vegetable • 1½ Meat • ½ Starch

CARB CHOICES: 1½

Speedy Hamburger Soup

If you're a busy stay-at-home mom or stressed-out student, you know that sometimes a recipe's greatest appeal is how fast you can yell, "Dinner's ready!" This one is meaty and quick, comfort food in a bowl that truly satisfies.   ☻   Serves 4 (1½ cups)

1 medium onion, peeled and cut into 6 wedges
8 ounces extra-lean ground sirloin beef or turkey breast
3 medium carrots, scraped and each cut into 2-inch pieces
4 medium stalks celery, trimmed and each cut into 2-inch pieces

1 (5-ounce) raw, unpeeled potato, cut into 4 wedges
1 (14-ounce) can Swanson Lower Sodium Fat Free Beef Broth
½ teaspoon Worcestershire sauce
3 tablespoons all-purpose flour
2 sprigs parsley, stems removed

Lock food processor bowl in position. Insert the steel knife blade. Drop onion wedges into the food processor bowl. Attach food chute cover and lock in place. Turn on processor and pulse 2 or 3 times or until onion is coarsely chopped. Transfer onion to a medium saucepan sprayed with butter-flavored cooking spray. Stir in meat. Brown for 5 minutes. Meanwhile, drop carrots through the food chute and pulse 2 or 3 times or until coarsely chopped. Stir chopped carrots into meat mixture. Repeat process with celery pieces and potato wedges. Remove cover. Place beef broth, Worcestershire sauce, flour, and parsley in food processor bowl. Re-cover and pulse 3 or 4 times or until mixture is smooth. Add broth mixture to meat mixture. Mix well to combine. Lower heat, cover, and simmer for 25 to 30 minutes or until vegetables are tender, stirring occasionally.

Each serving equals:

HE: 1½ Protein • 1½ Vegetable • ½ Bread • 8 Optional Calories

159 Calories • 3 gm Fat • 14 gm Protein • 19 gm Carbohydrate •
255 mg Sodium • 45 mg Calcium • 3 gm Fiber

DIABETIC EXCHANGES: 1½ Meat • 1½ Vegetable • 1 Starch

CARB CHOICES: 1

Superlative

Salads

Chop, chop, chop to your heart's delight—and good health! Salad-making has never been simpler or more fun than when you enlist your food processor in the process. Just read the tips up front carefully so you know how to get the best results from your machine for each different ingredient, and remember that some items need a lighter touch than others so they keep their shape and their crunch.

So many salads, so little time—well, not really, as you can choose to enjoy a different salad every day for quite some time when you dig deep into this chapter. Depending on the season, the occasion, and your mood, you might find yourself longing for the crisp pleasures of *Cauliflower Broccoli Raisin Salad.* Or you might be intrigued by my *Ranch Mushroom Salad* as a starter some summer evening. When planning a spicy night, put *Grande Gazpacho Pasta Salad* on the menu—and if you're in the mood for a fruity salad, try *Carrot Raisin Nut Toss* or *Walnut Waldorf Salad.*

King Coleslaw

The nursery rhyme tells us that the King was a "merry old soul" and I think I know why: He dined regularly on this dish of coleslaw royalty! ● Serves 6 (full ¾ cup)

    1 medium carrot, scraped and cut into 2-inch pieces
    2 medium stalks celery, trimmed and each cut into 2-inch
        pieces
    1 small onion, peeled and cut into 4 wedges
    4 red radishes, trimmed and each cut in half
    ½ small head cabbage, cut into 6 wedges
    ½ cup Kraft fat-free mayonnaise
    2 tablespoons white distilled vinegar
    2 tablespoons Splenda Granular
    ⅛ teaspoon black pepper

Lock food processor bowl in position. Insert the steel knife blade. Drop carrots, celery, onion, and radishes into the food processor bowl. Attach food chute cover and lock in place. Turn on processor and pulse 3 or 4 times or until vegetables are chopped. Transfer chopped vegetables to a large bowl. Remove steel knife blade from food processor and insert the slicer disc. Attach food chute cover and lock in place. Drop cabbage into the food chute. Position food pusher over cabbage. Turn on processor and use medium pressure to push cabbage through. Transfer sliced cabbage to vegetables in large bowl. Mix well to combine. Stir in mayonnaise, vinegar, Splenda, and black pepper. Cover and refrigerate for at least 30 minutes. Gently stir again just before serving.

Each serving equals:

HE: 1 Vegetable • 15 Optional Calories

---

40 Calories • 0 gm Fat • 1 gm Protein • 9 gm Carbohydrate •
191 mg Sodium • 42 mg Calcium • 2 gm Fiber

DIABETIC EXCHANGES: 1 Vegetable

CARB CHOICES: ½

Creamy Cucumber Salad

What a wonderful contrast this dish displays, between the silky, velvety sauce and the juicy crunch of the cucumbers! If summer has a taste of the garden, it's in this fresh blend.

◐ Serves 4 (½ cup)

> 2 medium unpeeled cucumbers, each cut in half lengthwise
>   and crosswise
> 1 small red bell pepper, stem and seeds removed and cut into
>   4 pieces
> ½ cup Kraft fat-free mayonnaise
> 1 tablespoon white distilled vinegar
> 1 tablespoon Splenda Granular

Lock food processor bowl in position. Insert the slicer disc. Attach food chute cover and lock in place. Drop cucumbers and red pepper into the food chute. Position food pusher over vegetables. Turn on processor and use light pressure to push vegetables through. Transfer sliced vegetables to a large bowl. Add mayonnaise, vinegar, and Splenda. Mix well to combine. Cover and refrigerate for at least 30 minutes. Mix well again just before serving.

Each serving equals:

HE: 1 Vegetable • ¼ Slider • 1 Optional Calorie

41 Calories • 1 gm Fat • 1 gm Protein • 7 gm Carbohydrate •
242 mg Sodium • 14 mg Calcium • 2 gm Fiber

DIABETIC EXCHANGES: 1 Vegetable

CARB CHOICES: ½

Country Cucumber Salad

How best to celebrate a bountiful harvest in your veggie garden? This is one of my happiest ideas, in which a piquant dressing "marries" the clean, bright flavors of a succulent summer vegetable.

♥ Serves 6 (¾ cup)

3 medium unpeeled cucumbers, each cut in half lengthwise and crosswise
1 medium onion, peeled and cut into 6 wedges
½ cup Kraft fat-free mayonnaise
2 tablespoons Grey Poupon Country Style Dijon Mustard
2 tablespoons Land O Lakes no-fat sour cream
2 sprigs parsley, stems removed
1 tablespoon Splenda Granular
⅛ teaspoon black pepper

Lock food processor bowl in position. Insert the slicer disc. Attach food chute cover and lock in place. Drop cucumber pieces into the food chute. Position food pusher over cucumber. Turn on processor and use light pressure to push cucumber through. Transfer sliced cucumber to a large bowl when full level is reached. Repeat process as necessary. Drop onion through food chute using medium pressure to push onion through. Transfer sliced onion to bowl with sliced cucumber. Remove slicer disc from food processor and insert the steel knife blade. Place mayonnaise, mustard, sour cream, parsley, Splenda, and black pepper into the food processor bowl. Attach food chute cover and lock in place. Position food pusher in chute to prevent ingredients from splashing out of bowl. Turn on processor and pulse 2 or 3 times or until mixture is smooth. Add dressing mixture to cucumber mixture. Mix gently just to combine. Cover and refrigerate for at least 30 minutes. Gently stir again just before serving.

Each serving equals:

HE: 1½ Vegetable • 19 Optional Calories

60 Calories • 0 gm Fat • 3 gm Protein • 12 gm Carbohydrate • 287 mg Sodium • 45 mg Calcium • 2 gm Fiber

DIABETIC EXCHANGES: 1½ Vegetable

CARB CHOICES: 1

Chilled Cauliflower and Green Bean Salad

Bright colors and appealing flavors make this crisp salad an inviting new tradition when you're serving supper on the patio!

◑ Serves 4 (1 cup)

½ small head cauliflower, broken into large pieces
1½ cups frozen cut green beans, thawed
2 cups water
1 small red onion, peeled and cut into 4 wedges

2 sprigs parsley, stems removed
½ cup Kraft Fat Free Italian Dressing
¼ cup Kraft fat-free mayonnaise
2 teaspoons Splenda Granular

In a large saucepan, combine cauliflower, green beans, and water. Cook over medium heat for 10 minutes or until vegetables are just tender. Drain and rinse under cold water for 1 minute. Separate cauliflower pieces into flowerettes that will fit into the food chute of food processor. Lock food processor bowl in position. Insert the slicer disc. Attach food chute cover and lock in place. Drop cauliflower into the food chute. Position food pusher over cauliflower. Turn on processor and use light pressure to push cauliflower through. Transfer sliced cauliflower to a large bowl. Stir in green beans. Remove slicer disc from food processor and insert the steel knife blade. Drop onion wedges and parsley into the food processor bowl. Attach food chute cover and lock in place. Turn on processor and pulse 2 or 3 times or until finely chopped. Stir onion mixture into cauliflower mixture. Add Italian dressing, mayonnaise, and Splenda. Mix well to combine. Cover and refrigerate for at least 30 minutes. Mix gently just before serving.

Each serving equals:

HE: 1½ Vegetable • ¼ Slider • 1 Optional Calorie

56 Calories • 0 gm Fat • 2 gm Protein • 12 gm Carbohydrate •
422 mg Sodium • 31 mg Calcium • 3 gm Fiber

DIABETIC EXCHANGES: 1½ Vegetable

CARB CHOICES: 1

Cauliflower Broccoli Raisin Salad

Cheers for the cruciferous vegetables, say lots of recent research studies. What does it all mean? Just that broccoli and cauliflower are G-O-O-D for you, especially when served crunchy and raw.

◐ Serves 6 (½ cup)

½ small head cauliflower, broken into flowerettes
½ small head broccoli, cut into flowerettes
1 small onion, peeled and cut into 4 wedges
½ cup seedless raisins
¼ cup Oscar Mayer or Hormel Real Bacon Bits
½ cup Kraft fat-free mayonnaise
2 tablespoons Splenda Granular
2 tablespoons white distilled vinegar

Lock food processor bowl in position. Insert the steel knife blade. Drop cauliflower flowerettes into the food processor bowl. Attach food chute cover and lock in place. Turn on processor and pulse 2 or 3 times or until cauliflower is coarsely chopped. Transfer chopped cauliflower to a medium bowl. Repeat process with broccoli and onion. Stir raisins and bacon bits into vegetable mixture. Add mayonnaise, Splenda, and vinegar. Mix well to combine. Cover and refrigerate for at least 15 minutes. Gently stir again just before serving.

Each serving equals:

HE: 1 Vegetable • ⅔ Fruit • ¼ Protein • 17 Optional Calories

85 Calories • 1 gm Fat • 3 gm Protein • 16 gm Carbohydrate • 286 mg Sodium • 24 mg Calcium • 2 gm Fiber

DIABETIC EXHANGES: 1 Vegetable • 1 Fruit

CARB CHOICES: 1

Ranch Mushroom Salad

On a day when you've visited the farmers' market and come home with one of those long baskets of fresh white mushrooms, you might just want to turn that breathtaking bounty into a dish fit for a queen!   ❍   Serves 6 (full ½ cup)

3 cups fresh whole mushrooms,
    each cut in half
1 medium carrot, scraped and
    cut into 2-inch pieces
1 small onion, peeled and cut
    into 4 wedges

½ cup Kraft Fat Free Ranch
    Dressing
2 tablespoons Land O Lakes
    no-fat sour cream
2 sprigs parsley, stems removed
2 teaspoons Splenda Granular

Lock food processor bowl in position. Insert the slicer disc. Attach food chute cover and lock in place. Drop mushrooms into the food chute. Position food pusher over mushrooms. Turn on processor and use light pressure to push mushrooms through. Transfer sliced mushrooms to a medium bowl. Remove slicer disc from food processor and insert the shredder disc. Attach food chute cover and lock in place. Drop carrot pieces and onion into the food chute. Position food pusher over vegetables. Turn on processor and use medium pressure to push vegetables through. Transfer sliced vegetables to bowl with mushrooms. Remove shredder disc from food processor and insert the steel knife blade. Place Ranch dressing, sour cream, parsley, and Splenda in food processor bowl. Attach food chute cover and lock in place. Position food pusher in chute to prevent ingredients from splashing out of bowl. Turn on processor and pulse 3 or 4 times or just until mixture is combined. Add dressing mixture to mushroom mixture. Mix gently just to combine. Cover and refrigerate for at least 15 minutes. Gently stir again just before serving.

Each serving equals:

HE: 1 Vegetable • ¼ Slider • 18 Optional Calories

56 Calories • 0 gm Fat • 2 gm Protein • 12 gm Carbohydrate •
251 mg Sodium • 20 mg Calcium • 1 gm Fiber

DIABETIC EXCHANGES: 1 Vegetable • ½ Other Carbohydrate

CARB CHOICES: 1

Tomato Mushroom Salad

Even if you have a small patch of grassy land, you can still grow a few tomato plants—but producing much of a harvest takes luck and time. So most people buy their luscious, ripe tomatoes at the market, which provides us with year-round delights.

◐ Serves 6 (⅔ cup)

6 large fresh whole mushrooms, each cut in half
4 medium tomatoes, each cut into 4 wedges
2 tablespoons olive oil
1 tablespoon Splenda Granular
1 tablespoon lemon juice
1½ teaspoons dried basil
¼ teaspoon black pepper

Lock food processor bowl in position. Insert the slicer disc. Attach food chute cover and lock in place. Drop mushrooms and tomatoes into the food chute. Position food pusher over vegetables. Turn on processor and use light pressure to push vegetables through. Transfer sliced vegetables to a large bowl. Add olive oil, Splenda, lemon juice, basil, and black pepper. Toss gently to combine. Cover and refrigerate for at least 1 hour. Gently stir again just before serving.

Each serving equals:

HE: 1 Fat • 1 Vegetable • 1 Optional Calorie

65 Calories • 5 gm Fat • 1 gm Protein • 4 gm Carbohydrate •
4 mg Sodium • 14 mg Calcium • 1 gm Fiber

DIABETIC EXCHANGES: 1 Fat • 1 Vegetable

CARB CHOICES: 0

Marinated Bean Salad

What's great about a three-bean salad like this one? Well, you can make it in advance and let the flavors soak in. And, it's colorful and a little crunchy as well as "beany." Your guests will enjoy it, your family will love it, and you won't be fussing in the kitchen during a party.   ☯   Serves 8 (¾ cup)

1 medium red onion, peeled and cut into 6 wedges
1 medium green bell pepper, stem and seeds removed
    and cut into 6 strips
1 medium red bell pepper, stem and seeds removed
    and cut into 6 strips
1 (15-ounce) can cut green beans, rinsed and
    drained
1 (15-ounce) can green lima beans, rinsed and
    drained
1 (15-ounce) can red kidney beans, rinsed and
    drained
¼ cup apple cider vinegar
2 tablespoons Kraft Fat Free French Dressing
2 tablespoons vegetable oil
2 tablespoons Splenda Granular
1 teaspoon prepared yellow mustard

Lock food processor bowl in position. Insert the slicer disc. Attach food chute cover and lock in place. Drop onion, green pepper, and red pepper into the food chute. Position food pusher over vegetables. Turn on processor and use medium pressure to push vegetables through. Transfer sliced vegetables to a large bowl when full level is reached. Repeat process as necessary. Add green beans, lima beans, and red kidney beans to vegetable mixture. Mix well to combine. In a small bowl, combine vinegar, French dressing, vegetable oil, Splenda, and mustard using a wire whisk. Pour mixture evenly over vegetables. Mix well to combine. Cover and refrigerate for at least 2 hours. Gently stir again just before serving.

Each serving equals:

HE: 1 Vegetable • ¾ Fat • ½ Bread • ½ Protein • 7 Optional Calories

136 Calories • 4 gm Fat • 5 gm Protein • 20 gm Carbohydrate •
148 mg Sodium • 22 mg Calcium • 6 gm Fiber

DIABETIC EXCHANGES: 1 Vegetable • 1 Fat • 1 Starch • ½ Meat

CARB CHOICES: 1

Tangy Copper Pennies Salad

I bet it was a child who first noticed that sliced carrots bear an astonishing resemblance (well, sort of) to shiny copper pennies delivered straight from the mint! This dish is vividly colored, and it's got a fresh, tangy flavor that is hard to forget.

○ Serves 8 (½ cup)

> 8 medium carrots, scraped and each cut into 2-inch pieces
> 1½ cups hot water
> 1 medium green bell pepper, stem and seeds removed and
>   cut into 8 strips
> 1 medium onion, peeled and cut into 6 wedges
> 1 (10¾-ounce) can Healthy Request Tomato Soup
> ¼ cup apple cider vinegar
> 2 tablespoons + 2 teaspoons vegetable oil
> ½ cup Splenda Granular
> 1½ teaspoons Worcestershire sauce
> 1 teaspoon prepared yellow mustard
> ¼ teaspoon black pepper

Lock food processor bowl in position. Insert the slicer disc. Attach food chute cover and lock in place. Drop carrots into the food chute. Position food pusher over carrots. Turn on processor and use medium pressure to push carrots through. Transfer sliced carrots to a medium saucepan when full level is reached. Repeat process as necessary. Pour hot water over carrots and cook over medium heat for 6 to 8 minutes or just until tender. Drain well. Meanwhile, remove slicer disc from food processor and insert the shredder disc. Attach food chute cover and lock in place. Drop green pepper and onion into the food chute. Position food pusher over vegetables. Turn on processor and use medium pressure to push vegetables through. Transfer shredded vegetables to a large bowl. Add tomato soup, vinegar, vegetable oil, Splenda, Worcestershire sauce, mustard, and black pepper. Mix well to combine. Stir in drained carrots. Cover and refrigerate for at least 2 hours. Gently stir again just before serving.

Each serving equals:

HE: 1½ Vegetable • 1 Fat • ¼ Slider • 13 Optional Calories

109 Calories • 5 gm Fat • 1 gm Protein • 15 gm Carbohydrate •
203 mg Sodium • 29 mg Calcium • 3 gm Fiber

DIABETIC EXCHANGES: 1½ Vegetable • 1 Fat • ½ Other Carbohydrate

CARB CHOICES: 1

Spicy Garden Salad

Tired of the same old, same old, when it comes to salad? Many dressings are smooth and creamy but also somewhat bland, so I decided to light a little fire to pour over this crunchy combo. If you enjoy life on the wild side, this is for you.

● Serves 6 (⅔ cup)

1 medium cucumber, cut in half lengthwise and crosswise
1 small onion, peeled and cut into 4 wedges
1 medium green pepper, stem and seeds removed and cut into 6 strips
2 medium stalks celery, trimmed and each cut into 2-inch pieces

2 medium tomatoes, each cut into 4 wedges
3 tablespoons white distilled vinegar
1 tablespoon vegetable oil
1 tablespoon Splenda Granular
½ teaspoon chili seasoning
2 or 3 drops hot pepper sauce

Lock food processor bowl in position. Insert the slicer disc. Attach food chute cover and lock in place. Drop cucumber and onion into the food chute. Position food pusher over vegetables. Turn on processor and use medium pressure to push vegetables through. Transfer sliced vegetables to a large bowl. Repeat process with green pepper, celery, and tomatoes. In a small bowl, combine vinegar, vegetable oil, Splenda, chili seasoning, and hot pepper sauce. Drizzle mixture evenly over vegetables. Toss gently just to combine. Cover and refrigerate for at least 15 minutes. Gently stir again just before serving.

HINT: If necessary, drain vegetables before serving.

Each serving equals:

HE: 1½ Vegetable • ½ Fat • 1 Optional Calorie

46 Calories • 2 gm Fat • 1 gm Protein • 6 gm Carbohydrate •
26 mg Sodium • 24 mg Calcium • 2 gm Fiber

DIABETIC EXCHANGES: 1½ Vegetable • ½ Fat

CARB CHOICES: ½

Savory Potato Salad

Are you one of the "Tater Team" who could eat potato salad every day if it was offered? I've met plenty of you in my travels, and I keep you in mind when it's time to create a new potato salad or two for my new books. This one is a bit vinegar-y and crunchy but oh-so-good! ☻ Serves 4 (1 cup)

3 (5-ounce) cooked unpeeled potatoes, and each cut into 4 wedges
2 medium stalks celery, trimmed and each cut into 2-inch pieces
1 small onion, peeled and cut into 4 wedges
½ cup Kraft fat-free mayonnaise
1 tablespoon white distilled vinegar
2 tablespoons Splenda Granular
2 sprigs parsley, stems removed
1 hard-boiled egg, cut into 4 pieces

Lock food processor bowl in position. Insert the slicer disc. Attach food chute cover and lock in place. Drop potatoes into the food chute. Position food pusher over potatoes. Turn on processor and use medium pressure to push potatoes through. Transfer sliced potatoes to a medium bowl. Repeat process with celery and onion. Remove food chute cover. Remove slicer disc and insert steel knife blade. Place mayonnaise, vinegar, Splenda, parsley, and egg pieces into food processor bowl. Re-cover and pulse 3 or 4 times or until mixture is blended. Add dressing mixture to potato mixture. Mix gently just to combine. Cover and refrigerate for at least 15 minutes. Gently stir again just before serving.

Each serving equals:

HE: ¾ Bread • ½ Vegetable • ¼ Protein • ¼ Slider • 3 Optional Calories

134 Calories • 2 gm Fat • 4 gm Protein • 25 gm Carbohydrate •
490 mg Sodium • 25 mg Calcium • 3 gm Fiber

DIABETIC EXCHANGES: 1½ Starch/Carbohydrate • ½ Vegetable

CARB CHOICES: 1½

Crunchy Tomato Aspic

Am I the only 21st-century recipe creator working to keep this glorious 1950s culinary tradition alive? Not exactly, but I think you'll agree that not many books still feature recipes for aspic, the savory gelled salad that looks so pretty on the plate. Here's one I think you'll love—even if you've never tried it before.

○ Serves 8

> 1 (4-serving) package Jell-O sugar-free lemon gelatin
> ¾ cup boiling water
> 1 cup reduced-sodium tomato juice
> 1 tablespoon Splenda Granular
> 1 medium stalk celery, trimmed and cut into 2-inch pieces
> 1 small onion, peeled and cut into 4 wedges
> 1 small green bell pepper, stem and seeds removed and cut
>   into 4 strips
> 1 small unpeeled cucumber, cut into 2-inch pieces

In a large bowl, combine dry gelatin and boiling water. Mix well to dissolve gelatin. Stir in tomato juice and Splenda. Lock food processor bowl in position. Insert the steel knife blade. Drop celery, onion, and green pepper into the food processor bowl. Attach food chute cover and lock in place. Turn on processor and pulse 3 or 4 times or until vegetables are coarsely chopped. Stir chopped vegetables into gelatin mixture. Repeat process with cucumber. Pour mixture into an 8-by-8-inch dish and refrigerate until firm, about 3 hours. Divide into 8 servings.

Each serving equals:

HE: ¾ Vegetable • 5 Optional Calories

20 Calories • 0 gm Fat • 2 gm Protein • 3 gm Carbohydrate •
49 mg Sodium • 12 mg Calcium • 1 gm Fiber

DIABETIC EXCHANGES: Free Food

CARB CHOICES: 0

Jelled Vegetable Salad

I remember hearing a little girl call a dish like this "see-through food"! Good for her, I thought, because it truly is. You can see all the good stuff you're going to be munching on, enrobed in a pale-colored gelatin that gives it a bright flavor.　　❤　Serves 8

2 (4-serving) packages
    Jell-O sugar-free lemon
    gelatin
1½ cups boiling water
1½ cups cold water
1 medium carrot, scraped and
    cut into 2-inch pieces
2 medium stalks celery,
    trimmed and each cut
    into 2-inch pieces

1 small green bell pepper, stem
    and seeds removed and
    cut into 6 strips
1 small onion, peeled and cut
    into 4 wedges
½ small head cabbage, cut into
    4 wedges
6 lettuce leaves
6 tablespoons Kraft fat-free
    mayonnaise

In a large bowl, combine dry gelatin and boiling water. Mix well to dissolve gelatin. Stir in cold water. Lock food processor bowl in position. Insert the steel knife blade. Drop carrots, celery, green pepper, and onion into the food processor bowl. Attach food chute cover and lock in place. Turn on processor and pulse 3 or 4 times or until vegetables are finely chopped. Stir chopped vegetables into gelatin mixture. Drop cabbage into the food processor bowl. Attach food chute cover and lock in place. Turn on processor and pulse 3 or 4 times or until cabbage is finely chopped. Stir cabbage into gelatin mixture. Pour mixture into an 8-by-8-inch dish. Refrigerate until firm, about 3 hours. Cut into 6 servings. When serving, place each piece on a lettuce leaf and top with 1 tablespoon mayonnaise.

Each serving equals:

HE: ¾ Vegetable • 10 Optional Calories

36 Calories • 0 gm Fat • 2 gm Protein • 7 gm Carbohydrate • 167 mg Sodium • 33 mg Calcium • 2 gm Fiber

DIABETIC EXCHANGES: 1 Vegetable

CARB CHOICES: ½

Walnut Waldorf Salad

This is one of those recipes that "begs" for a food processor—all that chopping of nuts, apples, and celery made oh-so-easy with your handy machine! ☯ Serves 6 (1 cup)

> ¼ cup walnuts
> 2 medium stalks celery, trimmed and each cut into 2-inch
>   pieces
> 4 medium unpeeled Red Delicious apples, cored and each cut
>   into 4 pieces
> ¼ cup seedless raisins
> ⅓ cup Kraft fat-free mayonnaise
> 1 tablespoon lemon juice
> 1 tablespoon Splenda Granular

Lock food processor bowl in position. Insert the slicer disc. Attach food chute cover and lock in place. Drop walnuts and celery into the food chute. Position food pusher over walnuts and celery. Turn on processor and use medium pressure to push walnuts and celery through. Transfer mixture to a large bowl. Repeat process for apples. Stir apples into nut mixture. Add raisins, mayonnaise, lemon juice, and Splenda. Mix well to combine. Cover and refrigerate for at least 15 minutes. Gently stir again just before serving.

HINT: To plump up raisins without "cooking," place in a glass measuring cup and microwave on HIGH for 20 seconds.

Each serving equals:

HE: 1 Fruit • ⅓ Fat • ¼ Vegetable • ¼ Slider • 1 Optional Calorie

111 Calories • 3 gm Fat • 1 gm Protein • 20 gm Carbohydrate • 118 mg Sodium • 20 mg Calcium • 3 gm Fiber

DIABETIC EXCHANGES: 1 Fruit • ½ Fat

CARB CHOICES: 1

Carrot Raisin Nut Toss

When I first typed the name of this recipe, I thought, "That sounds like some new kids' game, where you aim clumps of carrots, raisins, and nuts at a target!" See, making up names for recipes can make you think silly thoughts—but whatever you call this, it's a winner.   ☻   Serves 4 (½ cup)

4 large carrots, scraped and each cut into 2-inch pieces
¼ cup walnuts
¼ cup seedless raisins
½ cup Kraft fat-free mayonnaise
1 tablespoon lemon juice
1 tablespoon Splenda Granular

Lock food processor bowl in position. Insert the shredder disc. Attach food chute cover and lock in place. Drop carrots into food chute. Position food pusher over vegetables. Turn on processor and use medium pressure to push carrots through. Transfer shredded carrots to a large bowl. Remove shredder disc from food processor and insert the steel knife blade. Drop walnuts into the food processor bowl. Attach the food chute cover and lock in place. Position food pusher over walnuts. Turn on processor and pulse 6 or 8 times or until walnuts are coarsely chopped. Transfer walnuts to bowl with carrots. Stir in raisins. Add mayonnaise, lemon juice, and Splenda. Mix well to combine. Cover and refrigerate for at least 30 minutes. Gently stir again just before serving.

HINT: To plump up raisins without "cooking," place in a glass measuring cup and microwave on HIGH for 20 seconds.

Each serving equals:

HE: 1 Vegetable • ½ Fruit • ½ Fat • ¼ Protein • ¼ Slider • 1 Optional Calorie

129 Calories • 5 gm Fat • 2 gm Protein • 19 gm Carbohydrate • 299 mg Sodium • 30 mg Calcium • 2 gm Fiber

DIABETIC EXCHANGES: 1 Vegetable • 1 Fat • ½ Fruit • ½ Other Carbohydrate

CARB CHOICES: 1

Carrot Orange Jelled Salad

I know, I know, carrots and orange gelatin seem like perfect part-ners, but why stop at two ideal ingredients when you can create a more dazzling dish with a few others? "Orange" you glad I kept adding more sweet things to the mix?   ☻   Serves 6

1 (4-serving) package Jell-O sugar-free orange gelatin
1 cup boiling water
½ cup Diet Mountain Dew
1 (8-ounce) can crushed pineapple, packed in fruit juice,
*   undrained*
1 (11-ounce) can mandarin oranges, rinsed and drained
2 medium carrots, scraped and each cut into 2-inch pieces

In a large bowl, combine dry gelatin and boiling water. Mix well to dissolve gelatin. Stir in Diet Mountain Dew. Add undrained pineapple and mandarin oranges. Mix well to combine. Lock food processor bowl in position. Insert the shredder disc. Attach food chute cover and lock in place. Drop carrots into the food chute. Position food pusher over carrots. Turn on processor and use medium pressure to push carrots through. Stir shredded carrots into gelatin mixture. Evenly spread into an 8-by-8-inch dish. Refrigerate until firm, about 3 hours. Cut into 6 servings.

Each serving equals:

HE: ⅔ Fruit • ½ Vegetable • 6 Optional Calories

52 Calories • 0 gm Fat • 2 gm Protein • 11 gm Carbohydrate •
60 mg Sodium • 15 mg Calcium • 1 gm Fiber

DIABETIC EXCHANGES: 1 Fruit

CARB CHOICES: 1

Fruited Lemon Salad

There's just something glorious about sunshine-colored gelatin surrounding perfect strawberries and beautiful banana slices. I'd serve this at a card party or graduation luncheon with pride.

◑ Serves 6

> 2 (4-serving) packages Jell-O sugar-free lemon gelatin
> 2 cups boiling water
> 1 cup Diet Mountain Dew
> 2 cups fresh whole strawberries
> 2 medium bananas, each cut into 2-inch pieces

In a large bowl, combine dry gelatin and boiling water. Mix well to dissolve gelatin. Stir in Diet Mountain Dew. Refrigerate for 15 minutes. Lock food processor bowl in position. Insert the slicer disc. Attach food chute cover and lock in place. Drop strawberries into the food chute. Position food pusher over strawberries. Turn on processor and use light pressure to push strawberries through. Stir sliced strawberries into gelatin mixture. Repeat process with bananas. Mix well to combine. Pour mixture into an 8-by-8-inch dish. Refrigerate until firm, about 3 hours. Cut into 6 servings.

Each serving equals:

HE: 1 Fruit • 13 Optional Calories

60 Calories • 0 gm Fat • 2 gm Protein • 13 gm Carbohydrate •
78 mg Sodium • 9 mg Calcium • 2 gm Fiber

DIABETIC EXCHANGES: 1 Fruit

CARB CHOICES: 1

Creamy Mandarin Salad

Even if you've never "met" a raw mandarin orange, most of us have enjoyed those tiny canned orange sections since we were little children. I've rarely met an adult who doesn't still gobble those little citrusy slices with a smile, so why not "regress" to your childhood with a serving of this?   ❂   Serves 6

> 1 (4-serving) package Jell-O sugar-free orange gelatin
> 1 cup boiling water
> ¾ cup Diet Mountain Dew
> ¾ cup Land O Lakes no-fat sour cream
> ¼ cup flaked coconut
> 3 tablespoons pecans
> 1 medium banana, cut into 2-inch pieces
> 1 (11-ounce) can mandarin oranges, rinsed and drained

In a large bowl, combine dry gelatin and boiling water. Mix well to dissolve gelatin. Stir in Diet Mountain Dew. Refrigerate for 15 minutes. Add sour cream and coconut. Mix gently just to combine. Lock food processor bowl in position. Insert the steel knife blade. Drop pecans into the food processor bowl. Attach food chute and lock in place. Turn on processor and pulse 2 or 3 times or until pecans are coarsely chopped. Stir pecans into gelatin mixture. Remove steel knife blade from food processor and insert the slicer disc. Attach food chute cover and lock in place. Drop banana into the food chute. Position food pusher over banana. Turn on processor and use light pressure to push banana through. Pulse 2 or 3 times. Add banana slices and mandarin oranges to gelatin mixture. Mix gently just to combine. Spoon mixture into an 8-by-8-inch dish. Refrigerate until firm, about 3 hours. Cut into 6 servings.

Each serving equals:

HE: ½ Fruit • ½ Fat • ½ Slider • 10 Optional Calories

99 Calories • 3 gm Fat • 3 gm Protein • 15 gm Carbohydrate • 95 mg Sodium • 46 mg Calcium • 1 gm Fiber

DIABETIC EXCHANGES: ½ Fruit • ½ Fat • ½ Other Carbohydrate

CARB CHOICES: 1

Bountiful Blessings Fruit Salad

I passed a farm stand not long ago offering pears, apples, and grapes (the fall harvest) and thought, "We are so blessed to have this spectacular fresh fruit even when the temperature gets chilly outside!" Let's give thanks for these gifts with each and every bite.

♥ Serves 6 (⅔ cup)

> 2 medium unpeeled pears, cored and each cut into 4 wedges
> 2 medium unpeeled Red Delicious apples, cored and each cut
>   into 4 wedges
> 1 teaspoon lemon juice
> 1 cup seedless green grapes
> 3 tablespoons chopped pecans
> ½ cup Cool Whip Lite
> 2 tablespoons Kraft fat-free mayonnaise
> 1 tablespoon Splenda Granular

Lock food processor bowl in position. Insert the steel knife blade. Drop pear wedges into the food processor bowl. Attach food chute cover and lock in place. Turn on processor and pulse 2 or 3 times or until pears are coarsely chopped. Transfer chopped pears to a medium bowl. Repeat process with apple wedges. Stir in lemon juice. Fold in grapes and pecans. Add Cool Whip Lite, mayonnaise, and Splenda. Mix gently just to combine. Cover and refrigerate for at least 15 minutes. Gently stir again just before serving.

Each serving equals:

HE: 1 Fruit • ½ Fat • 18 Optional Calories

119 Calories • 3 gm Fat • 1 gm Protein • 22 gm Carbohydrate •
41 mg Sodium • 13 mg Calcium • 3 gm Fiber

DIABETIC EXCHANGES: 1 Fruit • ½ Fat • ½ Other Carbohydrate

CARB CHOICES: 1

Layered Summer Salad

This is sort of a picnic in a bowl, a pasta and veggie salad that includes tangy slices of pepperoni, too! If you don't own a pretty glass bowl, check out a few garage sales or search on eBay for just the right one. ☺ Serves 6 (1½ cups)

> 1 medium head romaine lettuce, stems removed and cut into
>   2-inch sections
> 1 large unpeeled cucumber, cut in half lengthwise, seeds
>   removed and each half cut into 2-inch pieces
> 1½ cups cooked elbow macaroni, rinsed and drained
> 1 (3.5-ounce) package Hormel reduced-fat pepperoni slices
> 1½ cups fresh or frozen cut green beans, cooked and cooled
> 1 cup Kraft fat-free mayonnaise
> ½ cup Land O Lakes no-fat sour cream
> 4 sprigs parsley, stems removed

Lock food processor bowl in position. Insert the slicer disc. Attach food chute cover and lock in place. Drop lettuce sections into the food chute. Position food pusher over lettuce. Turn on processor and use light pressure to push lettuce through. Transfer sliced lettuce to a large glass salad bowl. Repeat process with cucumber pieces. Evenly sprinkle macaroni over sliced cucumbers in salad bowl. Arrange pepperoni over macaroni and arrange cooked green beans evenly over top. Remove slicer disc from food processor and insert the steel knife blade. Place mayonnaise, sour cream, and parsley in food processor bowl. Attach food chute cover and lock in place. Position food pusher in chute to prevent ingredients from splashing out of bowl. Turn on processor and pulse 5 times or until parsley is chopped and mixture is blended. Using a rubber spatula, evenly spread mayonnaise mixture over top of salad. Cover and refrigerate for at least 2 hours. Gently toss together just before serving.

HINT: Usually 1 cup uncooked elbow macaroni cooks to about 1½ cups.

Each serving equals:

HE: 1½ Vegetable • ¾ Protein • ½ Bread • ½ Slider • 6 Optional Calories

160 Calories • 4 gm Fat • 9 gm Protein • 22 gm Carbohydrate •
573 mg Sodium • 120 mg Calcium • 3 gm Fiber

DIABETIC EXCHANGES: 1 Vegetable • 1 Starch/Carbohydrate • ½ Meat

CARB CHOICES: 1½

Rainbow Pasta Salad

Okay, so this festive dish may not contain all the colors of the rainbow (hard to find vegetables in indigo or violet, for instance) but you've got red, green, orange, plus whatever shade onions you buy, blended with brown-red bacon bits. Looks and tastes like a celebration to me! ◑ Serves 4 (1 cup)

> ½ small head of lettuce, cut into 4 wedges
> 2 medium carrots, scraped and each cut into
>   2-inch pieces
> 1 small onion, peeled and cut into 4 wedges
> 3 medium red radishes, trimmed and each cut in half
> ½ cup frozen peas
> 1½ cups cold cooked rotini pasta, rinsed and drained
> 2 tablespoons Oscar Mayer or Hormel Real Bacon Bits
> ½ cup Kraft Fat Free Thousand Island Dressing
> 2 tablespoons Land O Lakes no-fat sour cream
> 2 teaspoons Splenda Granular
> 2 sprigs parsley, stems removed

Lock food processor bowl in position. Insert the shredder disc. Attach food chute cover and lock in place. Drop lettuce into the food chute. Position food pusher over lettuce. Turn on processor and use medium pressure to push lettuce through. Transfer shredded lettuce to a large bowl. Drop carrots into the food chute. Position food pusher over carrots. Turn on processor and use medium pressure to push carrots through. Transfer shredded carrots to bowl with lettuce. Repeat process with onion and radishes. Add peas, rotini pasta, and bacon bits to vegetable mixture. Mix well to combine. Remove shredder disc from food processor and insert the steel knife blade. Place Thousand Island dressing, sour cream, Splenda, and parsley into the food processor bowl. Attach food chute cover and lock in place. Turn on processor and pulse 2 or 3 times or until mixture is blended. Add dressing mixture to salad mixture. Mix well to combine. Cover and refrigerate for at least 15 minutes. Gently stir again just before serving.

HINT: Usually 1 full cup uncooked rotini pasta cooks to about 1½ cups.

Each serving equals:

HE: 1¼ Vegetable • 1 Bread • ¼ Protein • ½ Slider • 7 Optional Calories

161 Calories • 1 gm Fat • 6 gm Protein • 32 gm Carbohydrate • 442 mg Sodium • 42 mg Calcium • 4 gm Fiber

DIABETIC EXCHANGES: 2 Starch/Carbohydrate • 1 Vegetable

CARB CHOICES: 2

Grande Gazpacho Pasta Salad

Instead of preparing the pasta salads that everyone else does, why not show up at the next office potluck with a bowl of this colorful and savory blend that takes a classic to the next level? It's zesty and fresh, featuring lots of different textures.

 ○ Serves 4 (1 cup)

2 medium tomatoes, peeled and each cut into 6 wedges

1 medium unpeeled cucumber, cut in half lengthwise and crosswise

2 medium stalks celery, trimmed and each cut into 2-inch pieces

1 small onion, peeled and cut into 4 wedges

1½ cups cold cooked rotini pasta, rinsed and drained

⅓ cup Kraft Fat Free Catalina Dressing

1 tablespoon vegetable oil

1 teaspoon chili seasoning

Lock food processor bowl in position. Insert the steel knife blade. Drop tomatoes into the food processor bowl. Attach food chute cover and lock in place. Turn on processor and pulse 2 or 3 times or until tomatoes are coarsely chopped. Transfer chopped tomatoes to a medium bowl. Repeat process with cucumber. Drop celery pieces into the food processor bowl. Attach food chute cover and lock in place. Turn on processor and pulse 2 or 3 times or until celery is coarsely chopped. Transfer chopped celery to bowl with other vegetables. Repeat process with onion. Stir rotini pasta into vegetable mixture. Add Catalina dressing, vegetable oil, and chili seasoning. Mix gently just to combine. Cover and refrigerate for at least 30 minutes. Gently stir again just before serving.

HINT: Usually 1 full cup uncooked rotini pasta cooks to about 1½ cups.

Each serving equals:

HE: 1½ Vegetable • ¾ Bread • ¾ Fat • ¼ Slider • 3 Optional Calories

164 Calories • 4 gm Fat • 4 gm Protein • 28 gm Carbohydrate • 254 mg Sodium • 37 mg Calcium • 4 gm Fiber

DIABETIC EXCHANGES: 1½ Vegetable • 1 Starch • 1 Fat

CARB CHOICES: 1½

Chicken and Orange Salad

This is a wonderful dish to make with leftover chicken or even a piece from the deli you pick up on the way home. Chicken seems to lend itself to sweet partnerships better than some other foods, don't you think?   ◐   Serves 4 (1 cup)

8 ounces cooked chicken breast, cut into 6 pieces
2 medium stalks celery, trimmed and each cut into 2-inch pieces
1 small green bell pepper, stem and seeds removed and cut into 4 strips
1 small onion, peeled and cut into 4 wedges
2 (11-ounce) cans mandarin oranges, rinsed and drained
½ cup Kraft fat-free mayonnaise
4 large lettuce leaves

Lock food processor bowl in position. Insert the steel knife blade. Drop chicken pieces into food processor bowl. Attach food chute cover and lock in place. Turn on processor and pulse 3 or 4 times or until chicken is chopped. Transfer chopped chicken to a large bowl. Remove steel knife blade from food processor and insert the slicer disc. Attach food chute cover and lock in place. Drop celery, green pepper, and onion into the food chute. Position food pusher over vegetables. Turn on processor and use medium pressure to push vegetables through. Transfer vegetables to bowl with chicken. Stir in mandarin oranges. Add mayonnaise. Mix gently to combine. For each serving, place a lettuce leaf on serving plate and spoon about 1 cup salad mixture over top.

HINT: If you don't have leftovers, purchase a chunk of cooked chicken breast from your local deli.

Each serving equals:

HE: 2 Protein • 1 Fruit • 1 Vegetable • ¼ Slider

151 Calories • 3 gm Fat • 18 gm Protein • 13 gm Carbohydrate • 304 mg Sodium • 33 mg Calcium • 2 gm Fiber

DIABETIC EXCHANGES: 2 Meat • 1 Fruit • 1 Vegetable

CARB CHOICES: 1

Hawaiian Chicken Salad

Perk up your next Sunday supper with a taste of Maui! Chicken salad can taste rich but a little dull, so add a little crunch and some juicy sweetness with this refreshing blend.

◐ Serves 4 (1 cup)

> ¼ cup walnuts
> 8 ounces cooked chicken breast, cut into 6 pieces
> 2 medium stalks celery, trimmed and each cut into
>   2-inch pieces
> ¼ small head iceberg lettuce, cut into 1-inch wedges
> 1 (8-ounce) can pineapple tidbits, packed in fruit juice,
>   drained and 1 tablespoon juice reserved
> ⅓ cup Kraft fat-free mayonnaise
> ⅛ teaspoon black pepper

Lock food processor bowl in position. Insert the steel knife blade. Drop walnuts into the food processor bowl. Attach food chute cover and lock in place. Turn on processor and pulse 3 or 4 times or until walnuts are chopped. Transfer chopped walnuts to a large bowl. Repeat process with chicken pieces. Chop celery using the food processor. Stir celery into walnut and chicken mixture. Remove steel knife blade from food processor and insert the slicer disc. Attach food chute cover and lock in place. Drop lettuce into the food chute. Position food pusher over lettuce. Turn on processor and use light pressure to push lettuce through. Transfer sliced lettuce into bowl with walnuts, chicken, and celery. Add pineapple. Mix well to combine. Add mayonnaise, reserved pineapple juice, and black pepper. Toss gently to combine. Serve at once.

HINTS: 1. If you don't have leftovers, purchase a chunk of cooked chicken breast from your local deli.

2. If you can't find pineapple tidbits, use chunk pineapple and coarsely chop.

Each serving equals:

HE: 2¼ Protein • 1 Vegetable • ½ Fruit • ½ Fat • 15 Optional Calories

195 Calories • 7 gm Fat • 19 gm Protein • 14 gm Carbohydrate • 219 mg Sodium • 35 mg Calcium • 2 gm Fiber

DIABETIC EXCHANGES: 2 Meat • 1 Vegetable • 1 Fat • ½ Fruit

CARB CHOICES: 1

Salmon Shoestring Salad

We've all had times that money was tight and we had to economize without letting our families know they were eating on a budget. Here's a dish that's as kind to your pocketbook as it is generous to your taste buds—it tastes rich but doesn't send you shopping for a loan! ◐ Serves 6 (¾ cup)

3 large carrots, scraped and each cut into 2-inch pieces
¼ medium head iceberg lettuce, cut into 1-inch wedges
1 small onion, peeled and cut into 4 wedges
1 (14.5-ounce) can pink salmon, drained, boned, and flaked
¾ cup Kraft fat-free mayonnaise
½ teaspoon prepared yellow mustard
1½ cups shoestring potatoes

Lock food processor bowl in position. Insert the steel knife blade. Drop carrot pieces into the food processor bowl. Attach food chute cover and lock in place. Turn on processor and pulse 3 or 4 times or until carrots are coarsely chopped. Transfer chopped carrots to a large bowl. Remove steel knife blade and insert the slicer disc. Attach food chute cover and lock in place. Drop lettuce and onion into the food chute. Position food pusher over vegetables. Turn on processor and use medium pressure to push vegetables through. Transfer sliced vegetables to bowl with carrots. Add salmon, mayonnaise, and mustard. Mix well to combine. Just before serving, stir in shoestring potatoes.

HINT: Don't add shoestring potatoes until ready to serve or they will get soggy.

Each serving equals:

HE: 2 Protein • 1 Bread • 1 Vegetable • ½ Fat • ¼ Slider

214 Calories • 10 gm Fat • 12 gm Protein • 19 gm Carbohydrate • 483 mg Sodium • 111 mg Calcium • 3 gm Fiber

DIABETIC EXCHANGES: 2 Meat • 1 Starch • 1 Vegetable • ½ Fat

CARB CHOICES: 1

Inspired

Vegetables

Now that we're encouraged to fill our plates with more veggies than meat, we need a little inspiration, and it's been my pleasure to provide you with fresh and exciting ideas for many of the vegetables you've been eating but perhaps not enjoying as much as you could. By varying your veggies and your cutting blades, you can fix some fabulous combinations without a lot of time or trouble.

Why not put the spotlight tonight on some *Garlic Sautéed Mushrooms*, an excellent "go-with" for almost any meat dish. Or experiment with an exhilarating way to prepare good old green beans with *Far East Green Bean Bake*. For a gorgeous touch of color, *Apricot Glazed Carrots* are a refreshing change, while you can enjoy a sizzling taste of Mexico with *South of the Border Veggie Skillet*. And when old-fashioned comfort food is what you desire, try *Broccoli-Corn Custard* and *Savory Onions au Gratin*.

Garlic Sautéed Mushrooms

It's good for your health, it's great for your taste buds, and it is also rumored to keep vampires away! Go for the garlic and you definitely go for the gusto. �𝗢 Serves 6 (⅓ cup)

2 cloves garlic, peeled
¼ cup I Can't Believe It's Not Butter! Light Margarine
4½ cups fresh whole mushrooms, each cut in half
1 teaspoon lemon pepper

Lock food processor bowl in position. Insert the steel knife blade. Drop garlic into the food processor bowl. Attach food chute cover and lock in place. Turn on processor and pulse 2 or 3 times or until garlic is minced. In a large skillet sprayed with butter-flavored cooking spray, melt margarine. Sauté garlic for 2 to 3 minutes. Meanwhile, remove steel knife blade from food processor and insert the slicer disc. Attach food chute cover and lock in place. Drop mushrooms into the food chute. Position food pusher over mushrooms. Turn on processor and use light pressure to push mushrooms through. Transfer mushrooms to skillet when full level is reached. Repeat process as necessary to slice mushrooms. Stir in lemon pepper. Sauté mushrooms for 4 to 5 minutes or just until tender.

Each serving equals:

HE: 1 Fat • ¾ Vegetable

56 Calories • 4 gm Fat • 2 gm Protein • 3 gm Carbohydrate •
364 mg Sodium • 3 mg Calcium • 1 gm Fiber

DIABETIC EXCHANGES: 1 Fat • 1 Vegetable

CARB CHOICES: 0

Savory Onions au Gratin

Talk about two that delight in a terrific tango, and you'd be talking about cheese and onions! This veggie recipe produces an inventive and tangy treat that will appeal to everyone, whether or not they are vegetable fans. ◐ Serves 4

> 2 medium onions, peeled and each cut into 6 wedges
> 4 slices reduced-calorie day-old white bread, torn into large
>   pieces
> 2 tablespoons I Can't Believe It's Not Butter! Light
>   Margarine
> ¼ cup shredded Kraft reduced-fat Cheddar cheese
> 2 eggs, or equivalent in egg substitute
> ½ cup Land O Lakes Fat Free Half & Half
> ¼ cup fat-free milk
> ¼ cup Kraft Reduced Fat Parmesan Style Grated Topping
> 1½ teaspoons Italian seasoning
> ⅛ teaspoon black pepper

Preheat oven to 350 degrees. Spray an 8-by-8-inch baking dish with butter-flavored cooking spray. Lock food processor bowl in position. Insert the slicer disc. Attach food chute cover and lock in place. Drop onions into the food chute. Position food pusher over onions. Turn on processor and use medium pressure to push onions through. Transfer sliced onions to a large skillet sprayed with butter-flavored cooking spray and sauté for 5 minutes. Lower heat, cover, and simmer for 10 minutes, stirring occasionally. Remove slicer disc from food processor and wipe food processor bowl with a clean cloth. Insert the steel knife blade. Place bread pieces and margarine in food processor bowl. Attach food chute cover and lock in place. Turn on processor and pulse 4 or 5 times or until bread is crumbly. Transfer to a small bowl. Stir in Cheddar cheese. Place eggs, half & half, milk, Parmesan cheese, Italian seasoning, and black pepper in food processor bowl. Attach food chute cover and lock in place. Turn on processor and pulse 3 times or until smooth. Spoon onions into prepared baking dish. Pour egg mixture over onions and evenly sprinkle crumb mixture over top.

Bake for 25 to 30 minutes. Place baking dish on a wire rack and let set for 5 minutes. Divide into 4 servings.

Each serving equals:

HE: 1 Vegetable • ¾ Protein • ¾ Fat • ½ Bread • ¼ Slider • 3 Optional Calories

193 Calories • 9 gm Fat • 10 gm Protein • 18 gm Carbohydrate • 440 mg Sodium • 186 mg Calcium • 1 gm Fiber

DIABETIC EXCHANGES: 1 Vegetable • 1 Meat • 1 Fat • ½ Starch

CARB CHOICES: 1

Baked Turnip Croquettes

My friend Barbara told me that her mother never prepared turnips when she was a child, and so now as an adult, she has no idea what to do with this sturdy and nutritious root vegetable. Here's one good idea, made easier with the food processor because it's so hard and awkward to slice.　　❍　　Serves 6 (2 each)

> *3 slices reduced-calorie day-old white bread, torn into large pieces*
> *6 medium turnips, cleaned, cooked, cooled, and each cut into 4 wedges*
> *2 tablespoons I Can't Believe It's Not Butter! Light Margarine*
> *1 egg, or equivalent in egg substitute*
> *½ cup shredded Kraft reduced-fat Cheddar cheese*

Preheat oven to 425 degrees. Spray a baking sheet with butter-flavored cooking spray. Lock food processor bowl in position. Insert the steel knife blade. Drop bread pieces into the food processor bowl. Attach food chute cover and lock in place. Turn on processor and pulse 20 or 25 times or until fine crumbs form. Transfer bread crumbs to a shallow bowl. Place turnips, margarine, egg, Cheddar cheese, and ⅓ of bread crumbs in food processor bowl. Attach food chute cover and lock in place. Turn on processor and pulse 3 or 4 times, or until mixture is blended. Shape mixture into 12 (1-inch) balls and roll each in remaining bread crumbs in shallow bowl. Evenly arrange on prepared baking sheet. Bake for 15 to 20 minutes. Serve at once.

Each serving equals:

HE: 1 Vegetable • ½ Protein • ½ Fat • ¼ Bread

92 Calories • 4 gm Fat • 6 gm Protein • 8 gm Carbohydrate • 213 mg Sodium • 107 mg Calcium • 2 gm Fiber

DIABETIC EXCHANGES: 1 Vegetable • ½ Meat • ½ Fat

CARB CHOICES: ½

Caraway Cabbage

These tiny seeds are just jam-packed with piquant flavor that adds so much to a loaf of rye bread or a side dish of cabbage you can prepare in minutes! Inspired by the way they're used in sauerkraut, this recipe uses a savory spice to bring out cabbage's best.

☻ Serves 4 (½ cup)

> 1 small head of cabbage, cut into 6 wedges
> 2 tablespoons I Can't Believe It's Not Butter! Light
>   Margarine
> 1 teaspoon caraway seeds
> 2 tablespoons Land O Lakes Fat Free Half & Half

Lock food processor bowl in position. Insert the slicer disc. Attach food chute cover and lock in place. Drop cabbage wedges into food chute. Position food pusher in chute. Turn on processor and use medium pressure to push cabbage through. Transfer sliced cabbage to a large bowl when full level is reached. Repeat process as necessary. In a large skillet sprayed with butter-flavored cooking spray, melt margarine. Stir in cabbage and caraway seeds. Cook on medium heat for 4 to 6 minutes or just until cabbage is tender, stirring often. Add half & half. Mix well to combine. Lower heat, cover, and simmer for 2 to 3 minutes, stirring occasionally.

Each serving equals:

HE: 1 Vegetable • ¾ Fat • 4 Optional Calories

63 Calories • 3 gm Fat • 2 gm Protein • 7 gm Carbohydrate • 99 mg Sodium • 65 mg Calcium • 2 gm Fiber

DIABETIC EXCHANGES: 1 Vegetable • 1 Fat

CARB CHOICES: ½

Crunchy Celery Bake

Oh, this was a fun recipe to make and taste test! (Maybe that's true of anything with potato chips on top—what do you think?) Combine two crunchy vegetables with some creamy soup, add a little color and a bit of spice, and then top with a good-for-you snack food, and you've got a year-round winner. ☻ Serves 6

> 8 medium stalks celery, trimmed and each cut into thick
>   diagonal pieces
> 1 (8-ounce) can water chestnuts, drained
> 1 (10¾-ounce) can Healthy Request Cream of Mushroom
>   Soup
> 1 (2-ounce) jar chopped pimiento, drained
> ⅛ teaspoon black pepper
> ¾ cup crushed Ruffles Light fat-free potato chips

Preheat oven to 375 degrees. Spray an 8-by-8-inch baking dish with butter-flavored cooking spray. Lock food processor bowl in position. Insert the slicer disc. Attach food chute cover and lock in place. Drop celery and water chestnuts into the food chute. Position food pusher over vegetables. Turn on processor and use medium pressure to push vegetables through. Transfer sliced vegetables to a large bowl when full level is reached. Repeat process as necessary. Add mushroom soup, pimiento, and black pepper to vegetables in large bowl. Mix well to combine. Evenly spread mixture into prepared baking dish. Sprinkle crushed potato chips evenly over top. Bake for 45 to 50 minutes. Place baking dish on a wire rack and let set for 5 minutes. Divide into 6 servings.

HINT: Add 1½ cups diced cooked chicken breast and change soup
    to Cream of Chicken Soup, and this side dish becomes a main
    dish!

Each serving equals:

HE: 1 Vegetable • ⅓ Bread • ¼ Slider • 8 Optional Calories

65 Calories • 1 gm Fat • 2 gm Protein • 12 gm Carbohydrate •
292 mg Sodium • 64 mg Calcium • 2 gm Fiber

DIABETIC EXCHANGES: 1 Vegetable • ½ Other Carbohydrate

CARB CHOICES: 1

Far-East Green Bean Bake

Here's a case where you do need to think in advance about what you're making for dinner, so you have time to thaw the frozen veggies. The good news is, it doesn't take all that long. Leave them out on a plate in the fridge in the morning, and you'll be all set to cook up a storm when you get home from work.

♥ Serves 6

> 1 (10-ounce) package frozen French-style green beans,
>   thawed
> 1 (10-ounce) package frozen cut broccoli, thawed
> 1 (4-ounce) can sliced mushrooms, drained
> 1 (8-ounce) can water chestnuts, well drained
> 1 (10¾-ounce) can Healthy Request Cream of Mushroom
>   Soup
> 2 tablespoons reduced-sodium soy sauce
> ⅛ teaspoon black pepper
> 1 cup coarsely broken chow mein noodles

Preheat oven to 375 degrees. Spray an 8-by-8-inch baking dish with butter-flavored cooking spray. In a large bowl, combine green beans, broccoli, and mushrooms. Lock food processor bowl in position. Insert the steel knife blade. Place water chestnuts, mushroom soup, soy sauce, and black pepper in food processor bowl. Position food pusher in chute to prevent ingredients from splashing out of bowl. Turn on processor and pulse 3 or 4 times or until water chestnuts are coarsely chopped and mixture is blended. Transfer soup mixture to large bowl with vegetables. Mix well to combine. Spread mixture into prepared baking dish. Evenly sprinkle chow mein noodles over top. Bake for 35 to 40 minutes or until vegetables are tender. Place baking dish on a wire rack and let set for 5 minutes. Divide into 6 servings.

HINT: Thaw vegetables by rinsing in a colander under hot water
    for 1 minute.

Each serving equals:

HE: 1½ Vegetable • ½ Bread • ¼ Slider • 8 Optional Calories

115 Calories • 3 gm Fat • 5 gm Protein • 17 gm Carbohydrate •
538 mg Sodium • 83 mg Calcium • 4 gm Fiber

DIABETIC EXCHANGES: 1½ Vegetable • 1 Starch/Carbohydrate

CARB CHOICES: 1

Zucchini-Sour Cream Sauté

Also known as green squash, zucchini is served peeled and unpeeled, but I recommend leaving the peel on for nutrition purposes—and also because it gives the dish more color! It's amazingly easy to whip up this creamy sauce and delight your family.

◐ Serves 4 (½ cup)

4 medium unpeeled zucchini, cut in half lengthwise and
   crosswise
1 small onion, peeled and cut into 4 wedges
2 tablespoons I Can't Believe It's Not Butter! Light
   Margarine
¼ cup Land O Lakes no-fat sour cream
½ teaspoon dried basil
⅛ teaspoon black pepper

Lock food processor in position. Insert the steel knife blade. Drop zucchini pieces into the food processor bowl. Attach food chute cover and lock in place. Turn on processor and pulse 4 or 5 times or until zucchini is finely chopped. Transfer zucchini to a large bowl when full level is reached. Repeat process as necessary. Repeat process with onion wedges. Turn on processor and pulse 3 or 4 times or until onion is finely chopped. In a large skillet sprayed with butter-flavored cooking spray, melt margarine. Stir in onion and sauté for 2 minutes. Add chopped zucchini. Mix well to combine. Sauté for 6 to 8 minutes or just until zucchini and onion are tender. Remove from heat. Stir in sour cream, basil, and black pepper. Serve at once.

Each serving equals:

HE: 1½ Vegetable • ¾ Fat • 15 Optional Calories

79 Calories • 3 gm Fat • 3 gm Protein • 10 gm Carbohydrate •
143 mg Sodium • 57 mg Calcium • 2 gm Fiber

DIABETIC EXCHANGES: 1 Vegetable • 1 Fat

CARB CHOICES: ½

Green Beans Oriental

I often tell you to cut vegetables into measured pieces, as in this dish. But good cooks know that cutting on the diagonal is a good choice in almost any recipe. Why? It allows the veggie a bigger surface to soak up a sauce or marinade, and it also looks pretty.

☻ Serves 4 (1 cup)

> 4 medium stalks celery, trimmed and each cut into 2-inch
>   pieces
> 1 tablespoon + 1 teaspoon I Can't Believe It's Not Butter!
>   Light Margarine
> 3 cups frozen cut green beans, thawed
> 2 tablespoons reduced-sodium soy sauce
> ⅛ teaspoon black pepper

Lock food processor bowl in position. Insert the slicer disc. Attach food chute cover and lock in place. Drop celery pieces into the food chute. Position food pusher over celery. Turn on processor and use medium pressure to push celery through. In a large skillet sprayed with butter-flavored cooking spray, melt margarine. Stir in celery. Sauté for 2 to 3 minutes. Add green beans. Mix well to combine. Stir in soy sauce and black pepper. Lower heat, cover, and simmer for 6 to 8 minutes or just until vegetables are tender, stirring occasionally.

HINT: Thaw green beans by rinsing in a colander under hot water
    for 1 minute.

Each serving equals:

HE: 2 Vegetable • ½ Fat

58 Calories • 2 gm Fat • 2 gm Protein • 8 gm Carbohydrate •
854 mg Sodium • 48 mg Calcium • 4 gm Fiber

DIABETIC EXCHANGES: 2 Vegetable • ½ Fat

CARB CHOICES: ½

Bountiful Carrot and Apple Sauté

Take a crunchy vegetable and a juicy fruit, add a bit of this and that, and you've got a dish you could proudly take to any potluck or office luncheon! We tested this with Granny Smith apples, which can be quite tart but wonderfully firm. If you've got a batch of some other firm apple, try it!   ☻   Serves 4 (½ cup)

4 medium carrots, scraped and each cut into 2-inch pieces
1 cup hot water
1 medium Granny Smith apple, cored, peeled, and cut into 4
*   wedges*
¼ cup walnuts
1 tablespoon + 1 teaspoon I Can't Believe It's Not Butter!
*   Light Margarine*
3 tablespoons orange marmalade spreadable fruit
¼ cup unsweetened apple juice

Lock food processor bowl in position. Insert the slicer disc. Attach food chute cover and lock in place. Drop carrot pieces into the food chute. Position food pusher over carrot pieces. Turn on processor and use medium pressure to push carrots through. Transfer sliced carrots to a large bowl when full level is reached. Repeat process as necessary. Place carrots in a medium saucepan with hot water. Cook over medium heat for 15 minutes or just until carrots are tender. Drain well. Meanwhile, drop apple wedges into the food chute. Position food pusher over apples. Turn on processor and use light pressure to push apple through. Transfer sliced apples into a medium bowl. Remove slicer disc from food processor and insert the steel knife blade. Place walnuts in food processor bowl. Attach food chute cover and lock in place. Turn on processor and pulse 3 or 4 times or until walnuts are coarsely chopped. In a large skillet sprayed with butter-flavored cooking spray, melt margarine. Sauté cooked carrots and apple slices for 5 minutes. Stir in walnuts. In a small bowl, combine spreadable fruit and apple juice. Add mixture to skillet with carrots. Mix well to combine. Continue sautéing for 6 to 8 minutes or until carrots and apple are coated and most of moisture is absorbed, stirring often.

Each serving equals:

HE: 1 Fruit • 1 Fat • 1 Vegetable • ¼ Protein

142 Calories • 6 gm Fat • 2 gm Protein • 20 gm Carbohydrate • 88 mg Sodium • 30 mg Calcium • 3 gm Fiber

DIABETIC EXCHANGES: 1 Fruit • 1 Fat • 1 Vegetable

CARB CHOICES: 1

Apricot-Glazed Carrots

The people who make spreadable fruit have already done a lot of the prep work for us (thank you!), which means that your glaze for these colorful carrots is ready in no time at all! I tested several flavors and thought this one worked best, though orange marmalade was a close second. ☾ Serves 6 (½ cup)

> 12 medium carrots, scraped and each cut into 2-inch pieces
> ½ cup hot water
> ¾ cup apricot spreadable fruit
> 2 tablespoons I Can't Believe It's Not Butter! Light
>   Margarine
> 1 teaspoon dried onion flakes
> 1 teaspoon dried parsley flakes

Lock food processor bowl in position. Insert the slicer disc. Attach food chute cover and lock in place. Drop carrot pieces into the food chute. Position food pusher over carrots. Turn on processor and use medium pressure to push carrots through. Transfer sliced carrots to a medium saucepan when full level is reached. Repeat process as necessary. Stir water into carrots. Cover and cook over medium heat for 20 minutes or just until carrots are tender. Drain well. In same saucepan, combine spreadable fruit, margarine, onion flakes, and parsley flakes. Add carrots. Mix well to combine. Continue cooking for 5 minutes or until mixture is heated through, stirring often.

Each serving equals:

HE: 2 Vegetable • 1 Fruit • ½ Fat

146 Calories • 2 gm Fat • 1 gm Protein • 31 gm Carbohydrate • 129 mg Sodium • 42 mg Calcium • 3 gm Fiber

DIABETIC EXCHANGES: 2 Vegetable • 1 Fruit • ½ Fat

CARB CHOICES: 2

Dilly Carrots

Of course, I could have named these "dilly" because one ingredient in the recipe is dill weed. But I could also have meant the other definition of "dilly": something that is remarkable or extraordinary. Taste it and see.   ☻   Serves 4 (¾ cup)

> 8 medium carrots, scraped and each cut into 2-inch pieces
> ¾ cup water
> ¼ cup Land O Lakes Fat Free Half & Half
> 2 tablespoons I Can't Believe It's Not Butter! Light
>   Margarine
> 1 teaspoon dried dill weed

Lock food processor bowl in position. Insert the slicer disc. Attach food chute cover and lock in place. Drop carrot pieces into the food chute. Position food pusher over carrots. Turn on processor and use medium pressure to push carrots through. Transfer sliced carrots to a medium saucepan when full level is reached. Repeat process as necessary. Stir water into carrots. Cover and cook over medium heat until carrots are tender, about 15 minutes. Drain carrots and return to saucepan. Add half & half, margarine, and dill weed. Mix well to combine. Continue cooking for 1 to 2 minutes, stirring often.

Each serving equals:

HE: 2 Vegetable • ¾ Fat • 4 Optional Calories

79 Calories • 3 gm Fat • 1 gm Protein • 12 gm Carbohydrate •
163 mg Sodium • 53 mg Calcium • 3 gm Fiber

DIABETIC EXCHANGES: 2 Vegetable • 1 Fat

CARB CHOICES: 1

Rising Sun Carrot Bake

It takes some baking to soften up carrots and bring out their full sweetness, but it's worth it! It also works to surround those carrots with glorious sauces that are delightfully lip-smacking good!

● Serves 6

> 6 medium carrots, scraped and each cut into 2-inch pieces
> 1 small green bell pepper, stem and seeds removed and cut
>   into 4 strips
> 1 medium onion, peeled and cut into 6 wedges
> 1 (10¾-ounce) can Healthy Request Tomato Soup
> 2 tablespoons reduced-sodium soy sauce
> 1¼ cups chow mein noodles

Preheat oven to 350 degrees. Spray an 8-by-8-inch baking dish with butter-flavored cooking spray. Lock food processor bowl in position. Insert the slicer disc. Attach food chute cover and lock in place. Drop carrot pieces into the food chute. Position food pusher over carrot pieces. Turn on processor and use medium pressure to push carrots through. Transfer sliced carrots to a large bowl when full level is reached. Repeat process as necessary. Repeat process with green pepper and onion wedges. Transfer shredded vegetables to large bowl with carrots. Add tomato soup and soy sauce. Mix well to combine. Evenly spread mixture into prepared baking dish. Bake for 30 minutes. Sprinkle chow mein noodles over top. Continue baking for 15 to 20 minutes or until vegetables are tender. Place baking dish on a wire rack and let set for 5 minutes. Divide into 6 servings.

Each serving equals:

HE: 1½ Vegetable • ½ Bread • ¼ Slider • 10 Optional Calories

127 Calories • 3 gm Fat • 3 gm Protein • 22 gm Carbohydrate •
488 mg Sodium • 28 mg Calcium • 3 gm Fiber

DIABETIC EXCHANGES: 1½ Vegetable • 1 Starch/Carbohydrate

CARB CHOICES: 1½

Sautéed Peppers and Mushrooms

Chop, chop, chop up a storm—and make all kinds of fabulous veggie dishes that you might have felt were just too much trouble before! This dish is tangy and moist, a wonderful accompaniment to any meaty entrée.   ☻   Serves 4 (½ cup)

> 1 medium onion, peeled and cut into 6 wedges
> 1 medium green bell pepper, stem and seeds removed and
>   cut into 6 strips
> 1 medium red bell pepper, stem and seeds removed and cut
>   into 6 strips
> 2 cups fresh whole mushrooms, each cut in half
> 2 tablespoons I Can't Believe It's Not Butter! Light
>   Margarine
> ¼ cup reduced-sodium ketchup
> 1 teaspoon Worcestershire sauce

Lock food processor bowl in position. Insert the slicer disc. Attach food chute cover and lock in place. Drop onion wedges into the food chute. Position food pusher over onion wedges. Turn on processor and use medium pressure to push onion through. Transfer sliced onion to a large bowl. Repeat process with green and red pepper. Drop mushroom halves into the food chute. Position food pusher over mushrooms. Turn on processor and use light pressure to push mushrooms through. Transfer sliced mushrooms to large bowl with other vegetables. In a large skillet sprayed with butter-flavored cooking spray, melt margarine. Add vegetables. Mix well to combine. Sauté for 8 to 10 minutes or just until vegetables are tender. Stir in ketchup and Worcestershire sauce. Continue to sauté for 2 to 3 minutes or until mixture is heated through, stirring occasionally.

Each serving equals:

HE: 2 Vegetable • ¾ Fat • 15 Optional Calories

83 Calories • 3 gm Fat • 2 gm Protein • 12 gm Carbohydrate •
89 mg Sodium • 21 mg Calcium • 2 gm Fiber

DIABETIC EXCHANGES: 1½ Vegetable • 1 Fat

CARB CHOICES: 1

Golden Gate Veggie Sauté

I've traveled from coast to coast (though not as much as my husband, Cliff!) and eaten well everywhere, but this dish just seemed to me to recall the colors and flavors of San Francisco, a city that celebrates great eating every day and night.

● Serves 4 (1 cup)

> 2 cups fresh whole mushrooms, each cut in half
> 1 medium red bell pepper, stem and seeds removed and cut into 8 strips
> 1 small onion, peeled and cut into 4 wedges
> 2 medium stalks celery, trimmed and each cut into 2-inch pieces
> 1 medium carrot, scraped and cut into 2-inch pieces
> 2 tablespoons I Can't Believe It's Not Butter! Light Margarine
> 2 cups frozen cut green beans, thawed
> 1 (14-ounce) can bean sprouts, rinsed and drained
> ¼ cup reduced-sodium soy sauce
> 6 tablespoons coarsely broken chow mein noodles

Lock food processor bowl in position. Insert the slicer disc. Attach food chute cover and lock in place. Drop mushrooms into the food chute. Position food pusher over mushrooms. Turn on processor and use medium pressure to push mushrooms through. Transfer mushrooms to a large bowl. Drop red pepper, onion, celery, and carrots into the food chute. Position food pusher over vegetables. Turn on processor and use medium pressure to push vegetables through. Transfer sliced vegetables into bowl with mushrooms. In a large skillet sprayed with butter-flavored cooking spray, melt margarine. Stir in sliced vegetables and green beans. Sauté over high heat for 5 minutes. Add bean sprouts. Mix well to combine. Continue sautéing for 2 to 3 minutes or just until vegetables are crisp. Stir in soy sauce. When serving, evenly sprinkle 1½ teaspoons chow mein noodles over top of each.

HINT: Thaw green beans by rinsing in a colander under hot water for 1 minute.

Each serving equals:

HE: 3 Vegetable • ¾ Fat • ¼ Bread

136 Calories • 4 gm Fat • 6 gm Protein • 19 gm Carbohydrate •
695 mg Sodium • 65 mg Calcium • 6 gm Fiber

DIABETIC EXCHANGES: 3 Vegetable • 1 Fat

CARB CHOICES: 1

California Vegetable Bake

This is pretty enough to serve to company, but it's the kind of thrifty dish you can also prepare for family at a moment's notice. My kids and grandkids love the crusty topping, and I bet yours will, too!   ❍   Serves 4

> 1 cup fresh whole mushrooms, each cut in half
> 1 small onion, peeled and cut into 4 wedges
> 2 teaspoons I Can't Believe It's Not Butter! Light
>   Margarine
> 1 (10-ounce) package frozen California Blend vegetables,
>   thawed
> 1 (10¾-ounce) can Healthy Request Cream of
>   Mushroom Soup
> 1 cup shredded Kraft reduced-fat Cheddar cheese
> 1 cup cornflake crumbs

Preheat oven to 350 degrees. Spray an 8-by-8-inch baking dish with butter-flavored cooking spray. Lock food processor bowl in position. Insert the slicer disc. Attach food chute cover and lock in place. Drop mushrooms and onion into the food chute. Position food pusher over vegetables. Turn on processor and use medium pressure to push vegetables through. In a large skillet sprayed with butter-flavored cooking spray, melt margarine. Add sliced mushrooms and onion to skillet. Mix well to combine. Sauté for 5 minutes. Stir in California Blend vegetables. Add mushroom soup and Cheddar cheese. Mix well to combine. Evenly spread mixture into prepared baking dish. Sprinkle cornflake crumbs evenly over top. Lightly spray top with butter-flavored cooking spray. Bake for 30 to 35 minutes or until vegetables are tender. Place baking dish on a wire rack and let set for 5 minutes. Divide into 4 servings.

HINT: Frozen carrots, broccoli, and cauliflower may be used in place of blended vegetables.

Each serving equals:

HE: 1½ Vegetable • 1 Bread • 1 Protein • ¼ Fat • ½ Slider •
1 Optional Calorie

239 Calories • 7 gm Fat • 13 gm Protein • 31 gm Carbohydrate •
777 mg Sodium • 288 mg Calcium • 2 gm Fiber

DIABETIC EXCHANGES: 2 Starch/Carbohydrate • 1 Meat • 1 Vegetable

CARB CHOICES: 2

South of the Border Veggie Skillet

Here's a fun, festive quick-fix dish that delivers all the sunny flavor of Mexico in every bite! It's easily doubled for a big crowd.

○ Serves 4 (¾ cup)

½ small head of cabbage, cut into 6 wedges
1 medium red bell pepper, stem and seeds removed and cut into 6 strips
1 medium onion, peeled and cut into 6 wedges
2 medium tomatoes, peeled and each cut into 4 wedges
2 tablespoons Splenda Granular
1 teaspoon chili seasoning

Lock food processor bowl in position. Insert the slicer disc. Attach food chute cover and lock in place. Drop cabbage wedges into the food chute. Position food pusher over cabbage. Turn on processor and use medium pressure to push cabbage through. Transfer sliced cabbage to a large bowl. Repeat process with red pepper and onion. Place vegetables in a large skillet sprayed with butter-flavored cooking spray. Sauté for 5 minutes. Meanwhile, remove slicer disc from food processor and insert the steel knife blade. Drop tomato wedges into the food processor bowl. Attach food chute cover and lock in place. Turn on processor and pulse 3 or 4 times or until tomatoes are finely chopped. Transfer chopped tomatoes to skillet with cabbage mixture. Mix well to combine. Stir in Splenda and chili seasoning. Lower heat and simmer for 10 minutes, stirring occasionally.

Each serving equals:

HE: 2 Vegetable • 3 Optional Calories

56 Calories • 0 gm Fat • 2 gm Protein • 12 gm Carbohydrate •
27 mg Sodium • 57 mg Calcium • 3 gm Fiber

DIABETIC EXCHANGES: 2 Vegetable

CARB CHOICES: 1

Tomato-Asparagus Sauté

The season for fresh asparagus isn't very long, so it's important to enjoy every bite while you can! This dish is a spectacular way to "show off" this enchanting vegetable. ☻ Serves 4 (¾ cup)

> 1 medium onion, peeled and cut into 6 wedges
> 12 fresh asparagus spears, cleaned and each cut into 2-inch
>   pieces
> 2 cups fresh whole mushrooms, each cut in half
> 2 tablespoons I Can't Believe It's Not Butter! Light Margarine
> 2 medium tomatoes, peeled and each cut into 6 wedges
> ¼ cup Kraft Fat Free French Dressing
> 2 tablespoons reduced-sodium soy sauce

Lock food processor bowl in position. Insert the slicer disc. Attach food chute cover and lock in place. Drop onion wedges into the food chute. Position food pusher over onion wedges. Turn on processor and use medium pressure to push onion through. Transfer sliced onions to a large bowl. Drop asparagus spears into the food chute. Position food pusher over asparagus. Turn on processor and use light pressure to push asparagus through. Transfer sliced asparagus into bowl with onion. Repeat process with mushrooms. In a large skillet sprayed with butter-flavored cooking spray, melt margarine. Stir in vegetable mixture. Sauté for 5 to 6 minutes. Meanwhile, drop tomato wedges into the food chute. Position food pusher over tomatoes. Turn on processor and use light pressure to push tomatoes through. Stir sliced tomatoes into skillet with vegetables. Add French dressing and soy sauce. Mix well to combine. Continue sautéing for 5 minutes or until tomatoes are soft, stirring often.

Each serving equals:

HE: 2 Vegetable • ¾ Fat • ¼ Slider • 2 Optional Calories

99 Calories • 3 gm Fat • 3 gm Protein • 15 gm Carbohydrate • 637 mg Sodium • 30 mg Calcium • 3 gm Fiber

DIABETIC EXCHANGES: 2 Vegetable • 1 Fat

CARB CHOICES: 1

Fresh Stewed Tomatoes with Rosemary

If you want a ready source of fresh herbs, you're a perfect candidate for a kitchen herb garden. Dried herbs are tasty, but you'll find that being able to snip off a bit of fresh rosemary, basil, or tarragon when you want it will change the way you eat!

❂ Serves 4 (½ cup)

> 2 medium stalks celery, trimmed and each cut into
> > 2-inch pieces
> 1 medium onion, peeled and cut into 6 wedges
> 1 tablespoon + 1 teaspoon I Can't Believe It's Not Butter!
> > Light Margarine
> 3 medium tomatoes, peeled and each cut into 4 wedges
> 2 tablespoons Splenda Granular
> ⅛ teaspoon black pepper
> 1 slice reduced-calorie white bread, toasted and cut into
> > 6 pieces
> 1 tablespoon fresh rosemary or 1 teaspoon dried
> > rosemary

Lock food processor bowl in position. Insert the steel knife blade. Drop celery pieces and onion wedges into the food processor bowl. Attach food chute cover and lock in place. Turn on processor and pulse 2 or 3 times or until vegetables are coarsely chopped. Transfer chopped vegetables to a medium saucepan sprayed with butter-flavored cooking spray. Stir in margarine. Sauté for 5 minutes. Meanwhile, drop tomato wedges into the food processor bowl. Attach food chute cover and lock in place. Turn on processor and pulse 2 or 3 times or until tomatoes are coarsely chopped. Add chopped tomatoes to vegetable mixture. Mix well to combine. Stir in Splenda and black pepper. Continue cooking for 5 minutes. Wipe food processor bowl clean. Place bread pieces and rosemary in food processor bowl. Attach food chute cover and lock in place. Turn on processor and pulse 2 or 3 times or until coarse crumbs are formed. Stir crumb mixture into tomato mixture. Lower heat and simmer for 4 to 5 minutes, stirring occasionally.

Each serving equals:

HE: 1½ Vegetable • ½ Fat • ¼ Bread • 3 Optional Calories

62 Calories • 2 gm Fat • 2 gm Protein • 9 gm Carbohydrate • 101 mg Sodium • 32 mg Calcium • 2 gm Fiber

DIABETIC EXCHANGES: 1½ Vegetable • ½ Fat

CARB CHOICES: ½

Cheesy Scalloped Celery and Carrots

Ever have one of those evenings where you open the refrigerator, and the only fresh vegetables you have on hand are some carrots, a couple stalks of celery, and a little old onion? This is *your* recipe—and your meal saver!   ♥   Serves 6

> 4 medium carrots, scraped and each cut into 2-inch pieces
> 2 medium stalks celery, trimmed and each cut into 2-inch
>   pieces
> 1 small onion, peeled and cut into 4 wedges
> 1½ cups hot water
> 1 (10¾-ounce) can Healthy Request Cream of Mushroom
>   Soup
> ¾ cup diced Velveeta Light processed cheese
> 15 Ritz Reduced Fat Crackers
> 1 tablespoon I Can't Believe It's Not Butter! Light Margarine
> 2 sprigs parsley, stem removed
> 2 tablespoons Oscar Mayer or Hormel Real Bacon Bits

Lock food processor bowl in position. Insert the slicer disc. Attach food chute cover and lock in place. Drop carrot pieces into the food chute. Position food pusher over carrots. Turn on processor and use medium pressure to push carrots through. Transfer sliced carrots to a medium saucepan when full level is reached. Repeat process as necessary. Repeat process with celery and onion. Stir water into saucepan. Cook over medium heat for 15 to 20 minutes or just until vegetables are tender. Preheat oven to 375 degrees. Spray an 8-by-8-inch baking dish with butter-flavored cooking spray. Drain vegetables and return to saucepan. Add mushroom soup and Velveeta cheese to vegetable mixture. Mix well to combine. Continue cooking for 3 to 4 minutes or just until cheese melts. Spoon hot mixture evenly into prepared baking dish. Wipe food processor bowl with a clean cloth. Remove slicer disc from food processor and insert the steel knife blade. Place crackers, margarine, and parsley in food processor bowl. Attach food chute and lock in place. Position food pusher in chute to prevent ingredients from splashing out of bowl. Turn on processor and pulse 3 or 4 times or until mixture is crumbly. Remove food chute cover and stir in bacon bits using a rubber spatula. Evenly sprinkle crumb mixture over vegetable mixture. Bake for 30 minutes. Place baking dish on a wire rack and let set for 5 minutes. Divide into 6 servings.

Each serving equals:

HE: 1 Vegetable • ⅔ Protein • ½ Bread • ¼ Fat • ¼ Slider • 8 Optional Calories

129 Calories • 5 gm Fat • 5 gm Protein • 16 gm Carbohydrate • 625 mg Sodium • 152 mg Calcium • 2 gm Fiber

DIABETIC EXCHANGES: 1 Vegetable • 1 Meat • 1 Starch

CARB CHOICES: 1

Sunday Best Asparagus Bake

The title tells you what I had in mind—an impressive family meal with everyone dressed up for a special occasion! Set up your food processor, lay out the ingredients, and you're good to go.

◐ Serves 4

> 1 (15-ounce) can asparagus spears, rinsed and drained
> 2 hard-boiled eggs
> 1 (12-fluid-ounce) can Carnation Evaporated Fat Free Milk
> 3 tablespoons all-purpose flour
> 2 tablespoons I Can't Believe It's Not Butter! Light
>   Margarine
> 1 (2.5-ounce) jar sliced mushrooms, drained
> 10 Ritz Reduced Fat Crackers, each broken in half
> ½ cup shredded Kraft reduced-fat Cheddar cheese

Preheat oven to 350 degrees. Spray an 8-by-8-inch baking dish with butter-flavored cooking spray. Evenly arrange asparagus spears in prepared baking dish. Lock food processor bowl in position. Insert the slicer disc. Attach food chute cover and lock in place. Drop eggs into the food chute. Position food pusher over eggs. Turn on processor and use light pressure to push eggs through. Evenly sprinkle egg slices over asparagus. Remove slicer disc from food processor and insert the steel knife blade. Add evaporated milk, flour, and margarine to processor bowl. Attach food chute cover and lock in place. Position food pusher in chute to prevent milk from splashing out of bowl. Turn on processor and pulse 10 or 12 times or until mixture is smooth. Transfer milk mixture to a medium saucepan sprayed with butter-flavored cooking spray. Stir in mushrooms. Cook over medium heat for 6 minutes or until mixture thickens, stirring often. Pour hot mixture evenly over asparagus and eggs. Wipe food processor bowl with a clean cloth. Add cracker halves and Cheddar cheese to food processor bowl. Attach food chute cover and lock in place. Pulse 2 or 3 times or until mixture is combined. Evenly sprinkle mixture over top of asparagus mixture. Bake for 25 to 30 minutes. Place baking dish on a wire rack and let set for 5 minutes. Divide into 4 servings.

HINT: Cooked fresh asparagus spears may be used in place of canned.

Each serving equals:

HE: 1 Protein • 1 Vegetable • ¾ Fat Free Milk • ¾ Bread • ¾ Fat

254 Calories • 10 gm Fat • 16 gm Protein • 25 gm Carbohydrate •
703 mg Sodium • 380 mg Calcium • 1 gm Fiber

DIABETIC EXCHANGES: 1 Meat • 1 Vegetable • 1 Fat Free Milk • 1 Fat •
½ Starch

CARB CHOICES: 1½

Broccoli-Corn Custard

Direct from Corn Country USA, here's a creative way to serve that good old standby, corn—a creamy baked casserole that no one will be able to resist. ❍ Serves 6

1 small onion, peeled and cut into 4 wedges
1 cup fresh or frozen cut broccoli, thawed
1 (8-ounce) can cream-style corn
2 eggs, or equivalent in egg substitute
¼ cup Land O Lakes Fat Free Half & Half
1 teaspoon prepared yellow mustard
2 tablespoons I Can't Believe It's Not Butter! Light
Margarine
⅛ teaspoon black pepper
2 cups frozen whole-kernel corn, thawed
2 tablespoons Oscar Mayer or Hormel Real
Bacon Bits

Preheat oven to 350 degrees. Spray an 8-by-8-inch baking dish with butter-flavored cooking spray. Lock food processor bowl in position. Insert the steel knife blade. Drop onion and broccoli into the food processor bowl. Attach food chute cover and lock in place. Turn on processor and pulse 4 times or until vegetables are coarsely chopped. Remove the food chute cover and add cream-style corn, eggs, half & half, mustard, margarine, and black pepper to processor bowl. Attach food chute cover and lock in place. Turn on processor and pulse 4 times or until mixture is well blended. Remove food chute cover. Stir in whole-kernel corn and bacon bits using a rubber spatula. Evenly spread mixture into prepared baking dish. Bake for 50 to 55 minutes or until center is firm when lightly touched. Place baking dish on a wire rack and let set for 5 minutes. Divide into 6 servings.

HINT: Thaw vegetables by rinsing in a colander under hot water for 1 minute.

Each serving equals:

HE: 1 Bread • ½ Protein • ½ Fat • ½ Vegetable • 6 Optional Calories

120 Calories • 4 gm Fat • 5 gm Protein • 16 gm Carbohydrate •
329 mg Sodium • 31 mg Calcium • 2 gm Fiber

DIABETIC EXCHANGES: 1 Starch • ½ Meat • ½ Fat • ½ Vegetable

CARB CHOICES: 1

Skillet Cabbage
and Peas au Gratin

I particularly like using the food processor for cabbage dishes—and I was always happy enough with a good knife. But I like the way the veggies look after they are chopped or shredded by machine—and I bet you will, too.　　☺　　Serves 4 (1 cup)

½ small head cabbage, cut into 8 wedges
*2 tablespoons I Can't Believe It's Not Butter! Light
   Margarine*
1 small onion, peeled and cut into 4 wedges
1 (12-fluid-ounce) can Carnation Evaporated Fat Free Milk
3 tablespoons all-purpose flour
1½ cups frozen peas, thawed
1 cup diced Velveeta Light processed cheese
½ teaspoon lemon pepper

Lock food processor bowl in position. Insert the steel knife blade. Drop cabbage wedges into the food processor bowl. Attach food chute cover and lock in place. Turn on processor and pulse 8 or 10 times or until cabbage is coarsely chopped. Transfer cabbage to a large bowl when full level is reached. Repeat process as necessary. In a large skillet sprayed with butter-flavored cooking spray, melt margarine. Place cabbage in skillet. Sauté for 1 to 2 minutes. Meanwhile, drop onion wedges into food processor bowl. Turn on processor and pulse 3 or 4 times or until finely chopped. Stir chopped onion into cabbage. Continue to sauté for 5 to 6 minutes or just until vegetables are tender. In a covered jar, combine milk and flour. Shake well to blend. Pour milk mixture into cabbage mixture. Add peas, Velveeta cheese, and black pepper. Mix well to combine. Continue cooking for 3 to 5 minutes or until mixture thickens and cheese melts, stirring often.

HINT: Thaw peas by rinsing in a colander under hot water for 1 minute.

Each serving equals:

HE: 1 Bread • 1 Protein • ¾ Fat Free Milk • ¾ Fat • ¾ Vegetable

246 Calories • 6 gm Fat • 16 gm Protein • 32 gm Carbohydrate •
690 mg Sodium • 462 mg Calcium • 5 gm Fiber

DIABETIC EXCHANGES: 1 Starch • 1 Meat • ½ Fat Free Milk • ½ Fat •
½ Vegetable

CARB CHOICES: 2

Tex-Mex Succotash

Succotash usually means a dish of corn and beans (often lima), but there's no reason why I can't create a combination dish inspired by that Native American favorite that features other available veggies. This sauce is zesty without being too hot for anyone.

◐ Serves 4 (1 cup)

> 1 medium unpeeled zucchini, cut in half lengthwise and crosswise
> 1 medium carrot, scraped and cut into 2-inch pieces
> 1 medium onion, peeled and cut into 6 wedges
> 2 medium tomatoes, peeled and each cut into 4 wedges
> 1½ cups frozen whole-kernel corn, thawed
> 3 tablespoons reduced-sodium ketchup
> 1 teaspoon chili seasoning
> ⅛ teaspoon black pepper

Lock food processor bowl in position. Insert the steel knife blade. Drop zucchini into the food processor bowl. Attach food chute cover and lock in place. Turn on processor and pulse 4 or 5 times or until zucchini is coarsely chopped. Transfer chopped zucchini to a large bowl. Repeat process with carrot and onion. Place vegetables in a large skillet sprayed with butter-flavored cooking spray and sauté for 5 minutes. Drop tomato wedges into the food chute. Turn on processor and pulse 2 or 3 times or until tomatoes are coarsely chopped. Transfer chopped tomatoes to skillet with sautéed vegetables. Add corn, ketchup, chili seasoning, and black pepper. Mix well to combine. Continue cooking for 5 minutes or just until vegetables are tender, stirring often.

HINT: Thaw corn by rinsing in a colander under hot water for 1 minute.

Each serving equals:

HE: 2 Vegetable • ¾ Bread • 12 Optional Calories

120 Calories • 0 gm Fat • 4 gm Protein • 26 gm Carbohydrate • 50 mg Sodium • 33 mg Calcium • 4 gm Fiber

DIABETIC EXCHANGES: 1½ Vegetable • 1 Starch

CARB CHOICES: 1½

Italian Tomato-Zucchini Bake

Want a terrific recipe to make good use of all those extra, end-of-summer zucchini you may find in your garden (or left on your back porch by a mystery giver!)? This savory, cheesy combo is scrumptious and oh-so-crusty-yum!   ◐   Serves 6 (⅔ cup)

4 small unpeeled zucchini, cut in half lengthwise and
crosswise
4 medium tomatoes, peeled and each cut into 4 wedges
1 medium green bell pepper, stem and seeds removed and
cut into 8 strips
1 small onion, peeled and cut into 4 wedges
1½ teaspoons Italian seasoning
1 tablespoon Splenda Granular
6 (¾-ounce) slices Kraft reduced-fat American cheese

Preheat oven to 350 degrees. Spray an 8-by-8-inch baking dish with butter-flavored cooking spray. Lock food processor bowl in position. Insert the slicer disc. Attach food chute cover and lock in place. Drop zucchini, tomatoes, green pepper, and onion into the food chute. Position food pusher over vegetables. Turn on processor and use medium pressure to push vegetables through. Transfer vegetables to a large bowl when full level is reached. Repeat process as necessary. Add Italian seasoning and Splenda to sliced vegetables. Mix well to combine. Evenly spoon half of vegetable mixture into prepared baking dish. Arrange 3 slices of cheese over vegetables. Repeat layers. Cover and bake for 45 to 50 minutes or until zucchini is tender. Place baking dish on a wire rack and let set for 5 minutes. Divide into 6 servings.

Each serving equals:

HE: 2 Vegetable • 1 Protein • 1 Optional Calorie

62 Calories • 2 gm Fat • 4 gm Protein • 7 gm Carbohydrate •
197 mg Sodium • 110 mg Calcium • 2 gm Fiber

DIABETIC EXCHANGES: 2 Vegetable • ½ Meat

CARB CHOICES: ½

Chuckwagon Beans

I watched a cowboy cooking contest on the Food Network not long ago, and I got to watch the contestants use actual chuckwagons to prepare the dishes they were competing with. These portable kitchens were used to feed dozens at every meal of a cattle drive, and the food had to be hearty and plentiful. This dish surely is!

❂ Serves 6 (full ½ cup)

> 1 small onion, peeled and cut into 4 wedges
> 2 medium tomatoes, peeled and each cut into 4 wedges
> ¼ cup reduced-sodium ketchup
> 1 teaspoon Worcestershire sauce
> 2 (15-ounce) cans Bush's pinto beans, rinsed and drained
> ¼ cup Oscar Mayer or Hormel Real Bacon Bits

Lock food processor bowl in position. Insert the steel knife blade. Drop onion wedges into the food processor bowl. Attach food chute cover and lock in place. Turn on processor and pulse 3 or 4 times or until onion is finely chopped. Place in a large skillet sprayed with butter-flavored cooking spray. Sauté for 5 minutes. Drop tomato wedges into the food processor bowl. Attach food chute cover and lock in place. Turn on processor and pulse 3 or 4 times or until tomatoes are finely chopped. Stir tomatoes into skillet with sautéed onion. Add ketchup, Worcestershire sauce, and pinto beans. Mix well to combine. Bring mixture to a boil. Stir in bacon bits. Lower heat and simmer for 15 minutes or until mixture thickens, stirring occasionally.

Each serving equals:

HE: 1 Protein • ½ Bread • ½ Vegetable • 10 Optional Calories

126 Calories • 2 gm Fat • 7 gm Protein • 20 gm Carbohydrate • 166 mg Sodium • 51 mg Calcium • 5 gm Fiber

DIABETIC EXCHANGES: 1 Meat • ½ Starch • ½ Vegetable

CARB CHOICES: 1

Creative Sides

Choosing the perfect side dish to complement your entrée won't be a chore anymore, now that you've got your super-duper chopping/slicing/shredding machine to start your engine! The question won't be just "potatoes or rice?" but what kind of exciting way can you prepare those old standbys (and a few other surprises) now?

When you want something a little glamorous and elegant on the side, try *Lyonnaise Potato Bake*—ooh-la-la! Your family will love my *Easy Supper Potato Pancakes* and race each other to the table when you're serving *Oven Baked Steak Chips*. Tasty casseroles in this section include *Cheesy Rice and Carrots* and my *Bountiful Garden Scalloped Corn*. And you don't have to wait for the fall holiday season to fix *Farmhouse Stuffing*, beloved by all!

Lyonnaise Potato Bake

In the style of the French town Lyon, this elegant baked potato dish is simple yet superlative in its flavors and texture. You'll be astonished how sweet an onion can taste when it naturally "caramelizes."

○ Serves 4

> 4 (5-ounce) raw potatoes, peeled and each cut into 4 wedges
> 1 medium onion, peeled and cut into 6 wedges
> 1 teaspoon lemon pepper
> 2 tablespoons I Can't Believe It's Not Butter! Light
>   Margarine
> 2 sprigs fresh parsley, stems removed

Preheat oven to 350 degrees. Spray an 8-by-8-inch baking dish with butter-flavored cooking spray. Lock food processor bowl in position. Insert the slicer disc. Attach food chute cover and lock in place. Drop potato pieces into the food chute. Position food pusher over potatoes. Turn on processor and use medium pressure to push potatoes through. Transfer sliced potatoes to prepared baking dish when full level is reached. Repeat process as necessary. Repeat process with onion wedges. Combine sliced potatoes, onion, and lemon pepper in baking dish. Drop margarine by teaspoonful over potato mixture. Remove slicer disc from food processor and insert the steel knife blade. Drop parsley sprigs into the food processor bowl. Turn on processor and pulse 2 or 3 times or until parsley is chopped. Evenly sprinkle over top. Cover and bake for 30 minutes. Uncover and continue baking for 30 minutes or until potatoes are tender. Place baking dish on a wire rack and let set for 5 minutes. Divide into 4 servings.

Each serving equals:

HE: 1 Bread • ¾ Fat • ½ Vegetable

135 Calories • 3 gm Fat • 2 gm Protein • 25 gm Carbohydrate • 188 mg Sodium • 13 mg Calcium • 2 gm Fiber

DIABETIC EXCHANGES: 1½ Starch • 1 Fat • ½ Vegetable

CARB CHOICES: 1½

Old-Fashioned
Scalloped Potatoes

Does your heart beat faster when you see a recipe that is described as "old-fashioned"? Mine does. I love old-time cooking, but I don't want to spend hours in the kitchen. This recipe shows that you can use easy cooking methods to prepare foods the way Mom and Grandma used to.   ☻   Serves 6

> 5 (5-ounce) raw potatoes, peeled and each cut into 4 wedges
> 1 small onion, peeled and cut into 4 wedges
> 3 tablespoons all-purpose flour
> 1 (12-fluid-ounce) can Carnation Evaporated Fat Free Milk
> 2 tablespoons I Can't Believe It's Not Butter! Light
>   Margarine
> 2 sprigs parsley, stems removed
> ⅛ teaspoon black pepper
> Dash paprika

Preheat oven to 350 degrees. Spray an 8-by-8-inch baking dish with butter-flavored cooking spray. Lock food processor bowl in position. Insert the slicer disc. Attach food chute cover and lock in place. Drop potato wedges into the food chute. Position food pusher over potatoes. Turn on processor and use medium pressure to push potatoes through. Transfer sliced potatoes to a large bowl when full level is reached. Repeat process as necessary. Transfer potatoes to prepared baking dish. Remove slicer disc from food processor and insert the steel knife blade. Drop onion wedges into the food processor bowl. Attach food chute cover and lock in place. Turn on processor and pulse 4 or 6 times or until onion is finely chopped. Remove cover. Add flour, evaporated milk, margarine, parsley, and black pepper. Re-cover and pulse 15 or 20 times or until mixture is smooth. Pour milk mixture evenly over potatoes. Sprinkle paprika evenly over top. Cover and bake for 45 minutes. Uncover and continue baking for 45 minutes or until potatoes are tender. Place baking dish on a wire rack and let set for 5 minutes. Divide into 6 servings.

Each serving equals:

HE: 1 Bread • ½ Fat Free Milk • ½ Fat

162 Calories • 2 gm Fat • 6 gm Protein • 30 gm Carbohydrate •
129 mg Sodium • 169 mg Calcium • 2 gm Fiber

DIABETIC EXCHANGES: 1½ Starch • ½ Fat Free Milk • ½ Fat

CARB CHOICES: 2

Scalloped Potatoes and Mushrooms

What a luscious and luxurious dish this is, and how sumptuous it looks when it comes bubbling to the table! It's a great go-with for all kinds of main dishes, and it's also a good idea for a buffet party, since it reheats well.   ☉   Serves 6

5 (5-ounce) raw potatoes, peeled and each cut into 4 wedges
1 medium onion, peeled and cut into 6 wedges
2 cups fresh whole mushrooms, each cut in half
3 tablespoons all-purpose flour
2 tablespoons I Can't Believe It's Not Butter! Light
*   Margarine*
2 sprigs parsley, stems removed
⅛ teaspoon black pepper
1 (12-fluid-ounce) can Carnation Evaporated Fat Free Milk
Dash paprika

Preheat oven to 350 degrees. Spray an 8-by-8-inch baking dish with butter-flavored cooking spray. Lock food processor bowl in position. Insert the slicer disc. Attach food chute cover and lock in place. Drop potato wedges into the food chute. Position food pusher over potatoes. Turn on processor and use medium pressure to push potatoes through. Transfer sliced potatoes to a large bowl when full level is reached. Repeat process as necessary. Repeat process with onion and mushrooms. Mix vegetables together and evenly arrange in prepared baking dish. Remove slicer disc from food processor and insert the steel knife blade. Place flour, margarine, parsley, and black pepper in food processor bowl. Cover and pulse 4 or 5 times or until blended. Pour evaporated milk through the food chute while processor is running. Pulse 5 times or until mixture is smooth. Transfer milk mixture to a medium saucepan sprayed with butter-flavored cooking spray. Cook over medium heat for 5 minutes or until mixture thickens, stirring constantly. Pour hot milk mixture evenly over potato mixture. Sprinkle paprika evenly over top. Bake for 55 to 65 minutes or until potatoes are tender and golden brown. Place baking dish on a wire rack and let set for 5 minutes. Divide into 6 servings.

Each serving equals:

HE: 1 Bread • 1 Vegetable • ½ Fat Free Milk • ½ Fat

178 Calories • 2 gm Fat • 7 gm Protein • 33 gm Carbohydrate •
350 mg Sodium • 175 mg Calcium • 3 gm Fiber

DIABETIC EXCHANGES: 1½ Starch • 1 Vegetable • ½ Fat Free Milk • ½ Fat

CARB CHOICES: 2

Summer Potato Scallop

Don't like to bake in the summer months? This dish will change your mind! It depends on sweet, ripe tomatoes, which as we all know are at their best in June, July, and August. The sauce is rich and cheesy, and the corn is the ultimate sweet touch. If you've got lots of fresh corn around, do use it.   ☻   Serves 6

> 4 (5-ounce) unpeeled raw potatoes, each cut into 4 wedges
> 2 medium tomatoes, peeled and each cut into 6 wedges
> 1 small onion, peeled and cut into 4 wedges
> ½ cup fat-free milk
> ¾ cup shredded Kraft reduced-fat Cheddar cheese
> ½ cup Land O Lakes Fat Free Half & Half
> 2 eggs, or equivalent in egg substitute
> 4 sprigs parsley, stems removed
> ⅛ teaspoon black pepper
> 1 cup fresh or frozen whole-kernel corn, thawed
> ¼ cup Kraft Reduced Fat Parmesan Style Grated Topping

Preheat oven to 350 degrees. Spray an 8-by-8-inch baking dish with butter-flavored cooking spray. Lock food processor bowl in position. Insert the slicer disc. Attach food chute cover and lock in place. Drop potatoes into the food chute. Position food pusher over potatoes. Turn on processor and use medium pressure to push potatoes through. Transfer sliced potatoes to a large bowl. Drop tomato wedges through food chute, using light pressure to push tomatoes through. Transfer sliced tomatoes to a medium bowl. Repeat process with onion. Remove slicer disc from food processor and insert the steel knife blade. Place milk, Cheddar cheese, half & half, eggs, parsley, and black pepper in food processor bowl. Attach food chute cover and lock in place. Turn on processor and pulse 3 or 4 times or until mixture is smooth. Place half of potatoes in prepared baking dish. Arrange tomatoes, onion, and corn evenly over potatoes. Top with remaining potato slices. Evenly pour milk mixture over potatoes. Sprinkle Parmesan cheese evenly over top. Bake for 60 to 65 minutes or until potatoes are tender. Place baking dish on a wire rack and let set for 5 minutes. Divide into 6 servings.

Each serving equals:

HE: 1 Bread • 1 Protein • ½ Vegetable • 19 Optional Calories

181 Calories • 5 gm Fat • 10 gm Protein • 24 gm Carbohydrate •
198 mg Sodium • 165 mg Calcium • 2 gm Fiber

DIABETIC EXCHANGES: 1½ Starch • 1 Meat • ½ Vegetable

CARB CHOICES: 1½

Baked German Potatoes

Each country has made its own unique magic with the classic spud, and Germany is no exception. German potato salad is more vinegary than mayonnaise-y, and this baked dish takes that flavor to a beautifully tangy level. ● Serves 6

> 1 medium onion, peeled and cut into 6 wedges
> 4 medium stalks celery, trimmed and each cut into 2-inch
>   pieces
> 3 sprigs parsley, stems removed
> 3 tablespoons apple cider vinegar
> ⅓ cup water
> 1 tablespoon Splenda Granular
> ⅛ teaspoon black pepper
> 6 (5-ounce) raw potatoes, peeled and each cut into 4 wedges
> 6 tablespoons Oscar Mayer or Hormel Real Bacon Bits

Preheat oven to 400 degrees. Spray an 8-by-8-inch baking dish with butter-flavored cooking spray. Lock food processor bowl in position. Insert the steel knife blade. Drop onion wedges, celery pieces, and parsley into the food processor bowl. Attach food chute cover and lock in place. Turn on processor and pulse 3 or 4 times or until vegetables are finely chopped. Transfer chopped vegetables to a large skillet sprayed with butter-flavored cooking spray. Sauté for 5 to 6 minutes. Stir in vinegar, water, Splenda, and black pepper. Lower heat and simmer while preparing potatoes. Remove steel knife blade from food processor and insert the slicer disc. Attach food chute cover and lock in place. Drop potatoes into the food chute. Position food pusher over potatoes. Turn on processor and use medium pressure to push potatoes through. Transfer sliced potatoes into skillet. Add bacon bits. Mix well to combine. Evenly spoon mixture into prepared baking dish. Cover with foil and bake for 55 to 60 minutes or until potatoes are tender. Uncover and place baking dish on a wire rack and let set for 5 minutes. Divide into 6 servings.

Each serving equals:

HE: 1 Bread • ½ Protein • ½ Vegetable • 1 Optional Calorie

125 Calories • 1 gm Fat • 5 gm Protein • 24 gm Carbohydrate •
177 mg Sodium • 22 mg Calcium • 3 gm Fiber

DIABETIC EXCHANGES: 1½ Starch • ½ Meat • ½ Vegetable

CARB CHOICES: 1½

Creamed Potatoes and Carrots

If you love potatoes (a lot!) and you also love carrots, you may love this dish more than you imagine! Tossed together tenderly in a luscious creamy sauce, they'll make your mouth water and your stomach rumble—and you know that's not bad!

❍ Serves 4 (1 cup)

> 3 (5-ounce) unpeeled raw potatoes, each cut into
> 4 wedges
> 2 medium carrots, scraped and each cut into
> 2-inch pieces
> 1 small onion, peeled and cut into 4 wedges
> 2 cups water
> 1 (12-fluid-ounce) can Carnation Evaporated Fat Free
> Milk
> 3 tablespoons all-purpose flour
> 1 tablespoon Splenda Granular
> 2 sprigs parsley, stems removed
> ⅛ teaspoon black pepper
> 1 tablespoon + 1 teaspoon I Can't Believe It's Not Butter!
> Light Margarine

Lock food processor bowl in position. Insert the steel knife blade. Drop potatoes into the food processor bowl. Attach food chute cover and lock in place. Turn on processor and pulse 2 or 3 times or until potatoes are coarsely chopped. Transfer chopped vegetables to a medium saucepan. Repeat process with carrots and onion. Add water to vegetables. Mix well to combine. Cook over medium heat for 10 to 12 minutes or until potatoes and carrots are tender. Drain well and let set in colander while preparing sauce. Remove food processor cover. Place evaporated milk, flour, Splenda, parsley, and black pepper in food processor bowl. Re-cover and pulse 3 or 4 times or until mixture is smooth. Pour milk mixture into same saucepan used to cook vegetables. Cook over medium heat for 2 to 3 minutes, stirring often. Stir in well-drained vegetables and margarine. Continue cooking for 5 minutes or until mixture thickens and is heated through, stirring often.

Each serving equals:

HE: 1 Bread • ¾ Fat Free Milk • ¾ Vegetable • ½ Fat • 2 Optional Calories

206 Calories • 2 gm Fat • 9 gm Protein • 38 gm Carbohydrate • 391 mg Sodium • 257 mg Calcium • 3 gm Fiber

DIABETIC EXCHANGES: 1½ Starch • 1 Fat Free Milk • 1 Vegetable • ½ Fat

CARB CHOICES: 2

Easy Supper Potato Pancakes

Are you one of those who could eat potatoes at every meal? (Go to Ireland—no one serves more potatoes in more ways than they do!) I think many people feel that potatoes are true comfort food, and these potato cakes, served nice and crisp, will make you feel good inside and out. ☻ Serves 4

3 (5-ounce) raw potatoes, peeled and each cut into 4 wedges
1 small onion, peeled and cut into 4 wedges
1 egg, or equivalent in egg substitute
3 tablespoons all-purpose flour
½ teaspoon baking powder
¼ teaspoon table salt
⅛ teaspoon black pepper

Lock food processor bowl in position. Insert the shredder disc. Attach food chute cover and lock in place. Drop potato wedges into the food chute. Position food pusher over potatoes. Turn on processor and use medium pressure to push potatoes through. Repeat process with onion. Remove shredder disc from food processor and insert the steel knife blade. Add egg, flour, baking powder, salt, and black pepper to the food processor bowl. Re-cover and process for 20 to 30 seconds or until mixture is smooth. Using a ½ cup measuring cup as a guide, drop batter onto a hot skillet or griddle sprayed with butter-flavored cooking spray to form 4 pancakes. Brown for 5 to 7 minutes on each side. Serve at once.

Each serving equals:

HE: 1 Bread • ¼ Protein • ¼ Vegetable

117 Calories • 1 gm Fat • 4 gm Protein • 23 gm Carbohydrate • 249 mg Sodium • 48 mg Calcium • 2 gm Fiber

DIABETIC EXCHANGES: 1½ Starch

CARB CHOICES: 1½

Oven-Baked Steak Chips

If you've gazed longingly at fried potato wedges in fast-food restaurants or takeout shops, I'm here to tell you the good news: You can make great-tasting potatoes in your oven that may make you forget about the high-fat version! It's all in the seasoning, the timing, and the food processing.   ❂   Serves 4 (¾ cup)

> 4 (5-ounce) raw potatoes, peeled and each cut into 4 wedges
> 2 tablespoons I Can't Believe It's Not Butter! Light
>   Margarine
> ½ teaspoon chili seasoning
> ⅛ teaspoon black pepper

Preheat oven to 400 degrees. Spray a baking sheet with butter-flavored cooking spray. Lock food processor bowl in position. Insert the slicer disc. Attach food chute cover and lock in place. Drop potato wedges into the food chute. Position food pusher over potatoes. Turn on processor and use medium pressure to push potatoes through. Transfer potatoes onto prepared baking sheet when full level is reached. Repeat process as necessary. In a small microwave-safe bowl, combine margarine, chili seasoning, and black pepper. Microwave on HIGH for 15 seconds or until margarine melts. Mix well. Brush mixture evenly over potatoes. Toss gently to coat. Bake for 30 to 35 minutes or until tops are golden brown.

Each serving equals:

HE: 1 Bread • ¾ Fat

119 Calories • 3 gm Fat • 2 gm Protein • 21 gm Carbohydrate • 75 mg Sodium • 8 mg Calcium • 2 gm Fiber

DIABETIC EXCHANGES: 1 Starch • 1 Fat

CARB CHOICES: 1

Dilled Potato Vegetable Bake

Some herbs capture your attention in a big way, while others just insinuate themselves into your consciousness so you hardly notice them—until you realize what a difference they make in the flavor of a dish. Dill is one of those—stirred into this dish, they make every veggie in it taste new. ☻ Serves 4

> 3 (5-ounce) unpeeled raw potatoes, each cut into
>   4 wedges
> 1 medium onion, peeled and cut into 6 wedges
> 2 medium stalks celery, trimmed and each cut into
>   2-inch pieces
> 2 medium tomatoes, peeled and each cut into
>   6 wedges
> 2 teaspoons dried dill weed
> ¼ teaspoon black pepper
> 1 tablespoon + 1 teaspoon I Can't Believe It's Not Butter!
>   Light Margarine

Preheat oven to 375 degrees. Spray an 8-by-8-inch baking dish with butter-flavored cooking spray. Lock food processor bowl in position. Insert the slicer disc. Attach food chute cover and lock in place. Drop potatoes into the food chute. Position food pusher over potatoes. Turn on processor and use medium pressure to push potatoes through. Transfer sliced potatoes onto a piece of waxed paper. Repeat process with onion, then with celery, and then with tomatoes, placing each on separate sheets of waxed paper after slicing. Evenly arrange half of potatoes, half of onion, half of celery, and half of tomatoes in prepared baking dish. Sprinkle 1 teaspoon dill weed and ⅛ teaspoon black pepper over top. Repeat layers. Drop margarine over top by teaspoonful. Cover and bake for 45 minutes. Uncover and continue baking for 15 to 20 minutes or until vegetables are tender. Place baking dish on a wire rack and let set for 5 minutes. Divide into 4 servings.

Each serving equals:

HE: 1 Vegetable • ¾ Bread • ½ Fat

154 Calories • 2 gm Fat • 3 gm Protein • 31 gm Carbohydrate •
76 mg Sodium • 35 mg Calcium • 3 gm Fiber

DIABETIC EXCHANGES: 1½ Starch • 1 Vegetable • ½ Fat

CARB CHOICES: 2

Maple Sweet Potato–Apple Bake ❄

Those Thanksgiving sweet potato casseroles might just need a bit of a makeover, and here's my candidate to replace them on your table! Baked with apples and maple syrup, these sweet potatoes will beguile your taste buds with an astonishing explosion of flavor.

◐ Serves 6

> 1 (15-ounce) can vacuum-packed sweet potatoes, drained and sliced
> 2 slices reduced-calorie white bread, torn into large pieces
> 3 medium baking apples, cored and peeled, each cut into 6 wedges
> ¼ cup I Can't Believe It's Not Butter! Light Margarine ☆
> ½ cup Log Cabin Sugar Free Maple Syrup

Preheat oven to 350 degrees. Spray an 8-by-8-inch baking dish with butter-flavored cooking spray. Evenly arrange sweet potato slices in prepared baking dish. Lock food processor bowl in position. Insert the steel knife blade. Drop bread pieces into the food processor bowl. Attach food chute cover and lock in place. Turn on processor and pulse 3 or 4 times or until fine crumbs form. Transfer bread crumbs to a small bowl. Drop apple wedges into the food processor bowl. Attach food chute cover and lock in place. Turn on processor and pulse 4 or 5 times or until apples are finely chopped. Add 2 tablespoons margarine and maple syrup. Pulse 10 or 15 times or until mixture is well blended. Pour apple mixture evenly over sweet potatoes. Evenly sprinkle bread crumbs over apple mixture and dot top with remaining 2 tablespoons margarine. Bake for 55 to 60 minutes. Place baking dish on a wire rack and let set for 5 minutes. Divide into 6 servings.

Each serving equals:

HE: 1 Bread • 1 Fat • ½ Fruit • 12 Optional Calories

168 Calories • 4 gm Fat • 2 gm Protein • 31 gm Carbohydrate •
200 mg Sodium • 23 mg Calcium • 4 gm Fiber

DIABETIC EXCHANGES: 1 Starch • 1 Fat • ½ Fruit

CARB CHOICES: 2

Rice Pilaf

I'm not a fan of plain white rice on your plate—it's just too pale and unexciting. Instead, why not whip up this easy rice pilaf that sparkles with color and crunch? It's simple, it's quick, and when you prepare it with chicken broth, it's intensely flavorful!

◑ Serves 4 (¾ cup)

1 medium onion, peeled and
    cut into 6 wedges
2 medium stalks celery,
    trimmed and each
    cut into 2-inch pieces
1 small red bell pepper,
    stem and seeds
    removed and cut into
    4 strips

2 tablespoons I Can't Believe
    It's Not Butter! Light
    Margarine
1 (14-ounce) can Swanson
    Lower Sodium Fat Free
    Chicken Broth
⅛ teaspoon black pepper
1⅓ cups uncooked Minute Rice
3 sprigs parsley, stems removed

Lock food processor bowl in position. Insert the steel knife blade. Drop onion into the food processor bowl. Attach food chute cover and lock in place. Turn on processor and pulse 3 or 4 times or until onion is finely chopped. Transfer onion to a medium bowl. Repeat process with celery and red pepper. In a large skillet sprayed with butter-flavored cooking spray, melt margarine. Sauté chopped vegetables for 5 minutes. Stir in chicken broth, black pepper, and uncooked instant rice. Bring mixture to a boil, stirring occasionally. Place parsley sprigs in food processor bowl. Cover and pulse 2 or 3 times or until minced. Stir parsley into rice mixture. Lower heat and simmer for 7 to 9 minutes or until rice is tender and liquid is absorbed, stirring occasionally.

Each serving equals:

HE: 1 Bread • 1 Vegetable • ¾ Fat • 8 Optional Calories

155 Calories • 3 gm Fat • 4 gm Protein • 28 gm Carbohydrate •
245 mg Sodium • 31 mg Calcium • 2 gm Fiber

DIABETIC EXCHANGES: 1½ Starch • 1 Vegetable • 1 Fat

CARB CHOICES: 2

Confetti Rice

Party time! Every night can be a celebration meal when you fill your plate with festive dishes like this one. It's a sort of healthy fried rice, with wonderful bits and pieces of tasty veggies stirred in.

🌑 Serves 4 (¾ cup)

1 medium carrot, scraped and
    cut into 2-inch pieces
2 medium stalks celery,
    trimmed and each cut
    into 2-inch pieces
1 small onion, peeled and cut
    into 4 wedges
1 small green bell pepper, stem
    and seeds removed and
    cut into 4 strips

1 small red bell pepper, stem
    and seeds removed and
    cut into 4 strips
2 tablespoons I Can't Believe
    It's Not Butter! Light
    Margarine
1½ cups cooked rice
2 tablespoons Land O Lakes
    Fat Free Half & Half
⅛ teaspoon black pepper

Lock food processor bowl in position. Insert the shredder disc. Attach food chute cover and lock in place. Drop carrot pieces into the food chute. Position food pusher over carrots. Turn on processor and use medium pressure to push carrots through. Transfer shredded carrots to a large bowl. Repeat process with celery, onion, green pepper, and red pepper. In a large skillet sprayed with butter-flavored cooking spray, melt margarine. Stir in shredded vegetables. Sauté for 5 to 6 minutes, stirring often. Add rice, half & half, and black pepper. Mix well to combine. Continue sautéing for 3 to 4 minutes or until vegetables are just tender and mixture is heated through.

HINT: Usually 1 cup uncooked instant or ¾ cup regular rice cooks to about 1½ cups.

Each serving equals:

HE: 1½ Vegetable • ¾ Bread • ¾ Fat • 4 Optional Calories

107 Calories • 3 gm Fat • 2 gm Protein • 18 gm Carbohydrate • 108 mg Sodium • 31 mg Calcium • 2 gm Fiber

DIABETIC EXCHANGES: 1½ Vegetable • 1 Starch • ½ Fat

CARB CHOICES: 1

Spanish Rice Side Dish

If you like your side dishes zesty and bright, serve this alongside a spicy, meaty entrée for a satisfying supper all year long! (And if you love your food hot-hot-hot like my husband, Cliff, add a bit more pepper and chili seasoning, to your taste.)

○ Serves 4 (1 cup)

1 medium green bell pepper, stem and seeds removed and cut into 6 strips
1 medium onion, peeled and cut into 6 wedges
2 medium stalks celery, trimmed and each cut into 2-inch pieces

2 medium tomatoes, peeled and each cut into 6 wedges
1 cup reduced-sodium tomato juice
2 tablespoons Splenda Granular
1 teaspoon chili seasoning
⅛ teaspoon black pepper
1 cup uncooked Minute Rice

Lock food processor bowl in position. Insert the steel knife blade. Drop green pepper strips into the food processor bowl. Attach food chute cover and lock in place. Turn on processor and pulse 4 or 5 times or until green pepper is finely chopped. Transfer chopped green pepper to a large bowl. Repeat process with onion and celery. Drop tomato wedges into processor bowl. Pulse 3 or 4 times or until finely chopped. Transfer chopped tomatoes to bowl with other vegetables. Place chopped vegetables in a large skillet sprayed with butter-flavored cooking spray. Sauté for 5 minutes. Add tomato juice, Splenda, chili seasoning, and black pepper. Mix well to combine. Stir in uncooked instant rice. Lower heat, cover, and simmer for 8 to 10 minutes or until rice is tender and most of liquid is absorbed, stirring occasionally.

Each serving equals:

HE: 2 Vegetable • ¾ Bread • 3 Optional Calories

128 Calories • 0 gm Fat • 4 gm Protein • 28 gm Carbohydrate • 65 mg Sodium • 42 mg Calcium • 3 gm Fiber

DIABETIC EXCHANGES: 2 Vegetable • 1 Starch

CARB CHOICES: 2

Broccoli and Rice Side Dish

What a cozy dish to serve on a cool fall night, so cheesy-creamy and tummy-filling! Sometimes I make extra rice on purpose, so I've got a container of leftover rice in the fridge ready for recipes like this one. ☻ Serves 6

> 1 medium onion, peeled and cut into 6 wedges
> 2 medium stalks celery, trimmed and each cut into
>   2-inch pieces
> 3 cups frozen chopped broccoli, thawed ☆
> 1 (10¾-ounce) can Healthy Request Cream of Mushroom
>   Soup
> ¾ cup diced Velveeta Light processed cheese
> 2 tablespoons Land O Lakes Fat Free Half & Half
> ⅛ teaspoon black pepper
> 1½ cups cooked rice

Preheat oven to 350 degrees. Spray an 8-by-8-inch baking dish with butter-flavored cooking spray. Lock food processor bowl in position. Insert the steel knife blade. Drop onion wedges into the food processor bowl. Attach food chute cover and lock in place. Turn on processor and pulse 3 or 4 times or until onion is finely chopped. Transfer chopped onion to a large bowl. Repeat process with celery. Remove cover. Place 1 cup thawed broccoli, mushroom soup, Velveeta cheese, half & half, and black pepper in food processor bowl. Re-cover and process for 5 seconds. Stir soup mixture into vegetable mixture. Add remaining 2 cups chopped broccoli and rice. Mix well to combine. Evenly spread mixture into prepared baking dish. Bake for 40 to 50 minutes. Place baking dish on a wire rack and let set for 5 minutes. Divide into 6 servings.

HINT: Usually 1 cup uncooked instant or ¾ cup regular rice cooks
    to about 1½ cups.

Each serving equals:

HE: 1½ Vegetable • ½ Bread • ½ Protein • ¼ Slider • 10 Optional Calories

143 Calories • 3 gm Fat • 7 gm Protein • 22 gm Carbohydrate •
451 mg Sodium • 170 mg Calcium • 4 gm Fiber

DIABETIC EXCHANGES: 1½ Vegetable • 1 Starch • ½ Meat

CARB CHOICES: 1

Cheesy Rice and Carrots

Rice-based casseroles are great for small households because they reheat beautifully in the microwave. You can keep the dish in the pan it was baked in, or you can divide it into plastic containers to be refrigerated or frozen as needed.   ☻   Serves 6

>   3 medium carrots, scraped and each cut into 2-inch pieces
>   1 small onion, peeled and cut into 4 wedges
>   1 (12-fluid-ounce) can Carnation Evaporated Fat Free Milk
>   2 eggs, or equivalent in egg substitute
>   1 tablespoon Splenda Granular
>   2 sprigs fresh parsley, stems removed
>   1½ cups cooked rice
>   1 cup diced Velveeta Light processed cheese
>   ½ teaspoon Worcestershire sauce
>   ⅛ teaspoon black pepper

Preheat oven to 350 degrees. Spray an 8-by-8-inch baking dish with butter-flavored cooking spray. Lock food processor bowl in position. Insert the shredder disc. Attach food chute cover and lock in place. Drop carrot pieces into the food chute. Position food pusher over carrots. Turn on processor and use medium pressure to push carrots through. Transfer shredded carrots to a large bowl. Repeat process with onion. Remove shredder disc from food processor and insert the steel knife blade. Place evaporated milk, eggs, Splenda, and parsley in food processor bowl. Attach food chute cover and lock in place. Position food pusher in chute to prevent milk from splashing out of bowl. Turn on processor and pulse 15 or 20 times or until mixture is well blended. Pour milk mixture into carrot mixture. Add rice, Velveeta cheese, Worcestershire sauce, and black pepper. Mix well to combine. Evenly spread mixture into prepared baking dish. Bake for 45 to 50 minutes. Place baking dish on a wire rack and let set for 5 minutes. Divide into 6 servings.

HINT: Usually 1 cup uncooked instant or ¾ cup regular rice cooks
    to about 1½ cups.

Each serving equals:

HE: 1 Protein • 1 Vegetable • ½ Fat Free Milk • ½ Bread • 1 Optional Calorie

172 Calories • 4 gm Fat • 11 gm Protein • 23 gm Carbohydrate • 425 mg Sodium • 293 mg Calcium • 2 gm Fiber

DIABETIC EXCHANGES: 1 Meat • 1 Vegetable • ½ Fat Free Milk • ½ Starch

CARB CHOICES: 1½

Corn Belt Corn and Rice

Corn is the mother vegetable of the Midwest, but how far does the Corn Belt stretch? It turns out that 50 percent of all corn grown in the USA comes from Iowa, Indiana, Ohio, and Illinois. Other big corn states include South Dakota, Nebraska, Kansas, Minnesota, Wisconsin, Michigan, Missouri, and Kentucky.

● Serves 6

3 medium stalks celery, trimmed and each cut into
    2-inch pieces
1 small onion, peeled and cut into 4 wedges
1 cup Land O Lakes Fat Free Half & Half
2 eggs, or equivalent in egg substitute
1 cup diced Velveeta Light processed cheese
2 sprigs parsley, stems removed
⅛ teaspoon black pepper
1½ cups frozen whole-kernel corn, thawed
1½ cups cooked rice

Preheat oven to 350 degrees. Spray an 8-by-8-inch baking dish with butter-flavored cooking spray. Lock food processor bowl in position. Insert the steel knife blade. Drop celery pieces into the food processor bowl. Attach food chute cover and lock in place. Turn on processor and pulse 3 or 4 times or until celery is finely chopped. Transfer celery to a large bowl. Repeat process with onion. Remove cover. Place half & half, eggs, Velveeta cheese, parsley, and black pepper into food processor bowl. Re-cover and pulse 6 or 8 times or until mixture is smooth. Pour mixture into a large bowl with vegetables. Add corn and rice. Mix well to combine. Evenly spread mixture into prepared baking dish. Bake for 40 to 50 minutes. Place baking dish on a wire rack and let set for 5 minutes. Divide into 6 servings.

HINTS: 1. Thaw corn by rinsing in a colander under hot water for 1 minute.
2. Usually 1 cup uncooked instant rice or ¾ cup regular rice cooks to about 1½ cups.

Each serving equals:

HE: 1 Bread • 1 Protein • ½ Vegetable • ¼ Slider • 3 Optional Calories

176 Calories • 4 gm Fat • 9 gm Protein • 26 gm Carbohydrate •
400 mg Sodium • 171 mg Calcium • 2 gm Fiber

DIABETIC EXCHANGES: 1½ Starch/Carbohydrate • 1 Meat • ½ Vegetable

CARB CHOICES: 1½

Corn and Celery Bake

Would it surprise you to know that there isn't any cream in the creamed corn that's sold in cans? What makes it "creamy" is the way the corn itself is prepared, and it's great for cooking. Here, I'm using two forms of corn to deepen the corn flavor of this hearty casserole. ◐ Serves 6

⅔ cup Carnation Nonfat Dry Milk Powder
1 cup water
1 medium onion, peeled and cut into 6 wedges
4 medium stalks celery, trimmed and each cut into
    2-inch pieces
14 small fat-free saltine crackers
2 sprigs parsley, stems removed
1 (8-ounce) can cream-style corn
1 cup frozen whole-kernel corn, thawed
1 tablespoon Splenda Granular
⅛ teaspoon black pepper

Preheat oven to 350 degrees. Spray an 8-by-8-inch baking dish with butter-flavored cooking spray. In a small bowl, combine dry milk powder and water. Set aside. Lock food processor bowl in position. Insert the steel knife blade. Drop onion wedges and celery pieces into the food processor bowl. Attach food chute cover and lock in place. Turn on processor and pulse 4 times or until vegetables are finely chopped. Transfer chopped vegetables to a large bowl. Wipe food processor bowl with a clean cloth. Place crackers and parsley in food processor bowl. Re-cover and pulse 25 to 30 times or until mixture is crumbly. Add crumb mixture to vegetables. Mix well to combine. Stir in milk mixture and cream-style corn. Add whole-kernel corn, Splenda, and black pepper. Mix well to combine. Evenly spread mixture into prepared baking dish. Bake for 45 to 50 minutes. Place baking dish on a wire rack and let set for 5 minutes. Divide into 6 servings.

HINT: Thaw corn by rinsing in a colander under hot water for 1 minute.

Each serving equals:

HE: 1 Bread • ½ Vegetable • ⅓ Fat Free Milk • 1 Optional Calorie

124 Calories • 0 gm Fat • 5 gm Protein • 26 gm Carbohydrate •
270 mg Sodium • 117 mg Calcium • 2 gm Fiber

DIABETIC EXCHANGES: 1½ Starch/Carbohydrate • ½ Vegetable

CARB CHOICES: 1½

Bountiful Garden Scalloped Corn

I've spent a lot of time these past several years studying to become a Master Gardener, but even before that, I devoted myself to creating a garden and orchards that fulfilled my dreams. And eating the bounty of my garden has always been a special gift from God.

Serves 8

> 1 medium carrot, scraped and cut into 2-inch pieces
> 1 small onion, peeled and cut into 4 wedges
> 1 small red bell pepper, stem and seeds removed and
>   cut into 4 strips
> 10 Ritz Reduced Fat Crackers
> ⅔ cup Carnation Nonfat Dry Milk Powder
> ⅓ cup water
> 2 eggs, or equivalent in egg substitute
> 1 cup frozen whole-kernel corn, thawed
> 1 (15-ounce) can cream-style corn
> 1 tablespoon Splenda Granular
> ⅛ teaspoon black pepper

Preheat oven to 350 degrees. Spray an 8-by-8-inch baking dish with butter-flavored cooking spray. Lock food processor bowl in position. Insert the shredder disc. Attach food chute cover and lock in place. Drop carrot pieces into the food chute. Position food pusher over carrots. Turn on processor and use medium pressure to push carrots through. Transfer carrots to a large bowl. Repeat process with onion and red pepper. Remove shredder disc from food processor and insert the steel knife blade. Place crackers, dry milk powder, water, and eggs in food processor bowl. Re-cover and pulse 3 or 4 times or until mixture is smooth. Add cracker mixture to vegetable mixture. Mix well to combine. Stir in whole-kernel corn. Add cream-style corn, Splenda, and black pepper. Mix well to combine. Evenly spread mixture into prepared baking dish. Bake for 35 to 45 minutes. Place baking dish on a wire rack and let set for 5 minutes. Divide into 8 servings.

Each serving equals:

HE: 1 Bread • ½ Vegetable • ¼ Fat Free Milk • ¼ Protein •
1 Optional Calorie

122 Calories • 2 gm Fat • 5 gm Protein • 21 gm Carbohydrate •
240 mg Sodium • 93 mg Calcium • 2 gm Fiber

DIABETIC EXCHANGES: 1 Starch • ½ Vegetable

CARB CHOICES: 1

Pasta-Pleasing
Broccoli Alfredo Side Dish

Some nights, when we've been testing recipes for hours, I look into the refrigerator and think about making dinner just from a few tasty side dishes. This is one of my recent favorites, and it's wonderfully soothing and filling after a busy day. ☽ Serves 4 (1 cup)

1 small onion, peeled and cut into 4 wedges
1 cup fresh whole mushrooms, each cut in half
2 cups frozen chopped broccoli, thawed
1½ cups hot cooked spaghetti, rinsed and drained
1 tablespoon + 1 teaspoon I Can't Believe It's Not Butter!
    Light Margarine
½ cup Land O Lakes Fat Free Half & Half
¼ cup fat-free milk
½ cup Kraft Reduced Fat Parmesan Style Grated
    Topping
1½ teaspoons Italian seasoning

Lock food processor bowl in position. Insert the steel knife blade. Drop onion into the food processor bowl. Attach food chute cover and lock in place. Turn on processor and pulse 3 or 4 times or until onion is finely chopped. Transfer onion to a large bowl. Repeat process with mushrooms. Remove lid. Place chopped broccoli in food processor bowl. Re-cover and pulse 3 or 4 times or until broccoli is finely chopped. Transfer chopped broccoli and onion mixture to a large skillet sprayed with butter-flavored cooking spray. Sauté over medium heat for 5 minutes. Stir in spaghetti. Add margarine, half & half, milk, Parmesan cheese, and Italian seasoning. Mix well to combine. Lower heat and simmer for 2 to 3 minutes or until mixture is heated through, stirring often.

HINT: Usually 1 full cup broken uncooked spaghetti cooks to about 1½ cups.

Each serving equals:

HE: 1½ Vegetable • ¾ Bread • ½ Protein • ½ Fat • ¼ Slider •
8 Optional Calories

222 Calories • 6 gm Fat • 9 gm Protein • 33 gm Carbohydrate •
490 mg Sodium • 200 mg Calcium • 5 gm Fiber

DIABETIC EXCHANGES: 1½ Vegetable • 1½ Starch • ½ Meat • ½ Fat

CARB CHOICES: 2

Rice-Vegetable Skillet

What *is* a water chestnut, and do they only grow in China? I've wondered, too, so I asked Google to help me find out, and here's what I learned: It's a tuber, the root of an aquatic plant that grows in Japan, China, Taiwan, Thailand, and Australia, where it's found in ponds, rivers, and lakes. I like them because they're firm, crispy, and crunchy.   ❂   Serves 6 (¾ cup)

1½ cups fresh whole
    mushrooms, each cut in
    half
2 medium stalks celery,
    trimmed and each cut
    into 2-inch pieces
1 (8-ounce) can water
    chestnuts, drained

1 small onion, peeled and cut
    into 4 wedges
¼ cup I Can't Believe It's Not
    Butter! Light Margarine
1½ cups cooked rice
¼ cup Land O Lakes no-fat
    sour cream
1½ teaspoons lemon pepper

Lock food processor bowl in position. Insert the slicer disc. Attach food chute cover and lock in place. Drop mushrooms, celery, water chestnuts, and onion into the food chute. Position food pusher over vegetables. Turn on processor and use medium pressure to push vegetables through. Transfer sliced vegetables to a large bowl when full level is reached. Repeat process as necessary. In a large skillet sprayed with butter-flavored cooking spray, melt margarine. Add sliced vegetables. Mix well to combine. Sauté vegetable's for 10 to 12 minutes or just until soft, stirring occasionally. Stir in rice, sour cream, and lemon pepper. Lower heat, cover, and simmer for 4 to 5 minutes, stirring occasionally.

HINT: Usually 1 cup uncooked instant or ¾ cup regular rice cooks to about 1½ cups.

Each serving equals:

HE: 1 Fat • ¾ Vegetable • ½ Bread • 10 Optional Calories

104 Calories • 4 gm Fat • 2 gm Protein • 15 gm Carbohydrate • 306 mg Sodium • 30 mg Calcium • 2 gm Fiber

DIABETIC EXCHANGES: 1 Fat • 1 Vegetable • ½ Starch

CARB CHOICES: 1

Noodle Basil-Tomato Side Dish

One of the things I love most about using a food processor is how it allows you to combine freshly chopped veggies and herbs together *easily* and chop them finely. There's just nothing like the flavor you get when you do it that way! ☻ Serves 4 (¾ cup)

> 2 medium tomatoes, peeled and each cut into 4 wedges
> 1 small onion, peeled and cut into 4 wedges
> 6 fresh basil leaves
> 1 tablespoon + 1 teaspoon I Can't Believe It's Not Butter!
>   Light Margarine
> 1 tablespoon Splenda Granular
> ⅛ teaspoon black pepper
> 2 cups hot cooked noodles, rinsed and drained

Lock food processor bowl in position. Insert the steel knife blade. Drop tomato and onion wedges into the food processor bowl. Attach food chute cover and lock in place. Turn on processor and pulse 3 or 4 times or until vegetables are chopped. Drop basil leaves through food chute. Pulse 1 or 2 times or until mixture is finely chopped. In a large skillet sprayed with butter-flavored cooking spray, melt margarine. Add tomato mixture, Splenda, and black pepper. Mix well to combine. Cook over medium heat for 5 minutes, stirring occasionally. Stir in noodles. Continue cooking for 3 to 4 minutes or until mixture is heated through, stirring often.

HINT: Usually 1¾ cups uncooked noodles cook to about 2 cups.

Each serving equals:

HE: 1 Bread • 1 Vegetable • ½ Fat • 2 Optional Calories

139 Calories • 3 gm Fat • 4 gm Protein • 24 gm Carbohydrate •
58 mg Sodium • 22 mg Calcium • 2 gm Fiber

DIABETIC EXCHANGES: 1½ Starch • 1 Vegetable • ½ Fat

CARB CHOICES: 1½

Spaghetti-Veggie Side Dish

This is a fun, made-from-leftovers combination that may surprise you with its original flavors and varied textures! Sometimes the most creative cooking happens when you least expect it.

�❍ Serves 4 (½ cup)

2 medium carrots, scraped and each cut into 2-inch pieces

2 medium stalks celery, trimmed and each cut into 2-inch pieces

1 medium onion, peeled and cut into 6 wedges

2 cups spinach leaves, stems removed and discarded

1½ cups cooked spaghetti, rinsed and drained

2 tablespoons reduced-sodium soy sauce

¼ cup reduced-sodium ketchup

⅛ teaspoon black pepper

Lock food processor bowl in position. Insert the shredder disc. Attach food chute cover and lock in place. Drop carrot pieces into the food chute. Position food pusher over carrots. Turn on processor and use medium pressure to push carrots through. Transfer shredded carrots to a large bowl. Repeat process with celery and onion. Place shredded vegetables in a large skillet sprayed with butter-flavored cooking spray. Sauté for 6 to 8 minutes. Remove shredder disc from food processor and insert the steel knife blade. Drop spinach leaves into the food processor bowl. Turn on processor and pulse 2 or 3 times or until spinach is coarsely chopped. Stir spaghetti and chopped spinach into sautéed vegetables. Add soy sauce, ketchup, and black pepper. Mix well to combine. Continue cooking for 3 to 4 minutes or until mixture is heated through, stirring often.

HINT: Usually a full 1 cup broken uncooked spaghetti cooks to about 1½ cups.

Each serving equals:

HE: 1½ Vegetable • ¾ Bread • 15 Optional Calories

120 Calories • 0 gm Fat • 4 gm Protein • 26 gm Carbohydrate • 319 mg Sodium • 46 mg Calcium • 3 gm Fiber

DIABETIC EXCHANGES: 1½ Vegetable • 1 Starch

CARB CHOICES: 1½

Farmhouse Stuffing

Did you know that stuffing is the dish highest in fat at most Thanksgiving feasts? It's true, usually because it contains a lot of butter. No one wants to give up enjoying stuffing, so I performed a bit of farmhouse "magic" to stir up a stuffing that won't "stuff" you!

◑ Serves 8

> 2 medium onions, peeled and each cut into 6 wedges
> 2 medium carrots, scraped and each cut into 2-inch pieces
> 4 medium stalks celery, trimmed and each cut into 2-inch
>   pieces
> 12 slices reduced-calorie bread, crumbled
> 1 tablespoon dried sage
> 1 teaspoon lemon pepper
> 1 (14-ounce) can Swanson Lower Sodium Fat Free Chicken
>   Broth
> ¼ cup water

Preheat oven to 350 degrees. Spray an 8-by-12-inch baking dish with butter-flavored cooking spray. Lock food processor bowl in position. Insert the steel knife blade. Drop onions, carrots, and celery into the food processor bowl. Attach food chute cover and lock in place. Turn on processor and pulse 6 or 8 times or until vegetables are coarsely chopped. Transfer chopped vegetables to a large bowl. Add crumbled bread, sage, and lemon pepper. Mix well to combine. Stir in chicken broth and water. Pour mixture into prepared baking dish. Bake for 45 to 50 minutes. Place baking dish on a wire rack and let set for at least 5 minutes. Divide into 8 servings.

Each serving equals:

HE: 1 Vegetable • ¾ Bread • 4 Optional Calories

84 Calories • 0 gm Fat • 5 gm Protein • 16 gm Carbohydrate •
336 mg Sodium • 56 mg Calcium • 2 gm Fiber

DIABETIC EXCHANGES: 1 Vegetable • 1 Starch

CARB CHOICES: 1

Veggie–Bread Stuffing Side Dish

If you're one of the stuffing fans who love lots of veggies blended in, this one's for you! You don't need a special occasion to put this saucy dish on the menu.   ❂   Serves 6

> 12 slices reduced-calorie white bread, toasted and each
>   cut into 6 pieces
> 1 large onion, peeled and cut into 8 wedges
> 2 medium carrots, scraped and each cut into
>   2-inch pieces
> 2 medium stalks celery, trimmed and each cut into
>   2-inch pieces
> 4 sprigs parsley, stems removed
> 1 (10¾-ounce) can Healthy Request Cream of Mushroom
>   Soup
> ½ cup water
> 1 teaspoon dried thyme
> ⅛ teaspoon black pepper

Preheat oven to 350 degrees. Spray an 8-by-8-inch baking dish with butter-flavored cooking spray. Lock food processor bowl in position. Insert the steel knife blade. Drop toast pieces into the food processor bowl. Attach food chute cover and lock in place. Turn on processor and pulse 5 or 6 times or until coarse crumbs form. Transfer bread crumbs to a large bowl. Re-cover and drop onion, carrots, celery, and parsley through food chute and pulse 4 or 5 times or until vegetables are coarsely chopped. Transfer chopped vegetables to bowl with crumbs when full level is reached. Repeat process as necessary. Add mushroom soup, water, thyme, and black pepper. Mix well to combine. Evenly spread mixture into prepared baking dish. Cover and bake for 45 minutes. Uncover and continue baking for 15 minutes. Place baking dish on a wire rack and let set for 5 minutes. Divide into 6 servings.

Each serving equals:

HE: 1 Bread • 1 Vegetable • ¼ Slider • 8 Optional Calories

130 Calories • 2 gm Fat • 6 gm Protein • 22 gm Carbohydrate •
452 mg Sodium • 96 mg Calcium • 2 gm Fiber

DIABETIC EXCHANGES: 1 Starch • 1 Vegetable

CARB CHOICES: 1

Italian Bread Stuffing Bake

I remember watching a commercial on TV that kept asking people whether they preferred rice or stuffing with their dinners, and lots of people smiled when they answered, "Stuffing." If you're one of them, here's a festive side dish good anytime at all!

● Serves 6

> 12 slices reduced-calorie Italian or white bread,
>   toasted and each cut into 6 pieces
> 1 large onion, peeled and cut into 6 wedges
> 1 medium unpeeled zucchini, cut in half lengthwise
>   and crosswise
> 2 medium carrots, scraped and each cut into
>   2-inch pieces
> 1 (15-ounce) can diced tomatoes, undrained
> ¼ cup reduced-sodium ketchup
> 1 teaspoon Italian seasoning

Preheat oven to 350 degrees. Spray an 8-by-8-inch baking dish with olive oil–flavored cooking spray. Lock food processor bowl in position. Insert the steel knife blade. Drop toast pieces into the food processor bowl. Attach food chute cover and lock in place. Turn on processor and pulse 12 or 15 times or until coarse crumbs form. Transfer bread crumbs to a large bowl. Remove steel knife blade from food processor and insert the shredder disc. Attach food chute cover and lock in place. Drop onion, zucchini, and carrots into the food chute. Position food pusher over vegetables. Turn on processor and use medium pressure to push vegetables through. Transfer shredded vegetables to large bowl with bread crumbs when full level is reached. Repeat process as necessary. Add undrained tomatoes, ketchup, and Italian seasoning. Mix well to combine. Evenly spread mixture into prepared baking dish. Cover and bake for 45 minutes. Uncover and continue baking for 15 minutes or until vegetables are tender. Place baking dish on a wire rack and let set for 5 minutes. Divide into 6 servings.

Each serving equals:

HE: 1½ Vegetable • 1 Bread • 10 Optional Calories

129 Calories • 1 gm Fat • 6 gm Protein • 24 gm Carbohydrate •
340 mg Sodium • 64 mg Calcium • 3 gm Fiber

DIABETIC EXCHANGES: 1½ Vegetable • 1 Starch

CARB CHOICES: 1½

Savory

Main Dishes

Testing the recipes in this book was a lot more fun than I expected, because preparation using the food processor was a culinary adventure! I took some new paths and explored some familiar places with new eyes because of it, and now I'm delighted to pass my discoveries on to you. I suspect you may banish some of your countertop appliances to a cabinet once you start stirring up some of these marvelous main dishes.

After a hard day at work or school, wouldn't it be lovely to come home and enjoy a steaming plate of *Chicken Cheddar Tetrazzini* or perhaps some luscious *Hamburger Stroganoff*? Instead of soup and sandwiches for Sunday supper, how about fixing *Pork Tenders Baked with Apple Stuffing* or maybe my *Golden Nugget Meat Loaf*? And when what you really long for is old-fashioned comfort food, try *Baked Layered Spaghetti* or a true melting-pot entrée, *Potato Kugel Shepherd's Pie*!

Crunchy Veggie-Cheese Sandwiches

These fun, open-faced treats are just a little spicy and wonderfully cheesy! You'll feel so speedy with your food processor "assembly line" as you drop the different veggies into the chute. Wouldn't it be great if everything in life was this easy? ☻ Serves 4

> 1 small onion, peeled and cut into 4 wedges
> 1 medium stalk celery, trimmed and cut into 2-inch pieces
> 1 medium carrot, scraped and cut into 2-inch pieces
> 1 medium tomato, peeled and cut into 6 wedges
> 1 cup shredded Kraft reduced-fat Cheddar cheese
> ¼ cup Kraft fat-free mayonnaise
> 1 teaspoon prepared horseradish sauce
> 4 slices reduced-calorie whole-wheat bread

Set oven temperature to broil. Lock food processor bowl in position. Insert the steel knife blade. Drop onion wedges, celery, and carrot into the food processor bowl. Attach food chute cover and lock in place. Turn on processor and pulse 3 or 4 times or until vegetables are chopped. Transfer chopped vegetables to a medium bowl. Repeat process with tomato wedges. Transfer chopped tomatoes to bowl with chopped vegetables. Stir in Cheddar cheese. Add mayonnaise and horseradish sauce. Mix well to combine. Place bread slices on a broiler pan sprayed with butter-flavored cooking spray. Evenly spread vegetable and cheese mixture over top of bread slices. Broil for 4 or 5 minutes or just until cheese melts, watching closely. Serve at once.

Each serving equals:

HE: 1 Protein • 1 Vegetable • ½ Bread • 10 Optional Calories

154 Calories • 6 gm Fat • 11 gm Protein • 14 gm Carbohydrate •
529 mg Sodium • 238 mg Calcium • 2 gm Fiber

DIABETIC EXCHANGES: 1 Meat • 1 Vegetable • ½ Starch

CARB CHOICES: 1

Cheesy Zucchini-Tomato Quiche

Remember when they used to say that "real men" didn't eat quiche? Well, they obviously didn't check with a lot of the men I know who will gladly gobble down a cheesy, custardy pie like this one! The way I make it, quiche isn't fussy food, just flavorful and fun.

○ Serves 6

> 2 medium unpeeled zucchini, cut in half lengthwise and
>   crosswise
> 2 medium tomatoes, peeled and each cut into 6 wedges
> 1 medium onion, peeled and cut into 6 wedges
> ½ cup shredded Kraft reduced-fat mozzarella cheese
> 1 (12-fluid-ounce) can Carnation Evaporated Fat Free Milk
> 3 eggs, or equivalent in egg substitute
> ¾ cup Bisquick Heart Smart Baking Mix
> ¼ cup Kraft Reduced Fat Parmesan Style Grated Topping
> 1 tablespoon Splenda Granular
> 1½ teaspoons Italian seasoning

Preheat oven to 400 degrees. Spray a deep-dish 10-inch pie plate with olive oil–flavored cooking spray. Lock food processor bowl in position. Insert the slicer disc. Attach food chute cover and lock in place. Drop zucchini into the food chute. Position food pusher over zucchini. Turn on processor and use medium pressure to push zucchini through. Transfer sliced zucchini to a large bowl. Repeat process with tomatoes and onion. Gently mix vegetables to combine. Spoon vegetables into prepared pie plate. Sprinkle mozzarella cheese evenly over top. Remove slicer disc from food processor and insert the steel knife blade. Place evaporated milk, eggs, baking mix, Parmesan cheese, Splenda, and Italian seasoning in food processor bowl. Attach food chute cover and lock in place. Position food pusher in chute to prevent milk from splashing out of bowl. Turn on processor and pulse 3 or 4 times or until mixture is smooth. Carefully pour mixture over vegetables. Bake for 30 to 35 minutes or until a knife inserted in center comes out clean. Place pie plate on a wire rack and let set for 10 minutes. Cut into 6 servings.

Each serving equals:

HE: 1½ Vegetable • 1 Protein • ½ Fat Free Milk • ½ Bread • 1 Optional Calorie

222 Calories • 6 gm Fat • 13 gm Protein • 29 gm Carbohydrate • 442 mg Sodium • 315 mg Calcium • 2 gm Fiber

DIABETIC EXCHANGES: 1 Vegetable • 1 Meat • 1 Starch • ½ Fat Free Milk

CARB CHOICES: 2

Cliff's Italian Baked Fish

Sometimes I'll create a very simple dish (like this one!) that takes very little work—and it will be the recipe that Cliff enjoys the most! That's a good reminder that we don't have to spend hours in the kitchen or the grocery store in order to please our loved ones.

○ Serves 4

⅓ cup Kraft Fat Free Italian Dressing
16 ounces white fish, cut into 4 pieces
2 slices reduced-calorie white bread, toasted and each cut
    into 6 pieces
¼ cup Kraft Reduced Fat Parmesan Style Grated Topping
⅛ teaspoon black pepper

Preheat oven to 375 degrees. Spray an 8-by-8-inch baking dish with butter-flavored cooking spray. Place Italian dressing in a shallow dish. Dip fish pieces on both sides in dressing. Evenly arrange fish pieces in prepared baking dish. Lock food processor bowl in position. Insert the steel knife blade. Drop toast pieces, Parmesan cheese, and black pepper into the food processor bowl. Attach food chute cover and lock in place. Turn on processor and pulse 20 or 30 times or until toast has turned into crumbs and mixture is combined. Evenly sprinkle about ¼ cup crumb mixture over top of each piece of fish. Bake for 25 to 30 minutes or until fish flakes easily with a fork. Serve at once.

Each serving equals:

HE: 2½ Protein • ¼ Bread • 7 Optional Calories

131 Calories • 3 gm Fat • 18 gm Protein • 8 gm Carbohydrate • 424 mg Sodium • 86 mg Calcium • 0 gm Fiber

DIABETIC EXCHANGES: 3 Meat • ½ Starch/Carbohydrate

CARB CHOICES: ½

Deluxe Tuna–Egg Salad Sandwiches

Why mix tuna and egg salad together, you may wonder? My first answer is, why not? But the other reason is also important. We eat so many sandwiches in our lives that we can get bored, and when we get bored, we tend to snack on unhealthy foods. By taking the familiar and transforming it just a little, I can recapture your attention—and win over your taste buds! ♥ Serves 4

> 1 small onion, peeled and cut into 4 wedges
> 1 medium stalk celery, trimmed and cut into 2-inch pieces
> 2 hard-boiled eggs
> 1 (6-ounce) can white tuna, packed in water, drained and
>   flaked
> ½ cup shredded Kraft reduced-fat Cheddar cheese
> ½ cup Kraft fat-free mayonnaise
> 2 tablespoons sweet pickle relish
> 4 lettuce leaves
> 8 slices reduced-calorie whole-wheat bread

Lock food processor bowl in position. Insert the steel knife blade. Drop onion and celery into the food processor bowl. Attach food chute cover and lock in place. Turn on processor and pulse 3 or 4 times or until vegetables are finely chopped. Transfer chopped vegetables to a medium bowl. Repeat process with eggs and tuna. Spoon egg mixture into bowl with chopped vegetables. Add Cheddar cheese, mayonnaise, and pickle relish. Mix well to combine. Evenly arrange lettuce leaves on 4 slices of bread. Spread about ½ cup filling mixture over lettuce and top with another slice of bread.

Each serving equals:

HE: 2 Protein • 1 Bread • ½ Vegetable • ¼ Slider • 10 Optional Calories

236 Calories • 8 gm Fat • 19 gm Protein • 22 gm Carbohydrate •
808 mg Sodium • 164 mg Calcium • 1 gm Fiber

DIABETIC EXCHANGES: 2 Meat • 1 Starch • ½ Vegetable

CARB CHOICES: 1½

Tuna Patties in Spanish Sauce

At first, you may feel that tuna patties are just a hamburger "substitute," a way to lower the number of meat servings we eat each week. But I bet that soon you'll decide that they're wonderful all by themselves, and when topped with a zesty sauce, they light up the room—or at least the plate!   ○   Serves 4

> 1 small onion, peeled and cut into 4 wedges
> 2 medium stalks celery, trimmed and each cut into
>   2-inch pieces
> 1 small red bell pepper, stem and seeds removed and
>   cut into 6 strips
> 1 (8-ounce) can Hunt's Tomato Sauce
> 1 tablespoon Splenda Granular
> ½ teaspoon chili seasoning
> 4 slices reduced-calorie white bread, toasted and each
>   cut into 6 pieces
> 1 (6-ounce) can white tuna, packed in water, drained
>   and flaked
> 1 egg, or equivalent in egg substitute
> 2 tablespoons Land O Lakes no-fat sour cream
> ⅛ teaspoon black pepper

Lock food processor bowl in position. Insert the steel knife blade. Drop onion, celery, and red pepper into the food processor bowl. Attach food chute cover and lock in place. Turn on processor and pulse 4 or 5 times or until vegetables are finely chopped. Transfer chopped vegetables to a medium skillet sprayed with butter-flavored cooking spray. Sauté vegetables for 5 minutes. Stir in tomato sauce, Splenda, and chili seasoning. Lower heat and simmer while preparing patties. Wipe food processor bowl with a clean cloth. Place toast pieces in the food processor bowl. Pulse 5 times or until toast is made into crumbs. In a large bowl, combine bread crumbs, tuna, egg, sour cream, and black pepper. Mix well to combine. Using a ½ cup measuring cup as a guide, form into 4 patties. Evenly arrange patties in a large skillet sprayed with butter-flavored cooking spray and brown for 5 minutes on each side. For each serving, place 1 patty on a plate and spoon about ⅓ cup sauce mixture over top.

Each serving equals:

HE: 2¼ Vegetable • 1¼ Protein • ½ Bread • 8 Optional Calories

139 Calories • 3 gm Fat • 12 gm Protein • 16 gm Carbohydrate •
609 mg Sodium • 59 mg Calcium • 2 gm Fiber

DIABETIC EXCHANGES: 2 Vegetable • 2 Meat • ½ Starch

CARB CHOICES: 1

Grandma's Salmon Casserole

Back when our grandmas were young, they were always trying to figure out clever ways to serve canned salmon. The women's magazines offered recipes for creamy salmon mousse and crunchy salmon loaf, all kinds of ideas to take advantage of this exotic canned fish. Here's a dish to make Grandma proud—and your family scrumptiously satisfied!   ◐   Serves 6

> 14 small fat-free saltine crackers, each broken
>   in half
> 4 sprigs parsley, stems removed
> 2 medium stalks celery, trimmed and each cut into
>   2-inch pieces
> 1 small onion, peeled and cut into 4 wedges
> 1 (14.5-ounce) can pink salmon, drained, boned,
>   and flaked
> ½ cup frozen peas, thawed
> 2 eggs, or equivalent in egg substitute
> ½ cup Land O Lakes Fat Free Half & Half
> 2 tablespoons Land O Lakes no-fat sour cream

Preheat oven to 350 degrees. Spray an 8-by-8-inch baking dish with butter-flavored cooking spray. Lock food processor bowl in position. Insert the steel knife blade. Drop crackers and parsley into the food processor bowl. Attach food chute cover and lock in place. Turn on processor and pulse 5 times or until crackers are coarsely chopped. Transfer cracker crumbs to a medium bowl. Repeat process with celery and onion. Layer half of cracker crumbs, half of salmon, half of peas, and half of chopped vegetables in prepared baking dish. Repeat layer. Place eggs, half & half, and sour cream in food processor bowl. Re-cover and pulse 6 or 8 times or until combined. Evenly pour mixture over top of casserole. Bake for 45 to 50 minutes or until set in center. Place baking dish on a wire rack and let set for 5 minutes. Divide into 6 servings.

Each serving equals:

HE: 2½ Protein • ½ Bread • ½ Vegetable • 17 Optional Calories

171 Calories • 7 gm Fat • 16 gm Protein • 11 gm Carbohydrate • 405 mg Sodium • 136 mg Calcium • 1 gm Fiber

DIABETIC EXCHANGES: 2½ Meat • 1 Starch

CARB CHOICES: 1

Skillet Salmon Patties

Salmon is so rich in nutrients, we're all supposed to eat it more often—but many people don't know what to do with it beyond grilling filets and steaks. Canned salmon is an inexpensive alternative and is splendidly succulent when shaped into patties like this and cooked in a skillet. I hope this is the year you're going to eat a lot of this rosy fish—a great, healthy protein source.

☺ Serves 6

> 1 small onion, peeled and cut into 4 wedges
> 1 medium carrot, scraped and cut into 2-inch pieces
> 1 (14½-ounce) can pink salmon, skin and bones removed,
>   and drained and flaked
> 2 eggs, or equivalent in egg substitute
> 2 tablespoons Land O Lakes no-fat sour cream
> 1½ cups cornflakes
> ⅛ teaspoon black pepper

Lock food processor bowl in position. Insert the steel knife blade. Attach food chute cover and lock in place. Drop onion and carrot pieces into the food processor bowl. Attach food chute cover and lock in place. Turn on processor and pulse 3 or 4 times or until vegetables are finely chopped. Remove cover. Add salmon, eggs, sour cream, cornflakes, and black pepper. Re-cover. Turn on processor and pulse 8 or 10 times or just until mixture is blended. Using a ⅔ cup measuring cup as a guide, form into 6 patties. Place patties on a hot griddle or skillet sprayed with butter-flavored cooking spray. Brown for 5 minutes on each side. Serve at once.

Each serving equals:

HE: 2¼ Protein • ½ Vegetable • ⅓ Bread • 5 Optional Calories

124 Calories • 4 gm Fat • 13 gm Protein • 9 gm Carbohydrate •
383 mg Sodium • 101 mg Calcium • 1 gm Fiber

DIABETIC EXCHANGES: 2 Meat • ½ Starch/Carbohydrate

CARB CHOICES: ½

Dilled Chicken Salad Sandwiches

I probably should have named this "Double Dill" because I've layered the dill in two forms—a relish and an herb! Each brings its own special charm to these sandwiches, which take a giant leap from the everyday kind into a culinary stratosphere.

◐ Serves 4

> 8 ounces cooked chicken breast, cut into 2-inch strips
> 1 medium stalk celery, trimmed and cut into 2-inch pieces
> ½ cup Kraft fat-free mayonnaise
> 2 tablespoons dill pickle relish
> ½ teaspoon dried dill weed
> 4 lettuce leaves
> 4 small hamburger buns

Lock food processor bowl in position. Insert the steel knife blade. Drop chicken pieces into the food processor bowl. Attach food chute cover and lock in place. Turn on processor and pulse 8 or 10 times or until chicken is finely chopped. Transfer chopped chicken to a medium bowl. Repeat process with celery. Add mayonnaise, pickle relish, and dill weed. Mix well to combine. For each sandwich, place a lettuce leaf on bottom half of hamburger bun, spoon about ⅓ cup mixture over lettuce, and arrange bun top over all.

HINT: If you don't have leftovers, purchase a chunk of cooked chicken breast from your local deli. Chicken can be chopped by hand or in the food processor.

Each serving equals:

HE: 2 Protein • 1 Bread • ¼ Vegetable • ¼ Slider • 9 Optional Calories

200 Calories • 4 gm Fat • 20 gm Protein • 21 gm Carbohydrate •
533 mg Sodium • 21 mg Calcium • 2 gm Fiber

DIABETIC EXCHANGES: 2 Meat • 1½ Starch/Carbohydrate

CARB CHOICES: 1½

Crunchy Chicken-Carrot Casserole

Don't let the list of ingredients worry you—this dish comes together pretty fast and bakes up in no time! What a great recipe to make with one of those rotisserie chickens from the grocery store— and what a healthy supper you can make in just one pan.

○ Serves 6

> 2 large carrots, scraped and each cut into 2-inch pieces
> 1 small onion, peeled and cut into 4 wedges
> 12 ounces cooked chicken breast, cut into 2-inch strips
> 1½ cups hot water ☆
> ¾ cup shredded Kraft reduced-fat Cheddar cheese
> 1 (10¾-ounce) can Healthy Request Cream of Chicken Soup
> ¼ cup Land O Lakes Fat Free Half & Half
> 1 (2-ounce) jar chopped pimiento, drained
> 2 tablespoons I Can't Believe It's Not Butter! Light
>   Margarine
> 2 cups purchased herb-seasoned stuffing mix

Preheat oven to 375 degrees. Spray an 8-by-8-inch baking dish with butter-flavored cooking spray. Lock food processor bowl in position. Insert the slicer disc. Attach food chute cover and lock in place. Drop carrots and onion into the food chute. Position food pusher over vegetables. Turn on processor and use medium pressure to push vegetables through. Transfer sliced vegetables to a medium saucepan. Add 1 cup hot water and cook for 12 minutes or until carrots are tender. Drain well. Remove slicer disc from food processor and insert the steel knife blade. Place chicken strips in food processor bowl. Attach food chute cover and lock in place. Turn on processor and pulse 8 or 10 times or until chicken is coarsely chopped. In a large bowl, combine carrot mixture, Cheddar cheese, and chicken soup. Add chicken, half & half, and pimiento. Mix well to combine. Evenly spread mixture into prepared baking dish. In same bowl, combine remaining ½ cup hot water and margarine. Stir in stuffing mix. Spread stuffing mixture evenly over chicken mixture. Bake for 30 minutes. Place baking dish on a wire rack and let set for 5 minutes. Divide into 6 servings.

HINTS: 1. If you don't have leftovers, purchase a chunk of cooked chicken breast from your local deli. Chicken can be chopped by hand or in the food processor.
2. Brownberry seasoned toasted bread cubes work great.

Each serving equals:

HE: 2½ Protein • 1 Bread • ¾ Vegetable • ½ Fat • ¼ Slider • 15 Optional Calories

264 Calories • 8 gm Fat • 25 gm Protein • 23 gm Carbohydrate • 657 mg Sodium • 150 mg Calcium • 2 gm Fiber

DIABETIC EXCHANGES: 2½ Meat • 1½ Starch/Carbohydrate • 1 Vegetable • ½ Fat

CARB CHOICES: 1½

Chicken Cacciatore and Rice Skillet

Skillet suppers are a busy cook's best friend, especially when they shimmer and shine with lush sauces like this savory Italian delight! You won't have to announce that dinner is served—your family will just follow their noses to the food.   ☻   Serves 4 (1 cup)

8 ounces cooked chicken breast, cut into 2-inch strips
1 medium onion, peeled and cut into 6 wedges
1 medium green bell pepper, stem and seeds removed and cut into 6 strips
1 medium red bell pepper, stem and seeds removed and cut into 6 strips
1 cup fresh whole mushrooms, each cut in half
2 medium tomatoes, peeled and each cut into 6 wedges
¼ cup pitted whole ripe olives
1 (8-ounce) can Hunt's Tomato Sauce
2 tablespoons Splenda Granular
1½ teaspoons Italian seasoning
⅛ teaspoon black pepper
1 cup cooked rice

Lock food processor bowl in position. Insert the steel knife blade. Drop chicken strips into the food processor bowl. Attach food chute cover and lock in place. Turn on processor and pulse 6 or 8 times or until chicken is coarsely chopped. Transfer chopped chicken to a small bowl and set aside. Remove steel knife blade and insert the slicer disc. Attach food chute cover and lock in place. Drop onion into the food chute. Position food pusher over onion. Turn on processor and use medium pressure to push onion through. Transfer sliced onion to a large bowl. Repeat process with green pepper, red pepper, and mushrooms. Place chopped vegetables in a large skillet sprayed with olive oil–flavored cooking spray. Sauté for 5 minutes. Meanwhile, drop tomato wedges into the food chute. Position food pusher over tomatoes. Turn on processor and use light pressure to push tomatoes through. Repeat process with olives. Stir tomatoes and olives into skillet with sautéed vegetables. Add tomato sauce, Splenda, Italian seasoning, and black pepper. Mix well to combine. Stir in chicken and rice. Lower heat and simmer for 5 or 6 minutes, stirring occasionally.

HINTS: 1. If you don't have leftovers, purchase a chunk of cooked chicken breast from your local deli. Chicken can be chopped by hand or in the food processor.

2. Usually ⅔ cup uncooked instant or ½ cup regular rice cooks to about 1 cup.

Each serving equals:

HE: 3½ Vegetable • 2 Protein • ¾ Bread • ¼ Fat • 3 Optional Calories

191 Calories • 3 gm Fat • 17 gm Protein • 24 gm Carbohydrate •
590 mg Sodium • 45 mg Calcium • 4 gm Fiber

DIABETIC EXCHANGES: 3 Vegetable • 2 Meat • 1 Starch

CARB CHOICES: 1½

Chicken Cheddar Tetrazzini

My family has always loved my varied versions of chicken tetrazzini, and this one scored high with them. It's wonderfully thick with vegetables, it's as creamy as it is cheesy, and the sauce coats the pasta perfectly. Mm-mm!   ●   Serves 4 (1 full cup)

> 2 medium stalks celery, trimmed and each cut into 2-inch
>   pieces
> 1 small onion, peeled and cut into 4 wedges
> 1 cup fresh whole mushrooms, each cut in half
> 6 ounces cooked chicken breast, cut into
>   2-inch strips
> 1 tablespoon + 1 teaspoon I Can't Believe It's
>   Not Butter! Light Margarine
> 1 (10¾-ounce) can Healthy Request Cream of
>   Chicken Soup
> ½ cup fat-free milk
> 2 sprigs parsley, stems removed
> ¾ cup shredded Kraft reduced-fat Cheddar cheese
> 1½ cups cooked spaghetti, rinsed and drained
> 1 (2-ounce) jar chopped pimiento
> ⅛ teaspoon black pepper

Lock food processor bowl in position. Insert the steel knife blade. Drop celery into the food processor bowl. Attach food chute cover and lock in place. Turn on processor and pulse 3 or 4 times or until celery is finely chopped. Transfer chopped celery to a large bowl. Repeat process with onion, mushrooms, and chicken. In a large skillet sprayed with butter-flavored cooking spray, melt margarine. Add chopped vegetables and chicken. Sauté for 6 to 8 minutes. Place chicken soup, milk, and parsley in food processor bowl. Cover and process for 3 seconds or until mixture is smooth. Stir soup mixture into chicken mixture. Add Cheddar cheese, spaghetti, pimiento, and black pepper. Mix well to combine. Lower heat and simmer for 5 to 6 minutes or until mixture is heated through and cheese is melted, stirring occasionally.

HINTS: 1. If you don't have leftovers, purchase a chunk of cooked chicken breast from your local deli. Chicken can be chopped by hand or in the food processor.

2. Usually 1½ cups broken uncooked spaghetti cooks to about 2 cups.

Each serving equals:

HE: 2¼ Protein • ¾ Bread • ¾ Vegetable • ½ Fat • ½ Slider • 15 Optional Calories

284 Calories • 8 gm Fat • 25 gm Protein • 28 gm Carbohydrate • 558 mg Sodium • 225 mg Calcium • 2 gm Fiber

DIABETIC EXCHANGES: 2 Meat • 1½ Starch/Carbohydrate • 1 Vegetable • ½ Fat

CARB CHOICES: 2

Chicken-Zucchini Casserole

I always recommend letting a casserole rest for at least five minutes before you try to cut it for serving, and I speak from experience. If you're in too much of a hurry, your beautiful creation will collapse and fall apart all over the plate (or worse, the table). So don't be swayed by cries of "I'm hungry *now*"—wait. Talk about the day, say grace, whatever it takes. ☻ Serves 4

1 medium unpeeled zucchini, cut in half lengthwise and
   crosswise
1 medium carrot, scraped and cut into 2-inch pieces
2 medium stalks celery, trimmed and each cut into 2-inch
   pieces
1 small onion, peeled and cut into 4 wedges
8 ounces cooked chicken breast, cut into 2-inch strips
1 (10¾-ounce) can Healthy Request Cream of Chicken Soup
¼ cup Land O Lakes no-fat sour cream
1½ cups unseasoned dried bread cubes
⅛ teaspoon black pepper
½ cup shredded Kraft reduced-fat Cheddar cheese

Preheat oven to 350 degrees. Spray an 8-by-8-inch baking dish with butter-flavored cooking spray. Lock food processor bowl in position. Insert the shredder disc. Attach food chute cover and lock in place. Drop zucchini pieces into the food chute. Position food pusher over zucchini. Turn on processor and use medium pressure to push zucchini through. Transfer shredded zucchini to a large bowl. Repeat process with carrot, celery, and onion. Remove shredder disc from food processor and insert the steel knife blade. Drop chicken into the food processor bowl. Attach food chute cover and lock in place. Turn on processor and pulse 3 times or until chicken is coarsely chopped. Add chicken soup and sour cream to vegetables. Mix well to combine. Stir in chicken, bread cubes, and black pepper. Evenly spoon mixture into prepared baking dish. Sprinkle Cheddar cheese evenly over top. Bake for 40 to 45 minutes. Place baking dish on a wire rack and let set for 5 minutes. Divide into 4 servings.

HINT: If you don't have leftovers, purchase a chunk of cooked chicken breast from your local deli. Chicken can be chopped by hand or in the food processor.

Each serving equals:

HE: 2½ Protein • 1¼ Vegetable • ½ Bread • ¾ Slider

234 Calories • 6 gm Fat • 25 gm Protein • 20 gm Carbohydrate • 494 mg Sodium • 170 mg Calcium • 2 gm Fiber

DIABETIC EXCHANGES: 2½ Meat • 1 Vegetable • 1 Starch/Carbohydrate

CARB CHOICES: 1

Baked Chicken Breast with Vegetables

Working with the food processor has provided lots of new inspiration for me as a creative cook. It's encouraged me to invent new sauces, it's led me to add extra vegetables to a dish (because I don't have to chop each one myself), and it's showed me fresh ways to think about basic dishes like chicken and veggies!

○ Serves 4

> 1 large onion, peeled and cut into 6 wedges
> 1 medium unpeeled zucchini, cut in half lengthwise and
>   crosswise
> 2 medium carrots, scraped and each cut into 2-inch pieces
> 2 (5-ounce) raw potatoes, peeled and each cut into 4 wedges
> 1 (10¾-ounce) can Healthy Request Tomato Soup ☆
> 3 tablespoons chili sauce ☆
> ⅛ teaspoon black pepper
> 16 ounces skinned and boned uncooked chicken breast, cut
>   into 4 pieces
> 2 sprigs parsley, stems removed
> 1 teaspoon prepared horseradish sauce

Preheat oven to 375 degrees. Spray an 8-by-8-inch baking dish with butter-flavored cooking spray. Lock food processor bowl in position. Insert the slicer disc. Attach food chute cover and lock in place. Drop onion, zucchini, carrots, and potatoes into the food chute. Position food pusher over vegetables. Turn on processor and use medium pressure to push vegetables through. Transfer sliced vegetables to a large bowl when full level is reached. Repeat process as necessary. Add ½ cup tomato soup, 1 tablespoon chili sauce, and black pepper. Mix well to combine. Evenly spoon vegetables into prepared baking dish. Arrange chicken pieces evenly over vegetables. Remove slicer disc from food processor and insert the steel knife blade. Add parsley, remaining tomato soup, remaining 2 tablespoons chili sauce, and horseradish sauce to food processor bowl. Attach food chute cover and lock in place. Position food pusher in chute to prevent ingredients from splashing out of bowl. Turn on processor and pulse 5 or 6 times or until blended. Pour mixture evenly over chicken. Cover and bake for 45 minutes. Uncover and continue baking for 15 to 20 minutes or until vegetables and chicken are tender. Place baking dish on a wire rack and let set for 5 minutes. Divide into 4 servings.

Each serving equals:

HE: 3 Protein • 1½ Vegetable • ¾ Bread • ¾ Slider • 2 Optional Calories

280 Calories • 4 gm Fat • 29 gm Protein • 32 gm Carbohydrate • 731 mg Sodium • 36 mg Calcium • 3 gm Fiber

DIABETIC EXCHANGES: 3 Meat • 1½ Vegetable • 1½ Starch/Carbohydrate

CARB CHOICES: 2

Potato-Crusted Chicken
over Veggies

If you're looking for a moist and juicy way to prepare chicken, dipping it in a dressing of some kind and then in a crust-making ingredient (like the potato flakes here) is a pretty sure thing! I tested several different kinds of dressing and liked them all but chose Ranch for this dish. It could be fun to try it with others.

○ Serves 4

> 1 medium onion, peeled and cut into 6 wedges
> 1 medium carrot, scraped and cut into 2-inch pieces
> 2 medium stalks celery, trimmed and each cut into
>   2-inch pieces
> ¼ cup Kraft Fat Free Ranch Dressing
> 2 tablespoons Kraft fat-free mayonnaise
> ⅔ cup instant potato flakes
> 16 ounces skinned and boned uncooked chicken breast,
>   cut into 4 pieces

Preheat oven to 350 degrees. Spray an 8-by-8-inch baking dish with butter-flavored cooking spray. Lock food processor bowl in position. Insert the steel knife blade. Drop onion, carrot, and celery into the food processor bowl. Attach food chute cover and lock in place. Turn on processor and pulse 3 or 4 times or until vegetables are coarsely chopped. Evenly arrange chopped vegetables in prepared baking dish. In a shallow saucer, combine Ranch dressing and mayonnaise. Place dry potato flakes in another shallow saucer. Coat chicken pieces first in dressing mixture, then in potato flakes. Evenly arrange coated chicken pieces over vegetables. Drizzle any remaining dressing mixture and potato flakes over top. Cover and bake for 45 minutes. Uncover and continue baking for 15 minutes or until vegetables and chicken are tender. Place baking dish on a wire rack and let set for 5 minutes. Divide into 4 servings.

Each serving equals:

HE: 3 Protein • 1 Vegetable • ½ Bread • ¼ Slider • 9 Optional Calories

208 Calories • 4 gm Fat • 28 gm Protein • 15 gm Carbohydrate •
332 mg Sodium • 36 mg Calcium • 1 gm Fiber

DIABETIC EXCHANGES: 3 Meat • 1 Vegetable • ½ Starch

CARB CHOICES: 1

South Seas
Sweet and Sour Chicken

Sometimes when I watch old movies set in faraway places, instead of getting caught up in the story, I notice what the people are eating. I start to dream about dishes made with ingredients on their tables, and I write them down. I can't recall if this one came from watching *Blue Hawaii*, *The Thorn Birds*, or *Mutiny on the Bounty!*

⭘ Serves 4 (1 cup)

> 2 medium carrots, scraped and each cut into 2-inch pieces
> 1 medium green bell pepper, stem and seeds removed and
>   cut into 6 strips
> 1 medium onion, peeled and cut into 6 wedges
> 1 tablespoon + 1 teaspoon I Can't Believe It's Not Butter!
>   Light Margarine
> 16 ounces skinned and boned uncooked chicken breast, cut
>   into bite-size pieces
> 1 (8-ounce) can Hunt's Tomato Sauce
> 1 (8-ounce) can pineapple tidbits, packed in fruit juice,
>   undrained
> ½ cup unsweetened orange juice
> 1½ tablespoons apricot spreadable fruit
> 2 tablespoons cornstarch
> 1 tablespoon Splenda Granular
> ½ teaspoon dried minced garlic

Lock food processor bowl in position. Insert the steel knife blade. Drop carrots into the food processor bowl. Attach food chute cover and lock in place. Turn on processor and pulse 3 or 4 times or until carrots are finely chopped. Transfer chopped carrots to a large bowl. Repeat process with green pepper and onion. In a large skillet sprayed with butter-flavored cooking spray, melt margarine. Add chicken and vegetables to skillet. Sauté for 5 to 6 minutes. Add tomato sauce and undrained pineapple. Mix well to combine. In a small bowl, combine orange juice, spreadable fruit, cornstarch,

Splenda, and garlic, using a wire whisk. Stir orange juice mixture into chicken mixture. Continue cooking for 5 minutes or until mixture thickens, stirring occasionally.

HINTS: 1. Good served over rice or as is.
2. If you can't find pineapple tidbits, purchase pineapple chunks, place undrained chunks in food processor, and pulse 1 or 2 times.

Each serving equals:

HE: 3 Protein • 3 Vegetable • 1 Fruit • ½ Fat • 16 Optional Calories

285 Calories • 5 gm Fat • 28 gm Protein • 32 gm Carbohydrate • 453 mg Sodium • 51 mg Calcium • 3 gm Fiber

DIABETIC EXCHANGES: 3 Meat • 3 Vegetable • 1 Fruit • ½ Fat

CARB CHOICES: 2

Turkey Hash

Leftover turkey is a fact of life, especially in November (and often December), so cooks are always asked for recipes to use up all that extra meat. I used to cook an extra-large bird on purpose, so I would have leftovers for dishes like this bountiful one. I'm sure you and yours will savor it any time of year.

● Serves 6 (1 cup)

> 4 (5-ounce) cooked potatoes, cooled, peeled, and
>   quartered
> 4 medium stalks celery, trimmed and each cut into
>   2-inch pieces
> 1 medium onion, peeled and cut into 6 wedges
> 16 ounces cooked turkey breast, cut into 2-inch strips
> 2 tablespoons I Can't Believe It's Not Butter! Light
>   Margarine
> 1 (10¾-ounce) can Healthy Request Cream of
>   Chicken Soup
> ¼ cup Land O Lakes Fat Free Half & Half
> 1 teaspoon dried sage
> ⅛ teaspoon black pepper

Lock food processor bowl in position. Insert the slicer disc. Attach food chute cover and lock in place. Drop potatoes into the food chute. Position food pusher over potatoes. Turn on processor and use light pressure to push potatoes through. Transfer sliced potatoes to a large bowl. Repeat process with celery. Transfer sliced celery to bowl with potatoes. Repeat process with onion. Remove slicer disc from food processor and insert the steel knife blade. Place turkey in food processor bowl. Attach food chute and lock in place. Turn on processor and pulse 8 or 10 times or until turkey is coarsely chopped. In a large skillet sprayed with butter-flavored cooking spray, melt margarine. Stir in potato mixture. Sauté for 5 minutes. Stir in chopped turkey. Meanwhile, place chicken soup, half & half, sage, and black pepper in food processor bowl. Cover and pulse 4 or 5 times or until mixture is smooth. Pour soup mixture into turkey mixture. Mix well to combine. Lower heat, cover, and simmer for 30 minutes, stirring occasionally.

HINT: If you don't have leftovers, purchase a chunk of turkey breast from your local deli. Turkey can be chopped by hand or in the food processor.

Each serving equals:

HE: 3 Protein • ⅔ Bread • ½ Fat • ½ Vegetable • ¼ Slider • 15 Optional Calories

219 Calories • 3 gm Fat • 26 gm Protein • 22 gm Carbohydrate • 305 mg Sodium • 44 mg Calcium • 2 gm Fiber

DIABETIC EXCHANGES: 2½ Meat • 1 Starch • ½ Fat • ½ Vegetable

CARB CHOICES: 1½

Classic Chicken Cacciatore

Why does a dish become a classic, and why does it stay on family menus for decades? With chicken cacciatore, I think it's because it features the best elements of a country's cuisine—the sweet and tangy tomatoes, the spirit of the herbs in the seasoning (especially the oregano and basil), and the ease of preparation.

○ Serves 4

2 teaspoons olive oil
16 ounces skinned and boned uncooked chicken breast, cut into 4 pieces
1 medium onion, peeled and cut into 6 wedges
1 medium green bell pepper, stem and seeds removed and cut into 6 strips

1 clove garlic, peeled
4 sprigs parsley, stems removed
1 (15-ounce) can diced tomatoes, undrained
2 tablespoons reduced-sodium ketchup
1½ teaspoons Italian seasoning
⅛ teaspoon black pepper

In a large skillet sprayed with olive oil–flavored cooking spray, heat olive oil. Arrange chicken pieces in prepared skillet. Brown for 3 to 4 minutes on each side. Meanwhile, lock food processor bowl in position. Insert the steel knife blade. Drop onion, green pepper, garlic, and parsley into the food processor bowl. Attach food chute cover and lock in place. Turn on processor and pulse 2 or 3 times or until vegetables are coarsely chopped. Add undrained tomatoes, ketchup, Italian seasoning, and black pepper. Re-cover and pulse 1 or 2 times. Pour mixture evenly over chicken pieces. Lower heat, cover, and simmer for 20 to 25 minutes or until chicken and vegetables are tender. When serving, evenly spoon sauce over chicken pieces.

Each serving equals:

HE: 3 Protein • 2 Vegetable • ½ Fat • 8 Optional Calories

201 Calories • 5 gm Fat • 28 gm Protein • 11 gm Carbohydrate • 201 mg Sodium • 42 mg Calcium • 2 gm Fiber

DIABETIC EXCHANGES: 3 Meat • 2 Vegetable • ½ Fat

CARB CHOICES: 1

Quick and Easy Meat Loaf

There are a zillion recipes for this American classic, and I've created plenty of them over the years. But now that I'm using a food processor to chop and blend, it's a whole new "ballgame" for me—a truly fun and creative one! ● Serves 6

> 3 slices reduced-calorie white bread, each cut into 4 pieces
> 1 medium onion, peeled and cut into 6 wedges
> 1 small green bell pepper, stem and seeds removed and cut
>   into 6 strips
> 1½ pounds extra-lean ground sirloin beef or turkey breast
> 6 tablespoons reduced-sodium ketchup ☆
> ¼ cup Land O Lakes Fat Free Half & Half
> 1½ teaspoons Worcestershire sauce
> ⅛ teaspoon black pepper

Preheat oven to 350 degrees. Spray a 9-by-5-inch loaf pan with butter-flavored cooking spray. Lock food processor bowl in position. Insert the steel knife blade. Drop bread pieces into the food processor bowl. Attach food chute cover and lock in place. Turn on processor and pulse 3 or 4 times or until coarse crumbs are formed. Transfer bread crumbs to a large bowl. Repeat process with onion and green pepper. Combine bread crumbs, onion, green pepper, meat, ¼ cup ketchup, half & half, Worcestershire sauce, and black pepper. Mix well to combine. Pat mixture into prepared loaf pan. Evenly spread remaining 2 tablespoons ketchup over top. Bake for 55 to 65 minutes. Place pan on a wire rack and let set for 5 minutes. Cut into 6 servings.

Each serving equals:

HE: 3 Protein • ½ Vegetable • ¼ Bread • ¼ Slider • 2 Optional Calories

185 Calories • 5 gm Fat • 24 gm Protein • 11 gm Carbohydrate •
154 mg Sodium • 27 mg Calcium • 1 gm Fiber

DIABETIC EXCHANGES: 3 Meat • ½ Vegetable • ½ Starch/Carbohydrate

CARB CHOICES: 1

Golden Nugget Meat Loaf

I hope this will become one of your most precious meat loaf recipes! A box of "old reliables" is a healthy cook's best friend—and this carrot-infused version is a mouthwatering one.

● Serves 6

> 3 slices reduced-calorie white bread, each cut into 4 pieces
> 2 medium carrots, scraped and each cut into 2-inch pieces
> 1 small onion, peeled and cut into 4 wedges
> 1 sprig parsley, stem removed
> 1½ pounds extra-lean ground sirloin beef or turkey breast
> ¼ cup fat-free milk
> ¼ cup reduced-sodium ketchup
> 1 teaspoon Worcestershire sauce
> ⅛ teaspoon black pepper

Preheat oven to 350 degrees. Spray a 9-by-5-inch loaf pan with butter-flavored cooking spray. Lock food processor bowl in position. Insert the steel knife blade. Drop bread pieces into the food processor bowl. Attach food chute cover and lock in place. Turn on processor and pulse 3 or 4 times or until coarse crumbs form. Transfer bread crumbs to a large bowl. Repeat process with carrot, onion, and parsley. Pulse 4 or 5 times or until vegetables are finely chopped. Stir vegetable mixture into crumb mixture. Add meat, milk, ketchup, Worcestershire sauce, and black pepper. Mix well to combine. Pat mixture into prepared loaf pan. Bake for 55 to 65 minutes. Place pan on a wire rack and let set for 5 minutes. Cut into 6 servings.

Each serving equals:

HE: 3 Protein • ½ Vegetable • ¼ Bread • 13 Optional Calories

157 Calories • 5 gm Fat • 19 gm Protein • 9 gm Carbohydrate • 131 mg Sodium • 31 mg Calcium • 1 gm Fiber

DIABETIC EXCHANGES: 3 Meat • ½ Vegetable

CARB CHOICES: ½

Florentine Meat Loaf

Everything in a meat loaf recipe adds texture, flavor, color—or all of the above. Here, you'll find fresh spinach (incredibly nutritious) and some oats (good for extra fiber) in addition to the meat. The result is delicious *and* nutritious, too!   ☻   Serves 6

> 2 cups spinach leaves, stems removed and discarded
> 1 medium onion, peeled and cut into 6 wedges
> 2 medium carrots, scraped and each cut into 2-inch pieces
> 16 ounces extra-lean ground sirloin beef or turkey breast
> ¾ cup quick oats
> ¼ cup Land O Lakes no-fat sour cream
> ⅓ cup reduced-sodium ketchup
> 1½ teaspoons Italian seasoning
> ⅛ teaspoon black pepper

Preheat oven to 375 degrees. Spray a 9-by-5-inch loaf pan with olive oil–flavored cooking spray. Lock food processor bowl in position. Insert the steel knife blade. Drop spinach leaves into the food processor bowl. Attach food chute cover and lock in place. Turn on processor and pulse 3 or 4 times or until spinach is finely chopped. Transfer chopped spinach to a large bowl. Remove steel knife blade from food processor and insert the shredder disc. Drop onion into the food chute. Position food pusher over onion. Turn on processor and use medium pressure to push onion through. Transfer shredded onion to bowl with spinach. Repeat process with carrots. Stir vegetables to combine. Add meat, oats, sour cream, ketchup, Italian seasoning, and black pepper. Mix well to combine. Pat mixture into prepared loaf pan. Bake for 55 to 60 minutes. Place pan on a wire rack and let set for 5 minutes. Divide into 6 servings.

Each serving equals:

HE: 2 Protein • 1 Vegetable • ½ Bread • ¼ Slider • 4 Optional Calories

168 Calories • 4 gm Fat • 17 gm Protein • 16 gm Carbohydrate •
82 mg Sodium • 40 mg Calcium • 2 gm Fiber

DIABETIC EXCHANGES: 2 Meat • 1 Vegetable • ½ Starch

CARB CHOICES: 1

Garden Patch Meat Loaf

Isn't it remarkable to serve six people with just a pound of meat—and no one feels deprived! This veggie-based entrée is impressively hearty and has great texture for a meat loaf. If you have a hard time getting your kids to eat their veggies, one of these veggie meat loaves will help you *sneak* some in. ☻ Serves 6

¼ small head of cabbage, cut into 4 wedges
2 medium carrots, scraped and each cut into 2-inch pieces
1 medium onion, peeled and cut into 6 wedges
3 slices reduced-calorie white bread, toasted and cut into quarters
1 (8-ounce) can Hunt's Tomato Sauce
2 tablespoons reduced-sodium ketchup
1 tablespoon Worcestershire sauce
2 sprigs parsley, stems removed
16 ounces extra-lean ground sirloin beef or turkey breast

Preheat oven to 350 degrees. Spray a 9-by-5-inch loaf pan with butter-flavored cooking spray. Lock food processor bowl in position. Insert the steel knife blade. Drop cabbage wedges into the food processor bowl. Attach food chute cover and lock in place. Turn on processor and pulse 4 or 5 times or until cabbage is finely chopped. Transfer chopped cabbage to a large bowl. Repeat process with carrots and onion. Wipe food processor bowl with a clean cloth. Place toast pieces in food processor bowl. Attach food chute cover and lock in place. Turn on processor and pulse 3 or 4 times or until crumbs form. Transfer crumbs to bowl with vegetables. Place tomato sauce, ketchup, Worcestershire sauce, and parsley in food processor bowl. Attach food chute cover and lock in place. Turn on processor and pulse 2 or 3 times. Pour ⅓ cup sauce mixture into bowl with vegetables. Add meat. Mix well to combine. Evenly pat meat mixture into prepared loaf pan. Bake for 30 minutes. Evenly spoon remaining sauce mixture over top of partially baked meat loaf. Continue baking for 20 to 25 minutes. Place pan on a wire rack and let set for 5 minutes. Divide into 6 servings.

Each serving equals:

HE: 2 Protein • 1½ Vegetable • ¼ Bread • 5 Optional Calories

148 Calories • 4 gm Fat • 14 gm Protein • 14 gm Carbohydrate •
353 mg Sodium • 44 mg Calcium • 2 gm Fiber

DIABETIC EXCHANGES: 2 Meat • 1½ Vegetable

CARB CHOICES: 1

Great Mushroom Meat Loaf

This meat loaf deserves lots of extravagant adjectives: marvelous, magnificent, mouthwatering, moist, and meaty! I think the mushrooms provide a savory flavor that really stands out.

⚫ Serves 6

1 clove garlic, peeled
1 medium onion, peeled
   and cut into
   6 wedges
1 cup fresh whole mushrooms,
   each cut in half
4 slices reduced-calorie
   white bread, toasted
   and each cut into
   6 pieces

16 ounces extra-lean ground
   sirloin beef or turkey
   breast
1 (10¾-ounce) can Healthy
   Request Cream of
   Mushroom Soup ☆
⅛ teaspoon black pepper
1 tablespoon Land O Lakes no-
   fat sour cream
2 tablespoons chili sauce

Preheat oven to 350 degrees. Spray a 9-by-5-inch loaf pan with butter-flavored cooking spray. Lock food processor bowl in position. Insert the steel knife blade. Drop garlic and onion into the food processor bowl. Attach food chute cover and lock in place. Turn on processor and pulse 6 or 8 times or until vegetables are chopped. Transfer chopped vegetables to a large bowl. Repeat process with mushrooms and toast pieces. Add meat, ¼ cup mushroom soup, and black pepper to vegetable mixture in large bowl. Mix well to combine. Pat mixture into prepared loaf pan. Bake for 20 minutes. In a small bowl, combine remaining mushroom soup, sour cream, and chili sauce. Evenly spoon mixture over partially baked meat loaf and continue baking for 30 to 40 minutes or until done. Place loaf pan on a wire rack and let set for 5 minutes. Cut into 6 servings.

Each serving equals:

HE: 2 Protein • ½ Vegetable • ⅓ Bread • ¼ Slider • 17 Optional Calories

165 Calories • 5 gm Fat • 17 gm Protein • 13 gm Carbohydrate •
535 mg Sodium • 62 mg Calcium • 1 gm Fiber

DIABETIC EXCHANGES: 2 Meat • 1 Starch/Carbohydrate • ½ Vegetable

CARB CHOICES: 1

Savory Beef and Noodles

My son Tommy watched me making this and asked if it was another of my cheeseburger skillet suppers, his favorites among my recipes. "Yes and no," I answered. It's got the burger and cheese ingredients, but the sauce and noodles take it in a different direction. Tommy pronounced it, "Really good." ☻   Serves 6 (1 cup)

> 1 medium onion, peeled and cut into 6 wedges
> 16 ounces extra-lean ground sirloin beef or turkey breast
> 1 (15-ounce) can diced tomatoes, undrained
> ¼ cup reduced-sodium ketchup
> ½ cup water
> 1 teaspoon chili seasoning
> 1½ cups uncooked noodles
> ¾ cup shredded Kraft reduced-fat Cheddar cheese

Lock food processor bowl in position. Insert the steel knife blade. Drop onion wedges into the food processor bowl. Attach food chute cover and lock in place. Turn on processor and pulse 4 or 5 times or until onion is finely chopped. In a large skillet sprayed with butter-flavored cooking spray, brown meat and chopped onion, stirring often. Add undrained tomatoes, ketchup, water, and chili seasoning. Mix well to combine. Stir in uncooked noodles. Bring mixture to a boil. Lower heat, cover, and simmer for 10 to 12 minutes or just until noodles are tender, stirring occasionally. Add Cheddar cheese. Mix well to combine. Continue simmering for 3 to 4 minutes or until cheese melts, stirring often.

Each serving equals:

HE: 2½ Protein • 1½ Vegetable • ½ Bread • 10 Optional Calories

198 Calories • 6 gm Fat • 21 gm Protein • 15 gm Carbohydrate •
293 mg Sodium • 124 mg Calcium • 2 gm Fiber

DIABETIC EXCHANGES: 2½ Meat • 1½ Vegetable • ½ Starch/Carbohydrate

CARB CHOICES: 2

Beef and Macaroni Supper

Why is it that kids just love elbow macaroni? This dish, with its creamy mushroom-tomato sauce and Italian-flavored beef, won the hearts of my grandkids, who kept slurping down the little noodles when their parents weren't watching! ❤ Serves 6 (1 cup)

> 1 medium onion, peeled and cut into 6 wedges
> 16 ounces extra-lean ground sirloin beef or turkey breast
> 1 (10¾-ounce) can Healthy Request Cream of Celery or
>   Mushroom Soup
> 1 (15-ounce) can diced tomatoes, undrained
> ½ cup water
> 1½ teaspoons Italian seasoning
> 2 medium unpeeled zucchini, cut in half lengthwise and
>   crosswise
> 1 cup uncooked elbow macaroni

Lock food processor bowl in position. Insert the steel knife blade. Drop onion wedges into the food processor bowl. Attach food chute cover and lock in place. Turn on processor and pulse 5 or 6 times or until onions are finely chopped. Transfer chopped onions to a large skillet sprayed with butter-flavored cooking spray. Brown onions and meat, stirring often. Add soup, undrained tomatoes, water, and Italian seasoning. Mix well to combine. Meanwhile, repeat chopping process with zucchini. Add chopped zucchini to skillet. Mix well to combine. Stir in uncooked macaroni. Lower heat, cover, and simmer for 10 minutes or until macaroni is tender, stirring occasionally.

Each serving equals:

HE: 2 Vegetable • ½ Bread • ¼ Slider • 8 Optional Calories

163 Calories • 3 gm Fat • 10 gm Protein • 24 gm Carbohydrate •
310 mg Sodium • 89 mg Calcium • 3 gm Fiber

DIABETIC EXCHANGES: 1½ Vegetable • 1½ Starch/Carbohydrate

CARB CHOICES: 1½

Supper Skillet Spaghetti

If it's been one of your goals to cook more with fresh vegetables instead of canned or frozen, this cookbook will definitely show you the way! This warm and welcoming spaghetti combo is old-fashioned in look and flavor but prepared in a way that's truly today!   ☻   Serves 4 (1½ cups)

1 medium onion, peeled and cut into 6 wedges	1 (15-ounce) can diced tomatoes, undrained
1 medium green bell pepper, stem and seeds removed and cut into 6 strips	1 (8-ounce) can Hunt's Tomato Sauce
1 cup fresh whole mushrooms, each cut in half	1 cup water
16 ounces extra-lean ground sirloin beef or turkey breast	1 tablespoon Splenda Granular
	1½ teaspoons Italian seasoning
	¾ cup broken uncooked spaghetti

Lock food processor bowl in position. Insert the slicer disc. Attach food chute cover and lock in place. Drop onion, green pepper, and mushrooms into the food chute. Position food pusher over vegetables. Turn on processor and use medium pressure to push vegetables through. Transfer sliced vegetables to a large skillet sprayed with olive oil–flavored cooking spray. Add meat. Mix well to combine. Brown vegetables and meat for 10 minutes, stirring often. Add undrained tomatoes, tomato sauce, water, Splenda, and Italian seasoning. Mix well to combine. Bring mixture to a boil, stirring often. Stir in broken uncooked spaghetti. Lower heat, cover, and simmer for 15 to 20 minutes or until spaghetti is tender, stirring often.

Each serving equals:

HE: 3 Protein • 3 Vegetable • ¾ Bread • 2 Optional Calories

265 Calories • 5 gm Fat • 27 gm Protein • 28 gm Carbohydrate • 502 mg Sodium • 38 mg Calcium • 4 gm Fiber

DIABETIC EXCHANGES: 3 Meat • 2 Vegetable • 1 Starch

CARB CHOICES: 2

Baked Layered Spaghetti

Not every layered Italian casserole has to be lasagna! If you're in the mood to pile up meat, cheese, pasta, sauce, and veggies, you have my blessing to substitute spaghetti noodles in this main dish "parfait"!   ☻   Serves 6

> 8 ounces extra-lean ground sirloin beef or turkey breast
> 1 medium onion, peeled and cut into 6 wedges
> 1 medium green bell pepper, stem and seeds removed and
>   cut into 6 strips
> 1 medium unpeeled zucchini, cut in half lengthwise and
>   crosswise
> 1 cup fresh whole mushrooms, each cut in half
> 2 medium tomatoes, peeled and each cut into 6 wedges
> 1 (10¾-ounce) can Healthy Request Tomato Soup
> 1½ teaspoons Italian seasoning
> 1½ cups cooked spaghetti, rinsed and drained
> ½ cup shredded Kraft reduced-fat Cheddar cheese
> ½ cup shredded Kraft reduced-fat mozzarella cheese

Preheat oven to 350 degrees. Spray an 8-by-8-inch baking dish with olive oil–flavored cooking spray. In a large skillet sprayed with olive oil–flavored cooking spray, brown meat. Meanwhile, lock food processor bowl in position. Insert the steel knife blade. Drop onion into the food processor bowl. Attach food chute cover and lock in place. Turn on processor and pulse 3 or 4 times or until onion is finely chopped. Transfer chopped onion to a large bowl. Repeat process with green pepper, zucchini, and mushrooms. Place chopped vegetables in another large skillet sprayed with olive oil–flavored cooking spray and sauté for 6 to 8 minutes. Meanwhile, drop tomatoes into the food processor bowl. Attach food chute cover and lock in place. Turn on processor and pulse 3 or 4 times or until finely chopped. Stir chopped tomatoes into skillet with browned meat. Continue cooking for 5 minutes. Stir in tomato soup and Italian seasoning. Layer half of spaghetti into prepared baking dish. Spoon half of vegetables and half of meat mixture over top. Repeat layers. Evenly sprinkle Cheddar cheese and mozzarella cheese over top. Bake for 30 to 35 minutes. Place baking dish on a wire rack and let set for 5 minutes. Divide into 6 servings.

HINT: Usually 1 cup broken uncooked spaghetti cooks to about 1½ cups.

Each serving equals:

HE: 1⅔ Protein • 1½ Vegetable • ½ Bread • ¼ Slider • 10 Optional Calories

206 Calories • 6 gm Fat • 16 gm Protein • 22 gm Carbohydrate • 376mg Sodium • 155 mg Calcium • 3 gm Fiber

DIABETIC EXCHANGES: 1½ Meat • 1 Vegetable • 1 Starch/Carbohydrate

CARB CHOICES: 2

Meatballs Baked with Zucchini-Tomato Sauce

If your favorite part of a spaghetti and meatballs meal is the meatballs, this recipe has your name on it! These moist and sturdy spheres may be some of the best you ever ate—and the sauce is rich with intense tomato flavor. ◐ Serves 6

> *3 slices reduced-calorie white bread, torn into quarters*
> *1 medium onion, peeled and cut into 6 wedges*
> *2 medium stalks celery, trimmed and each cut into 2-inch pieces*
> *16 ounces extra-lean ground sirloin beef or turkey breast*
> *1 tablespoon Worcestershire sauce*
> *⅛ teaspoon black pepper*
> *1 medium unpeeled zucchini, cut in half lengthwise and crosswise*
> *2 medium tomatoes, peeled and each cut into 6 wedges*
> *1½ teaspoons Italian seasoning*
> *1 tablespoon Splenda Granular*
> *1 cup reduced-sodium tomato juice*
> *1 tablespoon cornstarch*

Preheat oven to 350 degrees. Spray an 8-by-12-inch baking dish with olive oil–flavored cooking spray. Lock food processor bowl in position. Insert the steel knife blade. Drop bread pieces into the food processor bowl. Attach food chute cover and lock in place. Turn on processor and pulse 4 times or until fine crumbs form. Transfer bread crumbs to a large bowl. Drop onion wedges and celery pieces into the food processor bowl. Attach food chute cover and lock in place. Turn on processor and pulse 4 or 5 times or until vegetables are finely chopped. Transfer vegetables to bowl with bread crumbs. Add meat, Worcestershire sauce, and black pepper. Mix well to combine. Form into 18 (1½-inch) meatballs. Place meatballs in prepared baking dish. Bake for 20 minutes. Meanwhile, remove steel knife blade from food processor and insert the slicer disc. Attach food chute cover and lock in place. Drop zucchini pieces into the food chute. Position food pusher over zucchini. Turn on processor and use medium pressure to push zucchini through. Transfer sliced zucchini to a large skillet sprayed with olive oil–flavored cooking spray. Sauté while preparing tomatoes. Drop tomatoes into the food chute. Position food pusher over tomatoes. Turn on processor and use light pressure to push tomatoes through. Transfer sliced tomatoes to skillet. Stir in Italian seasoning and Splenda. Cover and simmer for 10 minutes. Add tomato juice and cornstarch. Mix well to combine. Continue cooking for 5 minutes or until mixture thickens. Spoon zucchini mixture evenly over meatballs. Continue baking for 10 minutes. When serving, place 3 meatballs on each plate and spoon a scant ½ cup zucchini sauce over top.

Each serving equals:

HE: 2 Protein • 1½ Vegetable • ¼ Bread • 5 Optional Calories

144 Calories • 4 gm Fat • 17 gm Protein • 10 gm Carbohydrate •
168 mg Sodium • 32 mg Calcium • 1 gm Fiber

DIABETIC EXCHANGES: 2 Meat • 1 Vegetable

CARB CHOICES: ½

Hungarian Hamburger Goulash

Goulash made the Hungarian way makes a star of the spice paprika, a seasoning made of sweet red peppers. Goulash usually features beef or sometimes veal. I chose to make mine with ground meat instead of chunks or slices of beef, with a tomato-based sauce that sparkles with the unique flavor of caraway seeds.

◑ Serves 6 (1 cup)

> 2 large onions, peeled and each cut into 6 wedges
> 2 medium carrots, scraped and each cut into 2-inch pieces
> 16 ounces extra-lean ground sirloin beef or turkey breast
> 1½ cups reduced-sodium tomato juice ☆
> 1 (15-ounce) can diced tomatoes, undrained
> 1 tablespoon paprika
> ¼ teaspoon caraway seeds
> 3 tablespoons all-purpose flour

Lock food processor bowl in position. Insert the steel knife blade. Drop onion wedges and carrot pieces into the food processor bowl. Attach food chute cover and lock in place. Turn on processor and pulse 5 or 6 times or until vegetables are finely chopped. In a large skillet sprayed with butter-flavored cooking spray, brown chopped vegetables and meat, stirring often. Stir in 1 cup tomato juice, undrained tomatoes, paprika, and caraway seeds. In a covered jar, combine flour and remaining ½ cup tomato juice. Shake well to blend. Add tomato juice mixture to meat mixture. Mix well to combine. Continue cooking for 6 to 8 minutes or until mixture thickens, stirring often.

HINT: Good "as is" or spooned over noodles.

Each serving equals:

HE: 2 Protein • 2 Vegetable • 14 Optional Calories

159 Calories • 3 gm Fat • 17 gm Protein • 16 gm Carbohydrate •
190 mg Sodium • 36 mg Calcium • 3 gm Fiber

DIABETIC EXCHANGES: 2 Meat • 2 Vegetable

CARB CHOICES: 1

Hamburger Stroganoff

Stroganoff sauce is one of the most velvety sauces ever created, a real synonym for luxurious flavor when it appears on a restaurant menu. Even when served with hamburger, it's a dish fit for the crème de la crème. ☻ Serves 4 (1 cup)

> 4 cups fresh whole mushrooms, each cut in half
> 1 large onion, peeled and cut into 8 wedges
> 16 ounces extra-lean ground sirloin beef or turkey breast
> 1 (14-ounce) can Swanson Lower Sodium Fat Free Beef
>   Broth
> 3 tablespoons all-purpose flour
> 1 teaspoon Worcestershire sauce
> ⅛ teaspoon black pepper
> ½ cup Land O Lakes no-fat sour cream

Lock food processor bowl in position. Insert the slicer disc. Attach food chute cover and lock in place. Drop mushrooms and onion wedges into the food chute. Position food pusher over vegetables. Turn on processor and use medium pressure to push vegetables through. In a large skillet sprayed with butter-flavored cooking spray, brown sliced mushrooms, onion, and meat, stirring occasionally. In a covered jar, combine beef broth and flour. Shake well to blend. Pour broth mixture into meat mixture. Mix well to combine. Stir in Worcestershire sauce and black pepper. Lower heat and simmer for 10 minutes or until mixture thickens, stirring occasionally. Remove from heat. Stir in sour cream. Serve at once.

HINT: Great served over noodles, potatoes, or toast.

Each serving equals:

HE: 3 Protein • 1½ Vegetable • ¼ Bread • ¼ Slider • 18 Optional Calories

217 Calories • 5 gm Fat • 26 gm Protein • 17 gm Carbohydrate •
277 mg Sodium • 64 mg Calcium • 3 gm Fiber

DIABETIC EXCHANGES: 3 Meat • 1½ Vegetable • ½ Starch/Carbohydrate

CARB CHOICES: 1

Mexican Casserole

A marvelous mélange of south-of-the-border ingredients, this "fiesta on a fork" will quickly become a family favorite. Whether you like it hot or not, you'll enjoy this delectable dish!

○ Serves 6

> 1 medium onion, peeled and cut into 6 wedges
> 1 medium green bell pepper, stem and seeds removed and
>   cut into 4 strips
> 16 ounces extra-lean ground sirloin beef or turkey breast
> 1 (15-ounce) can diced tomatoes, undrained
> 1 cup frozen whole-kernel corn, thawed
> 1 tablespoon Splenda Granular
> 1½ teaspoons chili seasoning
> ½ cup yellow cornmeal
> 6 tablespoons Bisquick Heart Smart Baking Mix
> 1½ teaspoons baking powder
> ¼ cup Land O Lakes Fat Free Half & Half
> 2 tablespoons Land O Lakes no-fat sour cream
> ½ cup Kraft fat-free mayonnaise

Preheat oven to 375 degrees. Spray an 8-by-8-inch baking dish with butter-flavored cooking spray. Lock food processor bowl in position. Insert the steel knife blade. Drop onion and green pepper into the food processor bowl. Attach food chute cover and lock in place. Turn on processor and pulse 3 or 4 times or until vegetables are finely chopped. Transfer chopped vegetables to a large skillet sprayed with butter-flavored cooking spray. Stir in meat. Sauté for 10 minutes or until meat is browned. Stir in undrained tomatoes, corn, Splenda, and chili seasoning. Continue to cook for 3 to 4 minutes, stirring occasionally. Spoon meat mixture into prepared baking dish. Wipe food processor bowl with a clean cloth. Place cornmeal, baking mix, baking powder, half & half, sour cream, and mayonnaise in food processor bowl. Cover and pulse 4 times or until mixture is blended. Evenly spread mixture over top of meat mixture. Bake for 17 minutes or until top is golden brown. Place baking dish on a wire rack and let set for 5 minutes. Divide into 6 servings.

Each serving equals:

HE: 2 Protein • 1 Bread • 1 Vegetable • ¼ Slider • 7 Optional Calories

229 Calories • 5 gm Fat • 18 gm Protein • 28 gm Carbohydrate • 459 mg Sodium • 103 mg Calcium • 4 gm Fiber

DIABETIC EXCHANGES: 2 Meat • 1 Starch • 1 Vegetable

CARB CHOICES: 2

Potato Kugel Shepherd's Pie

It's a bit of a wacky blend of cultures: Potato kugel is a Jewish/Eastern European specialty, while shepherd's pie came to us via Britain, probably Scotland, and was originally made with lamb (handy meat of shepherds, after all). The fact is, you're going to be eating meat and potatoes, and that's got to be good.   ❤   Serves 6

> 16 ounces extra-lean ground sirloin beef or
>   turkey breast
> ¼ cup reduced-sodium ketchup
> 1 (8-ounce) can peas and carrots, rinsed and drained
> 1 medium onion, peeled and cut into 6 wedges
> 3 (5-ounce) raw potatoes, peeled and each cut into
>   6 wedges
> 2 eggs, or equivalent in egg substitute
> 2 tablespoons Land O Lakes no-fat sour cream
> 1½ tablespoons all-purpose flour
> ½ teaspoon baking powder
> 2 sprigs parsley, stems removed
> ⅛ teaspoon black pepper

Preheat oven to 350 degrees. Spray an 8-by-8-inch baking dish with butter-flavored cooking spray. In a large skillet sprayed with butter-flavored cooking spray, brown meat. Stir in ketchup and peas and carrots. Lower heat and simmer while preparing topping. Lock food processor bowl in position. Insert the shredder disc. Attach food chute cover and lock in place. Drop onion into the food chute. Position food pusher over onion. Turn on processor and use medium pressure to push onion through. Repeat process with potatoes. Remove cover. Remove shredder disc from food processor and insert steel knife blade. Place eggs, sour cream, flour, baking powder, parsley, and black pepper in food processor bowl. Attach food chute cover and lock in place. Turn on processor and pulse 4 times or until mixture is smooth. Evenly spoon meat mixture into prepared baking dish. Pour potato mixture evenly over top. Bake for 55 to 65 minutes or until top is well browned and crisp. Place baking dish on a wire rack and let set for 5 minutes. Divide into 6 servings.

Each serving equals:

HE: 2⅓ Protein • 1 Bread • ½ Vegetable • ¼ Slider • 2 Optional Calories

209 Calories • 5 gm Fat • 19 gm Protein • 22 gm Carbohydrate • 113 mg Sodium • 54 mg Calcium • 3 gm Fiber

DIABETIC EXCHANGES: 2 Meat • 1 Starch • ½ Vegetable

CARB CHOICES: 1½

Grande Baked Sloppy Joes

Here's another American classic, reinvented for the twenty-first century in a way that makes serving a lot less messy! What a family-pleasing dish this has always been, and now you can adapt it to your taste and spiciness preference.   ☻   Serves 4 (2 each)

> 1 medium onion, peeled and cut into 6 wedges
> 8 ounces extra-lean ground sirloin beef or turkey breast
> 1 (8-ounce) can Hunt's Tomato Sauce
> 1 tablespoon all-purpose flour
> ½ cup chunky salsa (mild, medium, or hot)
> 1 tablespoon Splenda Granular
> ½ teaspoon chili seasoning
> 4 small hamburger buns
> 4 (¾-ounce) slices Kraft reduced-fat Cheddar cheese, each
>   cut in half diagonally

Preheat oven to 375 degrees. Lock food processor bowl in position. Insert the steel knife blade. Drop onion into the food processor bowl. Attach food chute cover and lock in place. Turn on processor and pulse 3 or 4 times or until onion is finely chopped. In a large skillet sprayed with butter-flavored cooking spray, brown meat and chopped onion. Add tomato sauce and flour. Mix well to combine. Stir in salsa, Splenda, and chili seasoning. Lower heat and simmer for 5 minutes. Meanwhile, spray a baking sheet with butter-flavored cooking spray. Spoon about ¼ cup meat mixture over each hamburger bun half and arrange on prepared baking sheet. Top each with a Cheddar cheese half. Bake for 10 minutes or until cheese melts. Serve at once.

Each serving equals:

HE: 2½ Protein • 1½ Vegetable • 1 Bread • 9 Optional Calories

225 Calories • 5 gm Fat • 19 gm Protein • 26 gm Carbohydrate • 751 mg Sodium • 103 mg Calcium • 2 gm Fiber

DIABETIC EXCHANGES: 2 Meat • 1½ Vegetable • 1 Starch

CARB CHOICES: 2

Cheesy Meat and Potatoes Bake

It's smart to have lots of healthy casseroles in your repertoire, especially if your family includes meat-and-potatoes men and kids. (Mine certainly does!) This one is simple but includes all you need to produce happy smiles at meal's end. Yum yum.

● Serves 4

1 small onion, peeled and cut into 4 wedges
8 ounces extra-lean ground sirloin beef or turkey breast
3 (5-ounce) unpeeled raw potatoes, each cut into 6 wedges
1 (10¾-ounce) can Healthy Request Cream of Mushroom
 Soup
¾ cup shredded Kraft reduced-fat Cheddar cheese

Preheat oven to 350 degrees. Spray an 8-by-8-inch baking dish with butter-flavored cooking spray. Lock food processor bowl in position. Insert the slicer disc. Attach food chute cover and lock in place. Drop onions into the food chute. Position food pusher over onions. Turn on processor and use medium pressure to push onions through. Transfer sliced onion to a large skillet sprayed with butter-flavored cooking spray. Stir in meat. Sauté for 5 to 6 minutes. Meanwhile, drop potato wedges into the food chute. Position food pusher over potato quarters. Turn on processor and use medium pressure to push potatoes through. Transfer sliced potatoes to prepared baking dish. Stir mushroom soup into browned meat mixture. Evenly spoon meat mixture over sliced potatoes. Sprinkle Cheddar cheese evenly over top. Bake for 35 to 45 minutes or until potatoes are tender. Place baking dish on a wire rack and let set for 5 minutes. Divide into 4 servings.

Each serving equals:

HE: 2¼ Protein • ¾ Bread • ¼ Vegetable • ½ Slider • 1 Optional Calorie

248 Calories • 8 gm Fat • 19 gm Protein • 25 gm Carbohydrate • 526 mg Sodium • 222 mg Calcium • 2 gm Fiber

DIABETIC EXCHANGES: 2 Meat • 1½ Starch/Carbohydrate

CARB CHOICES: 1½

Cabbage Beef Bake

Sometimes I wish I could include photos with my recipes, so you could see in advance just how luscious a dish will look when you finish preparing it. I always like to say that we eat with our eyes as well as our mouths, so making food look as good as it tastes is important—and this dish does that well.   ☻   Serves 8

1 medium onion, peeled and cut into 6 wedges
16 ounces extra-lean ground sirloin beef or turkey breast
½ small head cabbage, cut into 6 wedges
1 cup diced Velveeta Light processed cheese
⅛ teaspoon black pepper
1 (8-ounce) can Pillsbury Reduced Fat Crescent Rolls
1 (10¾-ounce) can Healthy Request Tomato Soup
1 (15-ounce) can diced tomatoes, undrained
2 sprigs parsley, stems removed
1 teaspoon Worcestershire sauce
1 teaspoon prepared yellow mustard

Preheat oven to 375 degrees. Lock food processor bowl in position. Insert the steel knife blade. Drop onion into the food processor bowl. Attach food chute cover and lock in place. Turn on processor and pulse 6 or 8 times or until onion is finely chopped. In a large skillet sprayed with butter-flavored cooking spray, brown meat and onion. Meanwhile, drop cabbage wedges into the food processor bowl. Attach food chute cover and lock in place. Turn on processor and pulse 6 or 8 times or until cabbage is finely chopped. Transfer chopped cabbage to a large bowl when full level is reached. Repeat process as necessary. Add chopped cabbage to browned meat mixture. Mix well to combine. Stir in Velveeta cheese and black pepper. Continue cooking for 5 to 6 minutes or until cabbage softens and cheese melts, stirring often. Remove from heat and let set for 15 minutes or until cooled. Unroll crescent rolls and place on an ungreased baking sheet. Pat into a 14-by-9-inch rectangle, being sure to seal perforations. Evenly spread filling mixture over rolls. Roll up like a jelly roll starting with long side. Seal edge well. Place sealed edge down. Gently make several slashes in top. Bake for 20 minutes. Meanwhile, add tomato soup, undrained tomatoes, parsley, Worcestershire sauce, and mustard to food processor bowl. Attach food chute cover and lock in place. Position food pusher in chute to prevent mixture from splashing out of bowl. Turn on processor and pulse 2 or 3 times just to combine, but tomatoes are still chunky. Transfer mixture to a medium saucepan and simmer while crescent roll is baking. Place baking sheet on a wire rack and let set for 5 minutes. Cut into 8 pieces. For each serving, place 1 piece of crescent roll on a plate and spoon about ¼ cup sauce over top.

Each serving equals:

HE: 1¾ Protein • 1 Bread • 1 Vegetable • ¼ Slider • 3 Optional Calories

228 Calories • 8 gm Fat • 14 gm Protein • 25 gm Carbohydrate • 694 mg Sodium • 112 mg Calcium • 2 gm Fiber

DIABETIC EXCHANGES: 2 Meat • 1 Starch/Carbohydrate • 1 Vegetable

CARB CHOICES: 1½

Beef and Zucchini Supper Skillet

Some of my recipes call for a pound of ground sirloin, while others need only eight ounces. What's the best way to handle this? I suggest that after every shopping trip, you divide your ground beef or turkey breast into eight-ounce packages, so you'll always be able to thaw as much as you need—but no more.

○ Serves 4 (1 cup)

> 1 medium onion, peeled and cut into 6 wedges
> 8 ounces extra-lean ground sirloin beef or
>   turkey breast
> 2 small unpeeled zucchini, each cut in half lengthwise
>   and crosswise
> 1 (10¾-ounce) can Healthy Request Tomato Soup
> 1 cup reduced-sodium tomato juice
> 2 tablespoons reduced-sodium soy sauce
> 1 cup uncooked Minute Rice

Lock food processor bowl in position. Insert the steel knife blade. Drop onion wedges into the food processor bowl. Attach food chute cover and lock in place. Turn on processor and pulse 3 or 4 times or until finely chopped. Transfer chopped onions to a large skillet sprayed with butter-flavored cooking spray. Brown onions and meat, stirring often. Meanwhile, remove steel knife blade from food processor and insert shredder disc. Attach food chute cover and lock in place. Drop zucchini pieces into the food chute. Position food pusher over zucchini. Turn on processor and use light pressure to push zucchini through. Transfer shredded zucchini into skillet with browned meat mixture and continue sautéing for 5 minutes. Add tomato soup, tomato juice, and soy sauce. Mix well to combine. Stir in uncooked instant rice. Lower heat, cover, and simmer for 10 minutes or just until rice and zucchini are tender, stirring occasionally.

Each serving equals:

HE: 1½ Protein • 1½ Vegetable • ¾ Bread • ½ Slider • 5 Optional Calories

240 Calories • 4 gm Fat • 15 gm Protein • 36 gm Carbohydrate •
602 mg Sodium • 27 mg Calcium • 2 gm Fiber

DIABETIC EXCHANGES: 1½ Starch/Carbohydrate • 1½ Meat • 1½ Vegetable

CARB CHOICES: 2½

Seven-Layer Casserole

The slow cooker is just great for layered dishes like this one. You've got a tall container, so there's plenty of room, and you can place each layer into the container as it comes from the food processor. "Building" a beautiful dinner makes you feel as if you've really accomplished something, too! ☻ Serves 6 (1 cup)

  16 ounces extra-lean ground sirloin beef or
      turkey breast
  3 medium carrots, scraped and each cut into
      2-inch pieces
  3 (5-ounce) unpeeled raw potatoes, each cut into
      6 wedges
  4 medium stalks celery, trimmed and each cut into
      2-inch strips
  1 large onion, peeled and cut into 6 wedges
  1½ cups frozen cut green beans, thawed
  1½ tablespoons Worcestershire sauce
  ⅛ teaspoon black pepper
  1 (10¾-ounce) can Healthy Request Tomato Soup

Spray a slow cooker container with butter-flavored cooking spray. In a large skillet sprayed with butter-flavored cooking spray, brown meat. Meanwhile, lock food processor bowl in position. Insert the slicer disc. Attach food chute cover and lock in place. Drop carrot pieces into the food chute. Position food pusher over carrots. Turn on processor and use medium pressure to push carrots through. Transfer sliced carrots to prepared slow cooker container. Repeat process with potatoes, celery, and onion. Transfer sliced vegetables to slow cooker. Sprinkle green beans evenly over onions. Spoon browned meat evenly over green beans. Stir Worcestershire sauce and black pepper into tomato soup. Spread soup mixture evenly over top. Cover and cook on LOW for 8 hours. Mix well before serving.

HINT: Thaw green beans by rinsing in a colander under hot water for 1 minute.

Each serving equals:

HE: 2 Protein • 1½ Vegetable • ½ Bread • ¼ Slider • 10 Optional Calories

212 Calories • 4 gm Fat • 17 gm Protein • 27 gm Carbohydrate •
291 mg Sodium • 43 mg Calcium • 4 gm Fiber

DIABETIC EXCHANGES: 2 Meat • 1½ Vegetable • 1 Starch/Carbohydrate

CARB CHOICES: 2

Slow-Cooker Shipwreck

Did I get your attention with this recipe title? Good, that was my plan. I know it makes it sound as if the dish will turn out a disaster, but what I had in mind was this: In times of trouble, just dump everything into the pot and feast on the result. It will fill you up, warm you up, and make facing the future better!

☻ Serves 6 (1⅓ cups)

> 16 ounces extra-lean ground sirloin beef or
>   turkey breast
> 1 medium onion, peeled and cut into 6 wedges
> 2 (5-ounce) raw potatoes, peeled and each cut into
>   6 wedges
> 2 medium stalks celery, trimmed and each cut into
>   2-inch pieces
> 3 medium carrots, scraped and each cut into
>   2-inch pieces
> 1 (15-ounce) can diced tomatoes, undrained
> 1 (10¾-ounce) can Healthy Request Tomato Soup
> 1½ teaspoons Worcestershire sauce
> ⅛ teaspoon black pepper
> ⅔ cup uncooked Minute Rice

In a large skillet sprayed with butter-flavored cooking spray, brown meat. Spray a slow cooker container with butter-flavored cooking spray. Lock food processor bowl in position. Insert the slicer disc. Attach food chute cover and lock in place. Drop onion into the food chute. Position food pusher over onion. Turn on processor and use medium pressure to push onion through. Transfer sliced onion to prepared slow cooker container. Repeat process with potatoes, celery, and carrots. Stir undrained tomatoes, tomato soup, Worcestershire sauce, and black pepper into slow cooker container. Add browned meat and uncooked instant rice. Mix well to combine. Cover and cook on LOW for 6 to 8 hours or until vegetables are tender. Mix well before serving.

Each serving equals:

HE: 2 Protein • 1½ Vegetable • ⅔ Bread • ¼ Slider • 10 Optional Calories

228 Calories • 4 gm Fat • 17 gm Protein • 31 gm Carbohydrate •
370 mg Sodium • 36 mg Calcium • 3 gm Fiber

DIABETIC EXCHANGES: 2 Meat • 1 Vegetable • 1 Starch

CARB CHOICES: 2

Sausage Pilaf

Traditional sausage is often high in fat, so I like to use the meat of my choice with just the right seasonings to convince you that you're enjoying the "real thing." Is it close enough to please your palate as you dine? I hope you agree that it is!

⭕ Serves 6 (1 cup)

> 1 medium onion, peeled and cut into 6 wedges
> 2 medium stalks celery, trimmed and each cut into
> 	2-inch pieces
> 2 medium carrots, scraped and each cut into
> 	2-inch pieces
> 1 small red bell pepper, stem and seeds removed and
> 	cut into 6 strips
> 16 ounces extra-lean ground sirloin beef or
> 	turkey breast
> 1¼ teaspoons poultry seasoning
> 1 teaspoon ground sage
> ¾ teaspoon garlic powder
> 1 (10¾-ounce) can Healthy Request Cream of Mushroom
> 	Soup
> 1 (12-fluid-ounce) can Carnation Evaporated Fat Free
> 	Milk
> 1 cup uncooked Minute Rice

Lock food processor bowl in position. Insert the shredder disc. Attach food chute cover and lock in place. Drop onion into the food chute. Position food pusher over onion. Turn on processor and use medium pressure to push onion through. Transfer onion to a large bowl. Repeat process with celery, carrots, and red pepper. In a large skillet sprayed with butter-flavored cooking spray, combine meat, poultry seasoning, sage, and garlic powder. Stir in shredded vegetables. Sauté for 6 to 8 minutes. Add mushroom soup and evaporated milk. Mix well to combine. Stir in uncooked instant rice. Lower heat, cover, and simmer for 8 to 10 minutes or until rice is tender, stirring occasionally.

Each serving equals:

HE: 2 Protein • 1 Vegetable • ½ Fat Free Milk • ½ Bread • ¼ Slider •
8 Optional Calories

245 Calories • 5 gm Fat • 21 gm Protein • 29 gm Carbohydrate •
347 mg Sodium • 227 mg Calcium • 2 gm Fiber

DIABETIC EXCHANGES: 2 Meat • 1 Vegetable • 1 Starch • ½ Fat Free Milk

CARB CHOICES: 2

Sausage Bistro Potatoes

If you had to choose between "meat" and "potatoes," are you one of those eaters who'd gladly choose the spuds? I'm a potato lover, too, and here's a substantial and satisfying dish that delivers just enough of both to keep us happy.　　● 　Serves 4

3 (5-ounce) unpeeled raw potatoes, each cut into 4 wedges
1 small onion, peeled and cut into 4 wedges
1 small green bell pepper, stem and seeds removed and cut
　　into 4 strips
1 cup fresh whole mushrooms, each cut in half
8 ounces extra-lean ground sirloin beef or turkey breast
¾ teaspoon poultry seasoning
½ teaspoon ground sage
¼ teaspoon garlic powder
1 (8-ounce) can tomatoes, undrained
⅛ teaspoon black pepper
¼ cup Land O Lakes no-fat sour cream

Preheat oven to 375 degrees. Spray a baking sheet with butter-flavored cooking spray. Lock food processor bowl in position. Insert the slicer disc. Attach food chute cover and lock in place. Drop potato wedges into the food chute. Position food pusher over potatoes. Turn on processor and use medium pressure to push potatoes through. Evenly arrange sliced potatoes on prepared baking sheet. Lightly spray tops with butter-flavored cooking spray. Bake for 20 to 25 minutes or until potatoes are crispy. Lower heat to 200 degrees to keep potatoes warm while preparing topping. Drop onion into the food chute. Position food pusher over onion. Turn on processor and use medium pressure to push onion through. Transfer sliced onion to a large bowl. Repeat process with green pepper and mushrooms. In a large skillet sprayed with butter-flavored cooking spray, combine meat, poultry seasoning, sage, and garlic powder. Stir in sliced vegetables. Sauté mixture for 8 to 10 minutes or until meat is browned and vegetables are just tender. Remove slicer disc from food processor and insert the steel knife blade. Place undrained tomatoes into food processor bowl. Attach food chute cover and lock in place. Turn on processor and pulse 4 times or just until tomatoes are coarsely chopped. Stir chopped tomatoes into meat mixture. Add black pepper. Mix well to combine. Continue cooking for 2 to 3 minutes or until mixture is heated through. For each serving, place a full ½ cup potatoes on a plate, spoon about ¾ cup meat mixture over potatoes, and top with 1 tablespoon sour cream.

Each serving equals:

HE: 1½ Protein • 1¼ Vegetable • ¾ Bread • 15 Optional Calories

183 Calories • 3 gm Fat • 14 gm Protein • 25 gm Carbohydrate • 295 mg Sodium • 46 mg Calcium • 3 gm Fiber

DIABETIC EXCHANGES: 1½ Meat • 1 Vegetable • 1 Starch

CARB CHOICES: 1½

Pork Chow Mein

A refreshing take on one of the dishes that symbolizes Americanized Chinese food, this chow mein recipe puts the emphasis on lean pork. For years, pork was considered a poor choice for health-conscious eaters, but these days, you can buy succulent pork that's better for you than many cuts of beef. ☻ Serves 6

> 16 ounces lean pork tenderloin, cut into bite-size
> pieces
> 4 medium stalks celery, trimmed and each cut into
> 3-inch pieces
> 1 large onion, peeled and cut into 6 wedges
> 1 (14-ounce) can bean sprouts, rinsed and
> drained
> 1¼ cups water ☆
> ¼ cup reduced-sodium soy sauce
> 2 tablespoons cornstarch
> 1½ cups chow mein noodles

In a large skillet sprayed with butter-flavored cooking spray, brown pork pieces. Meanwhile, lock food processor bowl in position. Insert the slicer disc. Attach food chute cover and lock in place. Drop celery and onion into the food chute. Position food pusher over vegetables. Turn on processor and use medium pressure to push vegetables through. Transfer sliced vegetables to skillet with pork. Mix well to combine. Continue browning for 5 minutes or just until vegetables are tender, stirring often. Stir in bean sprouts, 1 cup water, and soy sauce. In a small bowl, combine remaining ¼ cup water and cornstarch using a wire whisk. Add cornstarch mixture to pork mixture. Mix well to combine. Continue cooking for 2 to 3 minutes or until mixture thickens, stirring constantly. For each serving, place ¼ cup chow mein noodles on a plate and spoon about ⅔ cup pork mixture over top.

HINT: Do not overcook meat when browning, as it could become tough.

Each serving equals:

HE: 2 Protein • 1½ Vegetable • ¾ Bread • 10 Optional Calories

202 Calories • 6 gm Fat • 21 gm Protein • 16 gm Carbohydrate • 527 mg Sodium • 30 mg Calcium • 2 gm Fiber

DIABETIC EXCHANGES: 2 Meat • 1 Vegetable • 1 Starch

CARB CHOICES: 1

Pork Creole with Cornbread Topping

Sometimes a spectacular presentation will win over your family to a new dish, even before they taste it! This tangy dish, rich in tomato flavor, looks so appealing with its crusty topping, the applause may start early—and keep going! ☙ Serves 6

16 ounces lean pork tenderloins, cut into bite-size pieces
1 large onion, peeled and cut into 6 wedges
1 large green bell pepper, stem and seeds removed and cut into 6 strips
1 (15-ounce) can diced tomatoes, undrained
1 (8-ounce) can Hunt's Tomato Sauce
½ cup + 2 tablespoons Bisquick Heart Smart Baking Mix ☆
1 teaspoon chili seasoning
6 tablespoons yellow cornmeal
1 tablespoon Splenda Granular
2 teaspoons baking powder
1 egg, or equivalent in egg substitute
½ cup fat-free milk
2 tablespoons vegetable oil

Preheat oven to 375 degrees. Spray an 8-by-8-inch baking dish with butter-flavored cooking spray. In a large skillet sprayed with butter-flavored cooking spray, brown pork pieces. Meanwhile, lock food processor bowl in position. Insert the slicer disc. Attach food chute cover and lock in place. Drop onion and green pepper into the food chute. Position food pusher over vegetables. Turn on processor and use medium pressure to push vegetables through. Transfer sliced vegetables to skillet with pork. Mix well to combine. Continue cooking for 5 minutes. Stir in undrained tomatoes, tomato sauce, 2 tablespoons baking mix, and chili seasoning. Continue cooking for 5 minutes or until mixture thickens, stirring often. Spoon mixture into prepared baking dish. Wipe food processor bowl with a clean cloth. Remove slicer disc from food processor and insert the steel knife blade. Place remaining ½ cup baking mix, cornmeal, Splenda, baking powder, egg, milk, and vegetable oil in food processor bowl. Position food pusher in chute to prevent ingredients from splashing out of bowl. Turn on processor and pulse 5 times or just until mixture is smooth. Spoon batter evenly over pork mixture. Bake for 25 to 30 minutes or until golden brown.

HINTS: 1. Do not overcook meat when browning, as it could become tough.
2. When processing cornbread, do not overprocess, as it could make cornbread texture coarse.

Each serving equals:

HE: 2 Protein • 2 Vegetable • 1 Bread • 1 Fat • 8 Optional Calories

282 Calories • 10 gm Fat • 22 gm Protein • 26 gm Carbohydrate • 638 mg Sodium • 149 mg Calcium • 3 gm Fiber

DIABETIC EXCHANGES: 2 Meat • 2 Vegetable • 1 Starch • 1 Fat

CARB CHOICES: 1½

Pork Tenders and Potato Bake

What a simple weeknight supper this is, and how splendidly it will deliver that "Mm, I'm full," feeling every time! Keep your eyes open for specials on your favorite ingredients (like the mushroom soup and the pork tenderloins) and stock up!   ○   Serves 4

> 4 (4-ounce) lean tenderized pork tenderloins or
>   cutlets
> 3 (5-ounce) unpeeled raw potatoes, each cut into
>   4 wedges
> 1 medium onion, peeled and cut into 6 wedges
> 1 cup fresh whole mushrooms, each cut in half
> 1 (10¾-ounce) can Healthy Request Cream of Mushroom
>   Soup
> 1 teaspoon Worcestershire sauce
> ⅛ teaspoon black pepper

Preheat oven to 350 degrees. Spray an 8-by-8-inch baking dish with butter-flavored cooking spray. In a large skillet sprayed with butter-flavored cooking spray, brown pork tenderloins for 3 to 4 minutes on each side. Meanwhile, lock food processor bowl in position. Insert the slicer disc. Attach food chute cover and lock in place. Drop potatoes into the food chute. Position food pusher over potatoes. Turn on processor and use medium pressure to push potatoes through. Transfer sliced potatoes to prepared baking dish. Repeat process with onion wedges. Evenly arrange browned pork over potatoes and onion. Remove slicer disc from food processor and insert the steel knife blade. Place mushrooms in food processor bowl. Attach food chute cover and lock in place. Turn on processor and pulse 1 or 2 times or until mushrooms are coarsely chopped. In a medium bowl, combine mushroom soup, Worcestershire, black pepper, and chopped mushrooms. Spoon soup mixture evenly over browned pork. Cover with aluminum foil and bake for 1 hour. Uncover and continue baking for 15 minutes or until potatoes are tender. Place baking dish on a wire rack and let set for 5 minutes. Divide into 4 servings.

Each serving equals:

HE: 3 Protein • ¾ Bread • ¾ Vegetable • ½ Slider • 1 Optional Calorie

270 Calories • 6 gm Fat • 27 gm Protein • 27 gm Carbohydrate •
361 mg Sodium • 83 mg Calcium • 2 gm Fiber

DIABETIC EXCHANGES: 3 Meat • 1½ Starch/Carbohydrate • 1 Vegetable

CARB CHOICES: 2

Pork Tenders with Corn Dressing

The names "stuffing" and "dressing" are basically interchangeable here in the Midwest. Both tend to mean a bread-based, vegetable-infused side dish that goes beautifully with a meaty entrée. Here, I've used corn in two ways to create a delightfully appetizing "go-with."   ☻   Serves 4

> 4 (4-ounce) lean tenderized pork tenderloins or cutlets
> 1 small onion, peeled and cut into 4 wedges
> 1 small green bell pepper, stem and seeds removed and cut into 4 strips
> 3 slices reduced-calorie white bread, each cut into 4 strips
> 1 (8-ounce) can cream-style corn
> ½ cup frozen whole-kernel corn
> ⅛ teaspoon black pepper

Preheat oven to 350 degrees. Spray an 8-by-8-inch baking dish with butter-flavored cooking spray. In a large skillet sprayed with butter-flavored cooking spray, brown pork for 3 to 4 minutes on each side. Evenly arrange browned pork in prepared baking dish. Lock food processor bowl in position. Insert the steel knife blade. Drop onion into the food processor bowl. Attach food chute cover and lock in place. Turn on processor and pulse 3 or 4 times or until onion is finely chopped. Transfer chopped onion to a large bowl. Repeat process with green pepper. Remove cover. Drop bread pieces into the food processor bowl. Turn on processor and pulse 3 times or until coarse crumbs form. Transfer bread crumbs to bowl with vegetables. Add cream-style corn, whole-kernel corn, and black pepper. Mix well to combine. Evenly spoon about ½ cup dressing mixture over center of each tenderloin. Cover with foil and bake for 30 minutes. Uncover and continue baking for 15 minutes. Place baking dish on a wire rack and let set for 5 minutes.

HINT: Do not overcook meat when browning, as it could become tough.

Each serving equals:

HE: 3 Protein • 1 Bread • ½ Vegetable

245 Calories • 5 gm Fat • 28 gm Protein • 22 gm Carbohydrate •
297 mg Sodium • 26 mg Calcium • 2 gm Fiber

DIABETIC EXCHANGES: 3 Meat • 1 Starch • ½ Vegetable

CARB CHOICES: 1½

Pork Tenderloins
and Vegetable Bake

In the warmer months, some people prefer to use toaster ovens instead of their regular ones to heat up a casserole dish. Just remember to check your dish a little earlier in the cooking time, as often it will be ready a bit sooner. Let the top get crisp but not dried out. ☻ Serves 4

> 4 (4-ounce) lean tenderized pork tenderloins or cutlets
> 2 (5-ounce) unpeeled raw potatoes, each cut into 4 wedges
> 1 medium onion, peeled and cut into 6 wedges
> 1 cup fresh whole mushrooms, each cut in half
> 1 (15-ounce) can diced tomatoes, undrained
> 1 (10¾-ounce) can Healthy Request Cream of Mushroom Soup
> ⅛ teaspoon black pepper

Preheat oven to 350 degrees. Spray an 8-by-8-inch baking dish with butter-flavored cooking spray. In a large skillet sprayed with butter-flavored cooking spray, brown pork for 4 to 5 minutes on each side. Meanwhile, lock food processor bowl in position. Insert the slicer disc. Attach food chute cover and lock in place. Drop potatoes into the food chute. Position food pusher over potatoes. Turn on processor and use medium pressure to push potatoes through. Arrange browned pork in prepared baking dish. Evenly arrange potato slices over pork. Drop onion through food chute using medium pressure to push onion through. Sprinkle onion slices evenly over potatoes. Drop mushrooms into the food chute and use light pressure to push mushrooms through. Sprinkle sliced mushrooms evenly over onion. In a small bowl, combine undrained stewed tomatoes, mushroom soup, and black pepper. Spoon soup mixture evenly over top. Cover with foil and bake for 60 minutes. Uncover and continue baking for 15 minutes or until potatoes and pork are tender. Place baking dish on a wire rack and let set for 5 minutes. Divide into 4 servings.

HINT: Do not overcook meat when browning, as it could become tough.

Each serving equals:

HE: 3 Protein • 1½ Vegetable • ½ Bread • ½ Slider • 1 Optional Calorie

274 Calories • 6 gm Fat • 29 gm Protein • 26 gm Carbohydrate •
569 mg Sodium • 93 mg Calcium • 4 gm Fiber

DIABETIC EXCHANGES: 3 Meat • 1½ Vegetable • 1½ Starch/Carbohydrate

CARB CHOICES: 2

Pork Tenders
Baked with Apple Stuffing

Layering flavors is one of my best cooking tips, and you'll see that in this recipe, I not only use apples but also apple juice. Fruit juice provides a delectable intensity of flavor, produced as it is from a variety of fruits. You'll taste the difference every time.

Serves 4

> 2 medium stalks celery, trimmed and each cut into 2-inch
>   pieces
> 1 medium onion, peeled and cut into 6 wedges
> 4 sprigs parsley, stems removed
> 3 medium cooking apples, cored, peeled, and each cut into
>   quarters
> 6 slices reduced-calorie white bread, toasted and each cut
>   into 4 pieces
> 1 teaspoon dried sage
> ½ cup unsweetened apple juice
> 4 (4-ounce) lean pork tenderloins or cutlets

Preheat oven to 350 degrees. Spray an 8-by-8-inch baking dish with butter-flavored cooking spray. Lock food processor bowl in position. Insert the steel knife blade. Drop celery, onion, and parsley into the food processor bowl. Attach food chute cover and lock in place. Turn on processor and pulse 3 or 4 times or until vegetables are finely chopped. Transfer chopped vegetables to a large bowl. Drop apples into the food processor bowl. Pulse 3 or 4 times or until apples are finely chopped. Transfer chopped apples to bowl with vegetables. Place toast pieces in food processor bowl. Re-cover and pulse 4 or 5 times or until coarse crumbs form. Transfer bread crumbs to bowl with vegetables. Mix well to combine. Stir in sage and apple juice just until well moistened. Evenly spoon stuffing mixture into prepared baking dish. In a large skillet sprayed with butter-flavored cooking spray, brown tenderloins for 3 or 4 times on each side. Evenly arrange browned tenderloins over stuffing mixture. Cover and bake for 45 minutes. Uncover and continue baking for 15 minutes.

HINT: Do not overcook meat when browning, as it could become tough.

Each serving equals:

HE: 3 Protein • 1 Fruit • ¾ Bread • ¾ Vegetable

286 Calories • 6 gm Fat • 30 gm Protein • 28 gm Carbohydrate • 246 mg Sodium • 54 mg Calcium • 2 gm Fiber

DIABETIC EXCHANGES: 3 Meat • 1 Fruit • 1 Starch • ½ Vegetable

CARB CHOICES: 2

Pork Tenderloins
with Pear Cranberry Sauce

Why is it that pork goes so well with fruited sauces? I think it's mostly because its basic flavor is more bland, more willing to "partner up" with other flavors (in this case, a blend of pears, cranberries, and orange juice) to produce a tasty dish.   ❍   Serves 4

> 4 (4-ounce) lean tenderized pork tenderloins or cutlets
> 1 small onion, peeled and cut into 4 wedges
> 2 teaspoons I Can't Believe It's Not Butter! Light Margarine
> 3 medium Bartlett pears, cored, peeled, and each cut into 4
>   quarters
> 1/4 cup unsweetened orange juice
> 1/2 cup fresh or frozen whole cranberries
> 1/4 teaspoon ground cinnamon

In a large skillet sprayed with butter-flavored cooking spray, brown pork for 4 to 5 minutes on each side. Meanwhile, lock food processor bowl in position. Insert the steel knife blade. Drop onion into the food processor bowl. Attach food chute cover and lock in place. Turn on processor and pulse 3 or 4 times or until onion is finely chopped. Transfer chopped onion to a medium saucepan sprayed with butter-flavored cooking spray. Stir in margarine. Brown onion for 5 minutes. Meanwhile, drop pear quarters into the food processor bowl. Attach food chute cover and lock in place. Turn on processor and pulse 2 or 3 times or until pears are coarsely chopped. Transfer chopped pears to saucepan with onion. Stir in orange juice, cranberries, and cinnamon. Cook over medium heat for 3 to 5 minutes or just until cranberries soften. Spoon mixture evenly over browned tenderloins. Lower heat, cover, and simmer for 10 to 15 minutes or until pork is cooked through and tender. When serving, evenly spoon pear-cranberry sauce over top of tenderloins.

HINT: Do not overcook meat when browning, as it could become tough.

Each serving equals:

HE: 3 Protein • 1 Fruit • ¼ Fat • ¼ Vegetable

241 Calories • 5 gm Fat • 25 gm Protein • 24 gm Carbohydrate •
72 mg Sodium • 24 mg Calcium • 4 gm Fiber

DIABETIC EXCHANGES: 3 Meat • 1 Fruit

CARB CHOICES: 1½

Ham and Swiss Sandwich Bake

This oven-baked version of a grilled ham and cheese sandwich is a terrific choice for a Sunday supper, along with one of my aromatic and filling soups. There's no rule that says you can't eat sandwiches in the evening, and if you get home late from work, a lighter dinner is usually better for you. ☻ Serves 4 (2 each)

1 small onion, peeled and cut into 4 wedges
2 (3-ounce) slices Dubuque 97% fat-free ham or any extra-lean ham, each cut into 4 strips
4 (¾-ounce) slices Kraft reduced-fat Swiss cheese, each cut into 3 strips
⅓ cup Kraft fat-free mayonnaise
⅛ teaspoon black pepper
8 slices reduced-calorie white bread, toasted

Preheat oven to 375 degrees. Spray a baking sheet with butter-flavored cooking spray. Lock food processor bowl in position. Insert the steel knife blade. Drop onion and ham into the food processor bowl. Attach food chute cover and lock in place. Turn on processor and pulse 4 or 6 times or until onion and ham are finely chopped. Repeat process with Swiss cheese. Remove cover and add mayonnaise and black pepper. Re-cover and pulse 5 or 6 times or until mixture is blended. Evenly spread about ¼ cup mixture on each slice of toast and arrange on prepared baking sheet. Bake for 6 to 8 minutes or until mixture is bubbly. Serve at once.

HINT: A 3-ounce slice of ham is about ⅓ inch thick.

Each serving equals:

HE: 2 Protein • 1 Bread • ¼ Vegetable • 15 Optional Calories

220 Calories • 8 gm Fat • 18 gm Protein • 19 gm Carbohydrate • 703 mg Sodium • 263 mg Calcium • 1 gm Fiber

DIABETIC EXCHANGES: 2 Meat • 1 Starch

CARB CHOICES: 1

Octoberfest Ham Skillet

The leaves are changing to gold, orange, and red, there's a chill in the air, and fall is in full flower—it's definitely time for this savory ham, cabbage, and apple blend, heated in your skillet until the flavors begin to dance in unison. ☺ Serves 4 (1½ cups)

> 2 medium cooking apples, cored, peeled, and each cut into
>   4 quarters
> 1 medium onion, peeled and cut into 6 wedges
> ½ small head of cabbage, cut into 6 wedges
> 12 ounces Dubuque 97% fat-free ham or any extra-lean
>   ham, cut into 2-inch strips
> ½ cup unsweetened apple juice

Lock food processor bowl in position. Insert the steel knife blade. Drop apple quarters into the food processor bowl. Attach food chute cover and lock in place. Turn on processor and pulse 2 or 3 times or until apples are coarsely chopped. Transfer chopped apples to a large bowl. Repeat process with onion and cabbage. Place mixture in a large skillet sprayed with butter-flavored cooking spray. Sauté over medium heat while chopping ham. Drop ham strips into the food processor bowl. Attach food chute cover and lock in place. Turn on processor and pulse 2 or 3 times or until coarsely chopped. Stir chopped ham into skillet with sautéed apples and vegetables. Add apple juice. Mix well to combine. Lower heat and simmer for 5 minutes, stirring often.

Each serving equals:

HE: 1½ Protein • 1 Vegetable • ¾ Fruit

183 Calories • 3 gm Fat • 15 gm Protein • 24 gm Carbohydrate •
686 mg Sodium • 49 mg Calcium • 5 gm Fiber

DIABETIC EXCHANGES: 1½ Meat • 1 Vegetable • 1 Fruit

CARB CHOICES: 1½

Creamed Franks and Cabbage Dinner

This is an easy family meal, perfect for after your kids' soccer game or an all-day visit to a nearby flea market. It's rich and creamy but not at all fancy, so you can dine without guilt sitting at TV tables and watching your favorite reality show.   ○   Serves 4

> 8 ounces Oscar Mayer or Healthy Choice reduced-fat
>   frankfurters, cut into 2-inch pieces
> 1 medium onion, peeled and cut into 6 wedges
> ½ medium head of cabbage, cut into 6 wedges
> 1 (10¾-ounce) can Healthy Request Cream of Mushroom
>   Soup
> ¼ cup Land O Lakes no-fat sour cream
> ⅛ teaspoon black pepper
> 1½ cups hot cooked noodles, rinsed and drained

Lock food processor bowl in position. Insert the slicer disc. Attach food chute cover and lock in place. Drop frankfurters into food chute. Position food pusher over frankfurters. Turn on processor and use medium pressure to push frankfurters through. Transfer sliced frankfurters to a large bowl. Repeat process with onion and cabbage. In a large skillet sprayed with butter-flavored cooking spray, sauté frankfurters and vegetables for 10 minutes or just until cabbage is tender. Add mushroom soup, sour cream, and black pepper. Mix well to combine. Stir in noodles. Lower heat and simmer for 5 to 6 minutes or until mixture is heated through, stirring often.

HINTS: 1. 1½ cups diced Dubuque 97% fat-free ham or any extra-lean ham can be used instead of frankfurters.
2. Usually 1¼ cups uncooked noodles cook to about 1½ cups.

Each serving equals:

HE: 1⅓ Protein • 1 Vegetable • ¾ Bread • ½ Slider • 16 Optional Calories

237 Calories • 5 gm Fat • 13 gm Protein • 35 gm Carbohydrate •
858 mg Sodium • 154 mg Calcium • 1 gm Fiber

DIABETIC EXCHANGES: 1½ Starch/Carbohydrate • 1 Meat • 1 Vegetable

CARB CHOICES: 2

Kielbasa Sausage with Peppers and Onion

Kielbasa started out as a regional specialty but has quickly traveled around the USA, inviting people of all ethnic backgrounds to partake in its hearty, old-fashioned goodness. This recipe calls for green and red peppers, but if you've purchased one of those Costco pepper variety packs, you might add some yellow pepper, too, just for a little extra pizzazz!   ☻   Serves 4 (¾ cup)

> 8 ounces reduced-fat kielbasa or Polish sausage,
>   cut into 2-inch pieces
> 1 large onion, peeled and cut into 6 wedges
> 1 large green bell pepper, stem and seeds removed and
>   cut into 6 strips
> 1 large red bell pepper, stem and seeds removed and
>   cut into 6 strips
> ¼ cup reduced-sodium ketchup
> ¼ cup water

Lock food processor bowl in position. Insert the slicer disc. Attach food chute and lock in place. Drop kielbasa pieces into the food chute. Position food pusher over sausage pieces. Turn on processor and use medium pressure to push sausage through. Transfer sliced sausage to a large bowl. Drop onion wedges into the food chute. Position food pusher over onion. Turn on processor and use medium pressure to push onion through. Transfer sliced onion to bowl with sausage. Repeat process with green and red pepper. Place kielbasa and vegetable mixture in a large skillet sprayed with butter-flavored cooking spray. Sauté for 8 to 10 minutes. In a small bowl, combine ketchup and water. Stir mixture into kielbasa mixture. Lower heat and simmer for 2 to 3 minutes, stirring often.

HINT: Good "as is," spooned into a hot dog bun, or served over
    rice.

Each serving equals:

HE: 2 Protein • 2 Vegetable • 15 Optional Calories

122 Calories • 2 gm Fat • 8 gm Protein • 18 gm Carbohydrate • 486 mg Sodium • 37 mg Calcium • 2 gm Fiber

DIABETIC EXCHANGES: 2 Meat • 2 Vegetable

CARB CHOICES: 1

Delightful

Desserts

You might expect that a food processor won't have much impact on dessert-making, but you'd be wrong about that! I've found myself using lots of fantastically fresh ingredients—fruits, vegetables, nuts, and more—in my dessert recipes for this book. It's been fascinating to reconceive a classic recipe in a new way to take advantage of this spectacular kitchen "helper"!

If your favorite part of every meal is dessert, you're going to have so much fun stirring up the recipes in this chapter. Recipes that might have seemed like a lot of work will truly be easier than you expect—and the results absolutely scrumptious! Close your eyes and imagine tasting *Rhubarb Royale Swirl*, or maybe biting into a slice of *Strawberry Coconut Pizza*. There isn't a child anywhere (well, very few, anyway) who wouldn't love being treated to a piece of *Peanut Butter and Apple Scallop*—yum! And for any special occasion that demands an old-fashioned delight, serve my *Upside-Down Apple Cake* to great applause!

Zucchini Blondie Bars

Why stir a veggie like zucchini into a baked dessert such as a blondie? It adds moisture, texture, nutrition, and fiber—and you won't ever know that you're eating a green vegetable for dessert!

● Serves 12 (2 each)

> 2 medium unpeeled zucchini, cut in half lengthwise and
>   crosswise
> 1¾ cups Splenda Granular
> ½ cup I Can't Believe It's Not Butter! Light Margarine
> 2 eggs, or equivalent in egg substitute
> 2 tablespoons Land O Lakes Fat Free Half & Half
> 2 cups Bisquick Heart Smart Baking Mix
> 1 teaspoon ground cinnamon
> ½ cup mini chocolate chips

Preheat oven to 350 degrees. Spray a 9-by-13-inch cake pan with butter-flavored cooking spray. Lock food processor bowl in position. Insert the shredder disc. Attach food chute cover and lock in place. Drop zucchini into the food chute. Position food pusher over zucchini. Turn on processor and use medium pressure to push zucchini through. Transfer shredded zucchini to a medium bowl. In a large bowl, combine Splenda and margarine using a wire whisk. Stir in eggs and half & half. Add baking mix and cinnamon. Mix gently just to combine using a sturdy spoon. Fold in zucchini. Evenly spread batter into prepared cake pan. Sprinkle chocolate chips evenly over top. Bake for 18 to 26 minutes or until a toothpick inserted in center comes out clean. Place pan on a wire rack and allow to cool completely. Cut into 24 bars.

Each serving equals:

HE: 1 Fat • ¾ Bread • ⅓ Vegetable • ¾ Slider • 10 Optional Calories

172 Calories • 8 gm Fat • 3 gm Protein • 22 gm Carbohydrate •
339 mg Sodium • 33 mg Calcium • 1 gm Fiber

DIABETIC EXCHANGES: 1½ Starch/Carbohydrate • 1 Fat

CARB CHOICES: 1½

Strawberry-Coconut Delight

This was one of my favorite discoveries when I began using my food processor this time around—how magnificently it purées my beloved strawberries! Now it's astonishingly easy to produce a lovely finale to any meal.   ❍   Serves 4

> 2 cups fresh whole strawberries
> 1½ cups Dannon plain fat-free yogurt
> ½ teaspoon coconut extract
> 1 (4-serving) package Jell-O sugar-free instant vanilla
>   pudding mix
> ¼ cup Cool Whip Lite
> 1 tablespoon + 1 teaspoon flaked coconut

Lock food processor bowl in position. Insert the steel knife blade. Drop strawberries into the food processor bowl. Attach food chute cover and lock in place. Turn on processor and pulse 4 or 5 times or until strawberries are puréed. Remove food chute cover. Add yogurt, coconut extract, and dry pudding mix to food processor bowl. Attach food chute cover and lock in place. Turn on processor and pulse 5 or 6 times or until mixture is blended. Evenly spoon mixture into 4 dessert dishes. Top each with 1 tablespoon Cool Whip Lite and 1 teaspoon coconut.

Each serving equals:

HE: ½ Fat Free Milk • ½ Fruit • ½ Slider • 12 Optional Calories

129 Calories • 1 gm Fat • 7 gm Protein • 23 gm Carbohydrate •
405 mg Sodium • 196 mg Calcium • 2 gm Fiber

DIABETIC EXCHANGES: 1 Starch/Carbohydrate • ½ Fruit

CARB CHOICES: 1½

Blueberry Buckle

Can you make a true old-fashioned dessert using a "newfangled" appliance? You bet you can! This crumb-topped fruit dessert is like a time machine taking you back to the good old days of home baking. ◐ Serves 8

½ cup Land O Lakes Fat Free
   Half & Half
1 teaspoon lemon juice
¼ cup I Can't Believe It's
   Not Butter! Light
   Margarine
¾ cup Splenda Granular

1 egg, or equivalent in egg
   substitute
1½ cups all-purpose flour
2 teaspoons baking powder
½ teaspoon table salt
3 cups fresh or frozen
   blueberries

Preheat oven to 350 degrees. Spray a 9-by-9-inch cake pan with butter-flavored cooking spray. In a small bowl, combine half & half and lemon juice. Set aside. Lock food processor bowl in position. Insert the steel knife blade. Place margarine, Splenda, and egg in food processor bowl. Attach food chute cover and lock in place. Turn on processor and pulse 20 to 25 times or until mixture is smooth. Pour half & half mixture through the food chute. Continue to pulse 5 times. Add flour, baking powder, and salt to food processor bowl. Turn on processor and pulse 3 or 4 times to mix ingredients. Do not overprocess. Remove cover and stir in blueberries using a rubber spatula. Evenly spread batter into prepared cake pan. Bake for 35 to 45 minutes or until a toothpick inserted in center comes out clean. Place cake pan on a wire rack and let set for at least 10 minutes. Cut into 8 servings.

HINT: Good served warm with sugar- and fat-free vanilla ice cream or cold with Cool Whip Lite. If using, don't forget to count the additional calories.

Each serving equals:

HE: 1 Bread • ¾ Fat • ½ Fruit • ¼ Slider • 5 Optional Calories

168 Calories • 4 gm Fat • 4 gm Protein • 29 gm Carbohydrate • 344 mg Sodium • 85 mg Calcium • 2 gm Fiber

DIABETIC EXCHANGES: 1 Starch • 1 Fat • ½ Fruit

CARB CHOICES: 2

Rhubarb Royale Swirl

If you've always felt that fresh rhubarb tasted better than the frozen kind but required too much work, here's your chance to eat what you like without extra effort! This lusciously creamy dessert is fit for a king or queen. ☻ Serves 6

> 6 medium stalks rhubarb, trimmed and each cut into
>   2-inch pieces
> ¾ cup Splenda Granular ☆
> 1¾ cups water ☆
> 1 (4-serving) package Jell-O sugar-free strawberry
>   gelatin
> 1 (4-serving) package Jell-O sugar-free instant vanilla
>   pudding mix
> ⅔ cup Carnation Nonfat Dry Milk Powder
> ¾ cup Cool Whip Lite ☆
> 12 (2½-inch) graham cracker squares ☆

Lock food processor bowl in position. Insert the slicer disc. Attach food chute cover and lock in place. Drop rhubarb pieces into the food chute. Position food pusher over rhubarb. Turn on processor and use medium pressure to push rhubarb through. Transfer sliced rhubarb to a medium saucepan. Stir in ½ cup Splenda and ¼ cup water. Cover and cook over low heat for 10 to 12 minutes or until rhubarb softens, stirring occasionally. Remove from heat. Add dry gelatin. Mix well to combine. In a medium bowl, combine dry pudding mix, dry milk powder, and remaining 1½ cups water. Mix well using a wire whisk. Blend in 6 tablespoons Cool Whip Lite. Evenly arrange 9 graham crackers in a 9-by-9-inch cake pan. Carefully spread pudding mixture over graham crackers. Spoon rhubarb mixture evenly over top. Using a table knife, swirl rhubarb mixture into pudding mixture. Wipe food processor bowl with a clean cloth. Remove slicer disc from food processor and insert the steel knife blade. Coarsely break remaining 3 graham crackers and place in food processor bowl. Add remaining ¼ cup Splenda. Cover and pulse 6 or 7 times or until fine crumbs form. Evenly sprinkle crumb mixture over filling mixture. Refrigerate for at least 2 hours.

Divide into 6 servings. When serving, top each with 1 tablespoon Cool Whip Lite.

Each serving equals:

HE: ⅔ Bread • ½ Vegetable • ⅓ Fat Free Milk • ½ Slider • 14 Optional Calories

142 Calories • 2 gm Fat • 5 gm Protein • 26 gm Carbohydrate • 385 mg Sodium • 147 mg Calcium • 1 gm Fiber

DIABETIC EXCHANGES: 1½ Starch/Carbohydrate

CARB CHOICES: 2

Rhubarb–Banana Cream Dessert

You usually see rhubarb partnered with strawberries, but everyone (and everything) deserves a change of pace, right? So I've "invited" bananas to take a twirl around the dance floor with that Midwestern favorite, rhubarb. Wow!   ☾   Serves 6

12 (2½-inch) graham cracker squares ☆
3 tablespoons pecans
2 tablespoons Splenda Granular
6 medium stalks rhubarb, trimmed and each cut into 2-inch
*   pieces*
1 cup water
1 (4-serving) package Jell-O sugar-free strawberry gelatin
3 medium bananas, each cut into 2-inch pieces
1 (4-serving) package Jell-O sugar-free instant vanilla
*   pudding mix*
⅔ cup Carnation Nonfat Dry Milk Powder
¾ cup Cool Whip Free

Evenly arrange 9 graham crackers in a 9-by-9-inch cake pan. Lock food processor bowl in position. Insert the steel knife blade. Break remaining 3 graham crackers in half. Place graham cracker halves, pecans, and Splenda in food processor bowl. Attach food chute cover and lock in place. Turn on processor and pulse 3 or 4 times or until mixture is crumbly. Transfer to a small bowl. Wipe food processor bowl with a clean cloth. Remove steel knife blade from food processor and insert the slicer disc. Attach food chute cover and lock in place. Drop rhubarb pieces into the food chute. Position food pusher over rhubarb. Turn on processor and use medium pressure to push rhubarb through. In a medium saucepan, combine rhubarb and water. Cover and cook over medium heat for 10 minutes or until rhubarb softens. Remove from heat. Stir in dry gelatin. Place saucepan on a wire rack and allow to cool for 15 minutes. After rhubarb mixture has cooled, drop banana pieces into food chute and slice. Evenly arrange sliced bananas over graham crackers. Remove slicer disc from food processor and insert the steel knife blade. Add dry pudding mix, dry milk powder, and cooled rhubarb to food processor bowl. Attach food chute cover and lock in place. Position food pusher in chute to prevent ingredients from splashing out of bowl. Turn on processor and pulse 10 or 12 times or until mixture is smooth. Add Cool Whip Free. Pulse an additional 2 or 3 times. Evenly spread filling mixture over bananas. Sprinkle remaining graham cracker crumb mixture over top. Refrigerate for at least 30 minutes. Divide into 6 servings.

Each serving equals:

HE: 1 Fruit • ⅔ Bread • ½ Fat • ½ Vegetable • ⅓ Fat Free Milk • ¼ Slider • 19 Optional Calories

212 Calories • 4 gm Fat • 6 gm Protein •
38 gm Carbohydrate • 390 mg Sodium • 149 mg Calcium • 3 gm Fiber

DIABETIC EXCHANGES: 1½ Starch/Carbohydrate • 1 Fruit • ½ Fat

CARB CHOICES: 2½

Cliff's Rhubarb Crunch

My husband's mom always made rhubarb desserts for her family, so naturally Cliff still enjoys dining on treats starring those locally raised stalks. In this dish, he noticed the crunchy combination of textures on his tongue—and gave me a thumbs-up!

○ Serves 8

> 12 medium stalks fresh rhubarb, trimmed and each
>   cut into 2-inch pieces
> 1 cup quick oats
> ¾ cup all-purpose flour
> 2 cups Splenda Granular ☆
> ⅓ cup I Can't Believe It's Not Butter! Light
>   Margarine
> 1 cup water
> 2 tablespoons cornstarch
> 1 teaspoon vanilla extract

Preheat oven to 375 degrees. Spray a 9-by-9-inch cake pan with butter-flavored cooking spray. Lock food processor bowl in position. Insert the slicer disc. Attach food chute cover and lock in place. Drop rhubarb pieces into the food chute. Position food pusher over rhubarb. Turn on processor and use medium pressure to push rhubarb through. Transfer sliced rhubarb to a large bowl. Remove slicer disc from food processor and insert the steel knife blade. Place oats, flour, 1 cup Splenda, and margarine in food processor bowl. Attach food chute cover and lock in place. Position food pusher in chute to prevent ingredients from splashing out of bowl. Turn on processor and pulse 10 or 12 times or until mixture is crumbly. Evenly pat half of crumb mixture into prepared cake pan. Sprinkle rhubarb evenly over top. In a medium saucepan, combine water, remaining 1 cup Splenda, and cornstarch. Mix well using a wire whisk. Cook over medium heat for 2 to 3 minutes or until mixture thickens and starts to boil. Remove from heat. Stir in vanilla extract. Drizzle hot mixture evenly over rhubarb. Evenly sprinkle remaining crumb mixture over top. Bake for 45 to 50 minutes. Place cake pan on a wire rack and let set for at least 15 minutes. Divide into 8 servings.

Each serving equals:

HE: 1 Bread • 1 Fat • ¾ Vegetable • ¼ Slider • 11 Optional Calories

152 Calories • 4 gm Fat • 3 gm Protein • 26 gm Carbohydrate •
93 mg Sodium • 63 mg Calcium • 2 gm Fiber

DIABETIC EXCHANGES: 1½ Starch/Carbohydrate • 1 Fat

CARB CHOICES: 2

Peanut Butter and Apple Scallop

Were you one of those kids who liked to stick an apple slice into the nearest jar of chunky peanut butter? Join the club! This is a flavor combo that kids everywhere (and of any age!) just seem to love. This dessert won't last long, even if you have leftovers!

◑ Serves 6

> 15 (2½-inch) graham cracker squares ☆
> 4 medium cooking apples, cored, peeled, and each cut into quarters
> 1 (4-serving) package Jell-O sugar-free vanilla cook-and-serve pudding mix
> 1 cup unsweetened apple juice
> ½ cup water
> 3 tablespoons Bisquick Heart Smart Baking Mix
> ¼ cup Splenda Granular
> 6 tablespoons Peter Pan or Skippy reduced-fat peanut butter

Preheat oven to 350 degrees. Evenly arrange 9 graham crackers in a 9-by-9-inch cake pan. Lock food processor bowl in position. Insert the slicer disc. Attach food chute cover and lock in place. Drop apples into the food chute. Position food pusher over apples. Turn on processor and use medium pressure to push apples through. Evenly arrange apple slices over graham crackers. In a medium saucepan, combine dry pudding mix, apple juice, and water. Mix well using a wire whisk. Cook over medium heat for 6 to 8 minutes or until mixture thickens and starts to boil. Evenly spoon hot mixture over apples. Wipe food processor bowl with a clean cloth. Remove slicer disc from food processor and insert the steel knife blade. Break remaining 6 graham crackers into large pieces. Place graham cracker pieces in food processor bowl. Add baking mix, Splenda, and peanut butter. Turn on processor and pulse 4 or 5 times or until mixture is crumbly. Evenly sprinkle crumb mixture over top. Bake for 25 to 30 minutes. Place cake pan on a wire rack and let set for at least 15 minutes. Divide into 6 servings.

Each serving equals:

HE: 1 Bread • 1 Protein • 1 Fruit • 1 Fat • 17 Optional Calories

252 Calories • 8 gm Fat • 5 gm Protein • 40 gm Carbohydrate •
331 mg Sodium • 10 mg Calcium • 4 gm Fiber

DIABETIC EXCHANGES: 1½ Starch/Carbohydrate • 1 Fruit • 1 Fat • ½ Meat

CARB CHOICES: 2½

Country Apple Crisp

If you've just gone apple picking (and what a fun thing to do with the kids!) and you've got more apples than you know what to do with, here's a cozy, homemade dessert that will delight anyone lucky enough to stop by. ● Serves 6

> 6 medium cooking apples, cored, peeled, and each cut into
>   quarters
> 2 tablespoons lemon juice
> 1 cup quick oats
> ¾ cup Splenda Granular
> 6 tablespoons Bisquick Heart Smart Baking Mix
> 2 tablespoons + 2 teaspoons I Can't Believe It's Not Butter!
>   Light Margarine
> 1 teaspoon ground cinnamon

Preheat oven to 375 degrees. Spray an 8-by-8-inch baking dish with butter-flavored cooking spray. Lock food processor bowl in position. Insert the slicer disc. Attach food chute cover and lock in place. Drop apples into the food chute. Position food pusher over apples. Turn on processor and use medium pressure to push apples through. Transfer sliced apples to a large bowl when full level is reached. Repeat process as necessary. Evenly arrange sliced apples in prepared baking dish. Sprinkle lemon juice evenly over apples. Remove slicer disc from food processor and insert the steel knife blade. Add oats, Splenda, baking mix, margarine, and cinnamon to food processor bowl. Attach food chute cover and lock in place. Position food pusher in chute to prevent ingredients from splashing out of bowl. Turn on processor and pulse 10 or 12 times or until mixture is crumbly. Evenly spread crumb mixture over apples. Bake for 45 to 50 minutes or until apples are tender. Place baking dish on a wire rack and let set for at least 10 minutes. Divide into 6 servings.

HINT: Good served warm with sugar- and fat-free vanilla ice cream or cold with Cool Whip Lite. If using, don't forget to count the additional calories.

Each serving equals:

HE: 1 Bread • 1 Fruit • ⅔ Fat • 12 Optional Calories

184 Calories • 4 gm Fat • 3 gm Protein • 34 gm Carbohydrate •
148 mg Sodium • 25 mg Calcium • 3 gm Fiber

DIABETIC EXCHANGES: 1 Starch • 1 Fruit • 1 Fat

CARB CHOICES: 2

Strawberry-Coconut Pizza

Imagine a pizza meal from start to finish . . . Now, it's not hard to imagine the appetizer and main-dish recipes, but oh, what fun to come up with dessert pizzas that please! This beautiful, rosy-red delight is a truly grand finale. ☻ Serves 8

1 (8-ounce) can Pillsbury Reduced Fat Crescent Rolls
6 cups fresh whole strawberries ☆
2 (8-ounce) packages Philadelphia fat-free cream cheese
¼ cup Splenda Granular
1 teaspoon coconut extract
1 (4-serving) package Jell-O sugar-free vanilla cook-and-serve pudding mix
1 (4-serving) package Jell-O sugar-free strawberry gelatin
1½ cups water
¼ cup flaked coconut

Preheat oven to 375 degrees. Spray a rimmed 10-by-15-inch baking pan with butter-flavored cooking spray. Unroll crescent rolls and carefully pat into prepared pan, being sure to seal perforations. Bake for 8 to 10 minutes or until crust is golden brown. Place baking pan on a wire rack and allow to cool completely. Meanwhile, lock food processor bowl in position. Insert the steel knife blade. Drop 1 cup strawberries into the food processor bowl. Attach food chute cover and lock in place. Turn on processor and pulse 3 or 4 times or until strawberries are finely chopped. In a medium bowl, stir cream cheese with a sturdy spoon until softened. Add chopped strawberries, Splenda, and coconut extract. Mix well to combine. Evenly spread cream cheese mixture over cooled crust. Remove steel knife blade from food processor and insert the slicer disc. Attach food chute cover and lock in place. Drop remaining 5 cups strawberries into the food chute. Position food pusher over strawberries. Turn on processor and use light pressure to push strawberries through. Transfer sliced strawberries to a large bowl when full level is reached. Repeat process as necessary. Evenly sprinkle sliced strawberries over cream cheese mixture. In a medium saucepan, combine dry pudding mix, dry gelatin, and water. Mix well using a wire whisk. Cook over medium heat until mixture thickens and starts to boil, stirring constantly with a wire whisk. Drizzle hot mixture evenly over strawberries. Refrigerate for at least 1 hour. Evenly sprinkle coconut over top. Cut into 8 servings.

Each serving equals:

HE: 1 Bread • 1 Protein • ¾ Fruit • ¼ Slider • 9 Optional Calories

209 Calories • 5 gm Fat • 11 gm Protein • 30 gm Carbohydrate • 605 mg Sodium • 180 mg Calcium • 3 gm Fiber

DIABETIC EXCHANGES: 1 Starch • 1 Fruit • 1 Meat • 1 Fat

CARB CHOICES: 2

Apple-Walnut Cinnamon Crisp

You know that Columbus was searching for spices like aromatic cinnamon when he accidentally ended up in North America, right? Some men will go anywhere or do anything for a dessert that smells this good! ♥ Serves 6

4 medium cooking apples, cored, peeled, and each cut into quarters
¾ cup Splenda Granular ☆
1 teaspoon ground cinnamon
¼ cup unsweetened apple juice

12 (2½-inch) graham cracker squares
¼ cup walnuts
1 tablespoon + 1 teaspoon I Can't Believe It's Not Butter! Light Margarine

Preheat oven to 350 degrees. Spray an 8-by-8-inch baking dish with butter-flavored cooking spray. Lock food processor bowl in position. Insert the slicer disc. Attach food chute cover and lock in place. Drop apples into the food chute. Position food pusher over apples. Turn on processor and use medium pressure to push apples through. Place sliced apples in prepared baking dish. Evenly sprinkle ½ cup Splenda and cinnamon over apples. Drizzle apple juice evenly over top. Remove slicer disc from food processor and insert the steel knife blade. Break graham crackers in half. Add graham cracker halves, remaining ¼ cup Splenda, walnuts, and margarine to processor bowl. Attach food chute cover and lock in place. Position food pusher in chute to prevent ingredients from splashing out of bowl. Turn on processor and pulse 10 or 12 times or until mixture is crumbly. Evenly spread crumb mixture over apples. Cover with foil. Bake for 30 minutes. Uncover and continue baking for 15 minutes. Place baking dish on a wire rack and let set for 5 minutes. Divide into 6 servings.

Each serving equals:

HE: ¾ Fruit • ⅔ Bread • ⅔ Fat • ¼ Slider • 2 Optional Calories

145 Calories • 5 gm Fat • 2 gm Protein • 23 gm Carbohydrate • 76 mg Sodium • 15 mg Calcium • 3 gm Fiber

DIABETIC EXCHANGES: 1 Fruit • 1 Fat • ½ Starch

CARB CHOICES: 1½

Amazing Apple Crumb Pie

Remember how much work it is to slice apples for a pie? Now think how much easier it would be if you had a sous-chef, an assistant to do the repetitive stuff—and then realize that with a food processor, you *do*. ❂ Serves 8

1 Pillsbury refrigerated
    unbaked 9-inch pie crust
8 medium cooking apples,
    cored, peeled, and each
    cut into quarters
1½ cups Splenda Granular ☆

1½ teaspoons apple pie spice
¾ cup Bisquick Heart Smart
    Baking Mix ☆
2 tablespoons + 2 teaspoons
    I Can't Believe It's Not
    Butter! Light Margarine

Preheat oven to 375 degrees. Place pie crust in a 9-inch pie plate and flute edges. Lock food processor bowl in position. Insert the slicer blade. Attach food chute cover and lock in place. Drop apples into the food chute. Position food pusher over apples. Turn on processor and use light pressure to push apples through. Transfer sliced apples to a large bowl when full level is reached. Repeat process as necessary. Add 1 cup Splenda, apple pie spice, and ¼ cup baking mix to apple slices. Mix well to combine. Evenly spoon apple mixture into prepared pie crust. Wipe food processor bowl with a clean cloth. Remove slicer disc from food processor and insert the steel knife blade. Place remaining ½ cup baking mix, remaining ½ cup Splenda, and margarine in food processor bowl. Cover and pulse 3 or 4 times or until mixture is crumbly. Evenly sprinkle crumb mixture over apple mixture. Bake for 50 to 60 minutes or until apples are tender and topping is browned. Place pie plate on a wire rack and let set for 5 minutes. Cut into 8 servings.

Each serving equals:

HE: 1½ Bread • 1 Fruit • 1 Fat • 18 Optional Calories

270 Calories • 10 gm Fat • 1 gm Protein • 44 gm Carbohydrate •
276 mg Sodium • 16 mg Calcium • 4 gm Fiber

DIABETIC EXCHANGES: 1½ Starch/Carbohydrate • 1½ Fat • 1 Fruit

CARB CHOICES: 3

Apple-Raisin Crumb Pie

These days, many children (and plenty of adults) have no idea that raisins are actually dried grapes (or that prunes used to be plums!). Baking those wrinkled little guys brings out their best, especially in a lavish pie like this one. ☻ Serves 8

> 1 Pillsbury refrigerated unbaked 9-inch pie crust
> 5 medium cooking apples, cored, peeled, and each cut into
>   quarters
> 1 (4-serving) package Jell-O sugar-free vanilla cook-and-
>   serve pudding mix
> ½ cup Splenda Granular ☆
> ½ cup unsweetened apple juice
> ¼ cup water
> ¼ cup seedless raisins
> 1 teaspoon apple pie spice
> 6 tablespoons all-purpose flour
> 2 tablespoons + 2 teaspoons I Can't Believe It's Not Butter!
>   Light Margarine

Preheat oven to 400 degrees. Place pie crust in a 9-inch pie plate and flute edges. Lock food processor bowl in position. Insert the slicer disc. Attach food chute cover and lock in place. Drop apples into the food chute. Position food pusher over apples. Turn on processor and use light pressure to push apples through. Transfer sliced apples to a medium saucepan when full level is reached. Repeat process as necessary. In a small bowl, combine dry pudding mix, ¼ cup Splenda, apple juice, and water. Mix well using a wire whisk. Stir pudding mixture into apples using a sturdy spoon. Add raisins and apple pie spice. Mix well to combine. Cook over medium heat for 5 minutes or until apples soften, stirring often. Evenly spoon apple mixture into prepared pie crust. Wipe food processor bowl with a clean cloth. Remove slicer disc from food processor and insert the steel knife blade. Place flour, remaining ¼ cup Splenda, and margarine in food processor bowl. Cover and pulse 2 or 3 times or until mixture is crumbly. Evenly sprinkle crumb mixture over apple mixture. Bake for 35 to 40 minutes.

Place pie plate on a wire rack and allow to cool completely. Cut into 8 servings.

Each serving equals:

HE: 1¼ Bread • 1 Fruit • 1 Fat • 16 Optional Calories

233 Calories • 9 gm Fat • 1 gm Protein • 37 gm Carbohydrate • 204 mg Sodium • 11 mg Calcium • 2 gm Fiber

DIABETIC EXCHANGES: 1½ Starch • 1½ Fat • 1 Fruit

CARB CHOICES: 2½

Apple-Walnut Cream Pie

Do you remember that old ad campaign that suggested, "Sometimes you feel like a nut?" (and added that sometimes you don't?) For apple pie lovers who feel "like a nut," here's a dreamy dessert that adds wonderful walnuts for crunch. ☻ Serves 8

> 1 Pillsbury refrigerated unbaked 9-inch pie crust
> 6 medium cooking apples, cored, peeled, and each cut
>   into quarters
> ¼ cup walnuts
> 1 cup Land O Lakes Fat Free Half & Half
> 1 cup Splenda Granular
> 1 egg, or equivalent in egg substitute
> 3 tablespoons all-purpose flour
> 1 teaspoon vanilla extract
> 1 teaspoon apple pie spice

Preheat oven to 410 degrees. Place pie crust in a 9-inch pie plate and flute edges. Lock food processor bowl in position. Insert the slicer disc. Attach food chute cover and lock in place. Drop apples into the food chute. Position food pusher over apples. Turn on processor and use medium pressure to push apples through. Evenly arrange apple slices in pie crust. Remove slicer disc from food processor and insert the steel knife blade. Drop walnuts into the food processor bowl. Attach food chute cover and lock in place. Turn on processor and pulse 2 or 3 times or until walnuts are coarsely chopped. Transfer chopped walnuts to a small bowl. Add half & half, Splenda, egg, flour, vanilla extract, and apple pie spice to food processor bowl. Attach food chute cover and lock in place. Position food pusher in chute to prevent ingredients from splashing out of bowl. Turn on processor and pulse 10 or 12 times or until thoroughly mixed. Pour mixture evenly over apple slices. Evenly sprinkle walnuts over top. Bake for 10 minutes. Lower oven temperature to 350 degrees and continue baking for 35 to 40 minutes or until apples are tender. Place pie plate on a wire rack and allow to cool completely. Cut into 8 servings.

Each serving equals:

HE: 1 Bread • ¾ Fruit • ¾ Fat • ¼ Protein • ½ Slider • 1 Optional Calorie

250 Calories • 10 gm Fat • 3 gm Protein • 37 gm Carbohydrate •
152 mg Sodium • 38 mg Calcium • 3 gm Fiber

DIABETIC EXCHANGES: 1½ Starch/Carbohydrate • 1½ Fat • ½ Fruit

CARB CHOICES: 2½

Autumn Harvest Pie

What is the enchanting combination of flavors our taste buds link to the season of fall? For me, it's always been apples blended with pears and cranberries, just as in this spectacular pie. If you've got anything autumn to celebrate, this is it! ☯ Serves 8

1 Pillsbury refrigerated unbaked 9-inch pie crust
1 cup fresh or frozen whole cranberries
2 medium cooking apples, cored, peeled, and each
    cut into quarters
2 medium Bartlett pears, cored, peeled, and each
    cut into quarters
¾ cup Splenda Granular
6 tablespoons Bisquick Heart Smart Baking Mix
1 teaspoon apple pie spice
1 cup Ocean Spray reduced-calorie cranberry juice
    cocktail

Preheat oven to 425 degrees. Place pie crust in a 9-inch pie plate and flute edges. Lock food processor bowl in position. Insert the steel knife blade. Drop cranberries into the food processor bowl. Attach food chute cover and lock in place. Turn on processor and pulse 5 times or until cranberries are finely chopped. Transfer chopped cranberries to a large bowl. Remove steel knife blade from food processor and insert the slicer disc. Attach food chute cover and lock in place. Drop apples into the food chute. Position food pusher over apples. Turn on processor and use medium pressure to push apples through. Add sliced apples to chopped cranberries. Repeat process with pears. Mix well to combine. Stir in Splenda, baking mix, and apple pie spice. Add cranberry juice cocktail. Mix well to combine. Spoon mixture evenly into prepared pie crust. Bake for 15 minutes. Lower oven temperature to 350 degrees. Continue baking for 30 to 40 minutes. Place pie plate on a wire rack and allow to cool completely. Cut into 8 servings.

Each serving equals:

HE: 1¼ Bread • ¾ Fruit • ½ Fat • 9 Optional Calories

203 Calories • 7 gm Fat • 1 gm Protein • 34 gm Carbohydrate •
167 mg Sodium • 15 mg Calcium • 3 gm Fiber

DIABETIC EXCHANGES: 1 Starch • 1 Fruit • 1 Fat

CARB CHOICES: 2

Fresh Pineapple Pie

Do you know that a pineapple is probably ripe when you can easily pull a top leaf off? It's true, though I like the "sniff" test. Pick it up, bring your nose near the bottom, and inhale. If it smells sweet, it's oh-so-ready.   ◑   Serves 8

1 Pillsbury refrigerated unbaked 9-inch
    pie crust
1 ripe fresh pineapple
¾ cup Bisquick Heart Smart Baking Mix ☆
1 cup Splenda ☆
1 egg, or equivalent in egg substitute
1 teaspoon apple pie spice
2 tablespoons + 2 teaspoons I Can't Believe It's Not Butter!
    Light Margarine
2 tablespoons flaked coconut

Preheat oven to 375 degrees. Place pie crust in a 9-inch pie plate and flute edges. Cut top off of pineapple and cut lengthwise into fourths. Remove core and peel. Cut each piece in half and then each into 2-inch pieces. Lock food processor bowl in position. Insert the shredder disc. Attach food chute cover and lock in place. Drop pineapple into the food chute. Position food pusher over pineapple. Turn on processor and use medium pressure to push pineapple through. Transfer shredded pineapple to a large bowl. Add ¼ cup baking mix, ½ cup Splenda, egg, and apple pie spice. Mix gently just to combine. Evenly spoon mixture into prepared pie crust. Wipe food processor bowl with a clean cloth. Remove shredder disc from food processor and insert the steel knife blade. Add remaining ½ cup baking mix, remaining ½ cup Splenda, and margarine. Re-cover and pulse 4 or 5 times or until mixture is crumbly. Remove cover and gently stir in coconut using a rubber spatula. Sprinkle crumb mixture evenly over pineapple filling. Bake for 45 to 50 minutes. Place pie plate on a wire rack and let set for at least 15 minutes. Cut into 8 servings. Good warm or cold.

Each serving equals:

HE: 1½ Bread • 1 Fat • ½ Fruit • ¼ Slider • 6 Optional Calories

230 Calories • 10 gm Fat • 3 gm Protein • 32 gm Carbohydrate • 288 mg Sodium • 23 mg Calcium • 1 gm Fiber

DIABETIC EXCHANGES: 1½ Starch • ½ Fat • ½ Fruit

CARB CHOICES: 2

Open-Faced Pear Pie

Some pies just don't seem finished without a top crust while others look lovely with a latticework cover, and some are perfect without any top at all. By shining the spotlight on the pears in this pie, I've decided that no "cover-up" is just right.   ○   Serves 8

1 Pillsbury refrigerated unbaked 9-inch pie crust
1 cup Splenda Granular
2 tablespoons Land O Lakes Fat Free Half & Half
1 egg, or equivalent in egg substitute
1 teaspoon apple pie spice
8 medium Bartlett pears, cored, peeled, and each cut into
*   quarters*
2 tablespoons + 2 teaspoons I Can't Believe It's Not Butter!
*   Light Margarine*

Preheat oven to 350 degrees. Place pie crust in a 9-inch pie plate and flute edges. Lock food processor bowl in position. Insert the steel knife blade. Place Splenda, half & half, egg, and apple pie spice in food processor bowl. Attach food chute cover and lock in place. Turn on processor and pulse 3 times or until mixture is blended. Transfer mixture to a large bowl. Repeat process to coarsely chop pears. Transfer chopped pears to bowl with egg mixture when full level is reached. Repeat process as necessary. Add margarine to bowl. Mix well to combine. Evenly spoon pear mixture into prepared pie crust. Bake for 40 to 45 minutes or until filling is set. Place pie plate on a wire rack and let set for at least 10 minutes. Cut into 8 servings. Serve warm or cold.

Each serving equals:

HE: 1 Bread • 1 Fruit • 1 Fat • ¼ Slider • 3 Optional Calories

217 Calories • 9 gm Fat • 2 gm Protein • 32 gm Carbohydrate • 159 mg Sodium • 16 mg Calcium • 2 gm Fiber

DIABETIC EXCHANGES: 1½ Fat • 1 Starch • 1 Fruit

CARB CHOICES: 2

Cheyanne's Peach Crumb Pie

My daughter, Becky, is a peach lover, and now my grandchild has joined the club. Cheyanne had a chance to taste test this pie fresh from the oven. One big smile—and a quickly cleaned plate—told me all I needed to know.   ☉   Serves 8

> 1 Pillsbury refrigerated unbaked 9-inch pie crust
> 8 ripe medium peaches, peeled, pitted, and each cut into quarters
> ¾ cup all-purpose flour
> 1 cup Splenda Granular
> ¼ cup I Can't Believe It's Not Butter! Light Margarine

Preheat oven to 375 degrees. Place pie crust in a 9-inch pie plate and flute edges. Lock food processor bowl in position. Insert the slicer disc. Attach food chute cover and lock in place. Drop peaches into the food chute. Position food pusher over peaches. Turn on processor and use light pressure to push peaches through. Transfer sliced peaches to a large bowl when full level is reached. Repeat process as necessary. Wipe food processor bowl with a clean cloth. Remove slicer disc from food processor and insert the steel knife blade. Place flour, Splenda, and margarine in food processor bowl. Attach food chute cover and lock in place. Position food pusher in chute to prevent ingredients from splashing out. Turn on processor and pulse 10 or 15 times or until mixture is crumbly. Sprinkle half of crumb mixture into prepared pie crust. Evenly spoon sliced peaches over crumb mixture. Top with remaining crumb mixture. Bake for 45 to 55 minutes or until filling is bubbly and peaches are tender. Place pie plate on a wire rack and allow to cool completely. Cut into 8 servings.

Each serving equals:

HE: 1½ Bread • 1 Fruit • 1 Fat • 12 Optional Calories

238 Calories • 10 gm Fat • 3 gm Protein • 34 gm Carbohydrate • 168 mg Sodium • 3 gm Calcium • 2 gm Fiber

DIABETIC EXCHANGES: 1½ Starch/Carbohydrate • 1½ Fat • 1 Fruit

CARB CHOICES: 2

Peach-Coconut Meringue Pie

I don't think I've ever seen a peach meringue pie in a restaurant or even in a cookbook, yet I can't think of any reason not to make one! When peaches are ripe and sweet, there just isn't anything better. Topped with a special meringue, it's a recipe for pleasure.

○ Serves 8

> 1 Pillsbury refrigerated unbaked 9-inch pie crust
> 6 ripe medium peaches, peeled, pitted, and each cut into
>   quarters
> 1 cup Splenda Granular ☆
> ½ cup Diet Mountain Dew
> 1 tablespoon all-purpose flour
> 2 tablespoons cold water
> 6 egg whites
> ½ teaspoon coconut extract
> 3 tablespoons peach spreadable fruit
> 2 tablespoons flaked coconut

Preheat oven to 450 degrees. Place pie crust in a 9-inch pie plate and flute edges. Prick bottom and sides with tines of a fork. Bake for 5 to 7 minutes or just until lightly browned. Place pie plate on a wire rack and allow to cool. Lower oven temperature to 375 degrees. Lock food processor bowl in position. Insert the slicer disc. Attach food chute cover and lock in place. Drop peaches into the food chute. Position food pusher over peaches. Turn on processor and use light pressure to push peaches through. Transfer sliced peaches to a large bowl when full level is reached. Repeat process as necessary. Add ½ cup Splenda and Diet Mountain Dew to sliced peaches. Mix well to combine. Transfer mixture to a large saucepan and cook over medium heat for 10 to 12 minutes or until peaches soften, stirring often. In a small bowl, combine flour and water. Mix well using a wire whisk. Stir flour mixture into peach mixture. Continue cooking for 2 to 3 minutes or until mixture thickens, stirring often. Spoon peach mixture into cooled pie crust. In a large bowl, beat egg whites with an electric mixer on HIGH until soft peaks form. Add remaining ½ cup Splenda and coconut extract. Continue beating on HIGH until stiff peaks form. Gently fold in spreadable fruit. Spread meringue mixture evenly over filling mixture, being sure to seal to edges of pie crust. Evenly sprinkle coconut over top. Bake for 6 to 8 minutes or until meringue starts to turn golden brown. Place pie plate on a wire rack and let set for 30 minutes. Refrigerate for at least 2 hours. Cut into 8 servings.

HINTS: 1. Egg whites beat best when they are at room temperature.
2. Meringue pie cuts easily if you dip a sharp knife in warm water before slicing.

Each serving equals:

HE: 1 Bread • 1 Fruit • ½ Fat • ¼ Protein • ¼ Slider • 1 Optional Calorie

191 Calories • 7 gm Fat • 4 gm Protein • 28 gm Carbohydrate •
146 mg Sodium • 6 mg Calcium • 2 gm Fiber

DIABETIC EXCHANGES: 1 Starch • 1 Fruit • 1 Fat

CARB CHOICES: 2

Bountiful Blessings Pumpkin Pie

Most families have special traditions that make holiday meals even more meaningful. A couple of times each year, that means pumpkin pie on the feast table. Here's a glorious version of this holiday classic—a blue-ribbon recipe to enjoy!   ☻   Serves 8

> 1 Pillsbury refrigerated unbaked 9-inch pie crust
> 1 (15-ounce) can solid-packed pumpkin
> 1 cup Splenda Granular
> 2 eggs, or equivalent in egg substitute
> 1 (12-fluid-ounce) can Carnation Evaporated Fat Free Milk
> ⅓ cup Carnation Nonfat Dry Milk Powder
> 1 teaspoon pumpkin pie spice
> ½ teaspoon ground nutmeg

Preheat oven to 375 degrees. Place pie crust in a 9-inch pie plate and flute edges. Lock food processor bowl in position. Insert the steel knife blade. Place pumpkin, Splenda, eggs, evaporated milk, dry milk powder, and pumpkin pie spice in food processor bowl. Attach food chute cover and lock in place. Turn on processor and pulse 15 times or until mixture is smooth. Pour mixture into pie crust. Sprinkle nutmeg over top. Bake for 60 to 65 minutes or until filling is set in center. Place pie plate on a wire rack and allow to cool completely. Cut into 8 servings.

HINT: Good served with 1 tablespoon Cool Whip Lite, but don't forget to count the additional calories.

Each serving equals:

HE: 1 Bread • ½ Fat Free Milk • ½ Fat • ½ Vegetable • ¼ Protein • 12 Optional Calories

212 Calories • 8 gm Fat • 7 gm Protein • 28 gm Carbohydrate • 195 mg Sodium • 174 mg Calcium • 2 gm Fiber

DIABETIC EXCHANGES: 1½ Starch/Carbohydrate • 1 Fat • ½ Fat Free Milk

CARB CHOICES: 2

Orange-Raisin Cake

There's something so refreshing about an orange-flavored cake, as if sunshine had been baked right into it! Now, don't be alarmed about using the peel in this recipe—just make sure you scrub it well before using. ☻ Serves 8

1 cup Splenda Granular
¼ cup I Can't Believe It's Not
   Butter! Light Margarine
¼ cup Land O Lakes no-fat
   sour cream
2 eggs, or equivalent in egg
   substitute
1 teaspoon baking powder

1 medium unpeeled orange,
   quartered and seeds
   removed
1½ cups Bisquick Heart Smart
   Baking Mix
½ cup fat-free milk
¾ cup seedless raisins
¼ cup chopped walnuts

Preheat oven to 350 degrees. Spray a 9-by-9-inch cake pan with butter-flavored cooking spray. Lock food processor bowl in position. Insert the steel knife blade. Place Splenda, margarine, sour cream, eggs, and baking powder in food processor bowl. Attach food chute cover and lock in place. Turn on processor and drop orange pieces through food chute with processor running. Pulse 5 or 6 times or until orange is chopped and mixture is blended. Remove food chute cover. Add baking mix, milk, raisins, and walnuts to food processor bowl. Attach food chute cover and lock in place. Position food pusher in chute to prevent ingredients from splashing out of bowl. Turn on processor and pulse 2 or 3 times or until mixture is blended. Evenly spread batter into prepared cake pan. Bake for 30 to 40 minutes or until cake springs back when lightly touched in center. Place pan on a wire rack and let set for at least 10 minutes. Cut into 8 servings.

Each serving equals:

HE: 1 Bread • 1 Fruit • 1 Fat • ⅓ Protein • ¼ Slider • 4 Optional Calories

232 Calories • 8 gm Fat • 5 gm Protein • 35 gm Carbohydrate •
415 mg Sodium • 107 mg Calcium • 2 gm Fiber

DIABETIC EXCHANGES: 1½ Starch/Carbohydrate • 1 Fruit • 1 Fat

CARB CHOICES: 2

Basic Cheesecake

Here's one of those recipes that every cook should have on hand because, once you do, you can make just about any flavor you like! "Basic" here means just a starting point, not something ordinary, I can promise you that. ○ Serves 12

18 (2½-inch) graham cracker squares, broken into
    large pieces
⅓ cup + 2 teaspoons I Can't Believe It's Not Butter!
    Light Margarine
1¼ cups Splenda Granular ☆
½ teaspoon ground cinnamon
3 (8-ounce) packages Philadelphia fat-free
    cream cheese
3 eggs, or equivalent in egg substitute
1½ teaspoons vanilla extract
1½ cups Cool Whip Lite

Preheat oven to 375 degrees. Spray a 9-inch springform pan with butter-flavored cooking spray. Lock food processor bowl in position. Insert the steel knife blade. Drop graham cracker pieces into the food processor bowl. Attach food chute cover and lock in place. Turn on processor and pulse 3 or 4 times or until coarse crumbs are formed. Remove cover and add margarine, 2 tablespoons Splenda, and cinnamon. Re-cover and pulse 5 or 6 times or until mixture is blended. Pat crumb mixture into prepared pan. Wipe food processor bowl and blade with a clean cloth. Place cream cheese, eggs, 1 cup + 2 tablespoons Splenda, and vanilla extract in food processor bowl. Re-cover and pulse 6 or 8 times or until mixture is well blended and creamy, scraping down bowl as necessary with a rubber spatula. Evenly spread filling mixture over crumb crust in springform pan. Bake for 30 to 35 minutes or until center is set. Turn oven off and partially open door to oven. Leave cheesecake set in oven for 1 hour or until cool. Refrigerate for at least 4 hours. Run a knife along inside edges of pan. Remove sides. Spread whipped topping evenly over cheesecake. Cut into 12 servings.

HINTS: 1. Top of cheesecake may crack, but Cool Whip will cover any "flaws."
2. Garnish with fruit or spreadable fruit of your choice.

Each serving equals:

HE: 1¼ Protein • ¾ Fat • ½ Bread • ¼ Slider • 10 Optional Calories

175 Calories • 7 gm Fat • 11 gm Protein • 17 gm Carbohydrate •
429 mg Sodium • 171 mg Calcium • 1 gm Fiber

DIABETIC EXCHANGES: 1½ Meat • 1 Fat • 1 Starch/Carbohydrate

CARB CHOICES: 1

Aloha Carrot Cake

I wonder, if I lived in Hawaii, would I eat fresh pineapple every single day (and maybe at every meal!)? It's possible, especially when I have recipes like this one to stir up and serve. We're lucky that Hawaii and other islands export plenty of pineapples, so we can enjoy this whenever we like.   ♥   Serves 8

3 medium carrots, scraped and each cut into
    2-inch pieces
1 cup Splenda Granular
¼ cup I Can't Believe It's Not Butter! Light
    Margarine
½ cup unsweetened applesauce
2 eggs, or equivalent in egg substitute
1 teaspoon baking powder
1 teaspoon ground cinnamon
1½ cups Bisquick Heart Smart Baking Mix
1 (8-ounce) can crushed pineapple, packed in
    fruit juice, undrained

Preheat oven to 350 degrees. Spray an 8-by-8-inch baking dish with butter-flavored cooking spray. Lock food processor bowl in position. Insert the shredder disc. Attach food chute cover and lock in place. Drop carrot pieces into the food chute. Position food pusher over carrots. Turn on processor and use medium pressure to push carrots through. Remove shredder disc from food processor and insert the steel knife blade. Add Splenda, margarine, applesauce, eggs, baking powder, and cinnamon to processor bowl. Attach food chute cover and lock in place. Position food pusher in chute to prevent ingredients from splashing out of bowl. Turn on processor and pulse 6 to 8 times or until mixture is blended. Add baking mix and pulse 15 times to combine. Add undrained pineapple and pulse 2 or 3 times or just until mixed. Spread batter evenly into prepared pan. Bake for 35 to 45 minutes or until top springs back when lightly touched in center. Place pan on a wire rack and let set for at least 10 minutes. Cut into 8 servings.

HINT: This is a very moist cake.

Each serving equals:

HE: 1 Bread • ¾ Fat • ⅓ Fruit • ⅓ Vegetable • ¼ Protein •
12 Optional Calories

169 Calories • 5 gm Fat • 4 gm Protein • 27 gm Carbohydrate •
415 mg Sodium • 71 mg Calcium • 2 gm Fiber

DIABETIC EXCHANGES: 1 Starch • 1 Fat • ½ Fruit

CARB CHOICES: 2

Apple Mocha Cake

Okay, I admit it's an odd combination, but everything about this cake is just so good. Coffee—just a little bit—deepens and enriches the flavor of a cake, bringing out a special intensity, especially when chocolate is part of the mix.   ☕   Serves 8

⅓ cup cold coffee
¾ teaspoon baking soda
2 medium cooking apples, cored, peeled, and each cut into
*   quarters*
¼ cup walnuts
¼ cup I Can't Believe It's Not Butter! Light Margarine
2 tablespoons Land O Lakes no-fat sour cream
¾ cup Splenda Granular
1 egg, or equivalent in egg substitute
1 cup + 2 tablespoons Bisquick Heart Smart Baking Mix
1 teaspoon ground cinnamon
¼ cup mini chocolate chips
1 cup Cool Whip Lite

Preheat oven to 350 degrees. Spray a 9-by-9-inch cake pan with butter-flavored cooking spray. In a small bowl, combine coffee and baking soda. Set aside. Lock food processor bowl in position. Insert the steel knife blade. Drop apples into the food processor bowl. Attach food chute cover and lock in place. Turn on processor and pulse 3 or 4 times or until apples are finely chopped. Transfer sliced apples to a medium bowl. Repeat process with walnuts. Transfer walnuts to a small bowl. Add margarine, sour cream, Splenda, egg, and coffee mixture to food processor bowl. Attach food chute cover and lock in place. Position food pusher in chute to prevent ingredients from splashing out of bowl. Turn on processor and pulse 30 times or until mixture is blended. Add baking mix and cinnamon. Pulse 15 times to combine. Remove food chute cover. Fold in apples, chocolate chips, and walnuts. Evenly spread batter into prepared cake pan. Bake for 22 to 26 minutes or until a tooth-pick inserted in center comes out clean. Place pan on a wire rack and allow to cool completely. Cut into 8 servings. When serving, top each piece with 2 tablespoons Cool Whip Lite.

Each serving equals:

HE: 1 Fat • ¾ Bread • ¼ Fruit • ¼ Protein • ½ Slider •
19 Optional Calories

197 Calories • 9 gm Fat • 3 gm Protein • 26 gm Carbohydrate •
396 mg Sodium • 34 mg Calcium • 2 gm Fiber

DIABETIC EXCHANGES: 1½ Fat • 1½ Starch/Carbohydrate

CARB CHOICES: 1½

Upside-Down Apple Cake

Do you have to count the calories if you eat dessert while standing on your head? Good question. That reminds me of the comment that broken cookie pieces have no calories—now, wouldn't that be a reason to drop the bag when unpacking your groceries? The calories do count in this, but one bite will assure you that every one is worth it. ❍ Serves 8

¼ cup I Can't Believe It's Not Butter! Light Margarine
¼ cup walnuts
1 cup Splenda Granular ☆
2 tablespoons graham cracker crumbs
½ teaspoon ground cinnamon
4 medium cooking apples, cored, peeled, and each cut
*   into quarters*
1 cup Bisquick Heart Smart Baking Mix
½ cup Land O Lakes Fat Free Half & Half
¼ cup Land O Lakes no-fat sour cream
1 egg, or equivalent in egg substitute
1½ teaspoons baking powder
½ teaspoon table salt
½ teaspoon vanilla extract

Preheat oven to 350 degrees. Melt 2 tablespoons margarine and evenly pour into a 9-inch round cake pan. Lock food processor bowl in position. Insert the slicer disc. Attach food chute cover and lock in place. Drop walnuts into the food chute. Position food pusher over walnuts. Turn on processor and use medium pressure to push walnuts through. Transfer sliced walnuts to a small bowl. Add ½ cup Splenda, graham cracker crumbs, and cinnamon to walnuts. Mix well to combine. Evenly sprinkle mixture over melted margarine in cake pan. Drop apples into food chute. Position food pusher over apples. Turn on processor and use medium pressure to push apples through. Arrange sliced apples over crumb mixture. Remove slicer disc from food processor and insert the steel knife blade. Add baking mix, remaining ½ cup Splenda, half & half, remaining 2 tablespoons margarine, sour cream, egg, baking powder, salt, and vanilla extract to food processor bowl. Position food pusher in chute to prevent ingredients from splashing out of bowl. Turn on processor and pulse 25 or 30 times or until mixture is smooth. Evenly spoon batter over apples. Bake for 35 to 40 minutes or until cake springs back when lightly touched. Loosen sides of cake and invert onto serving platter. Cut into 8 servings.

HINT: Good warm with sugar- and fat-free vanilla ice cream or cold with Cool Whip Lite. If using, don't forget to count the additional calories.

Each serving equals:

HE: 1 Fat • ¾ Bread • ½ Fruit • ¼ Protein • ¼ Slider • 8 Optional Calories

175 Calories • 7 gm Fat • 3 gm Protein • 25 gm Carbohydrate •
511 mg Sodium • 96 mg Calcium • 1 gm Fiber

DIABETIC EXCHANGES: 1 Fat • 1 Starch • ½ Fruit

CARB CHOICES: 1½

Buttermilk Pecan Banana Cake

We made this cake on a day we were celebrating a bunch of birthdays at the office of Healthy Exchanges, and all the "birthday girls" agreed they'd love to have it as a birthday cake—or anytime at all! I just call it a "real sweetie!" ◗ Serves 8

½ cup Land O Lakes Fat Free Half & Half
2 teaspoons white distilled vinegar
2 tablespoons pecans
2 ripe medium bananas, each cut into 2-inch pieces
¼ cup I Can't Believe It's Not Butter! Light Margarine
½ cup Splenda Granular
2 eggs, or equivalent in egg substitute
1 teaspoon vanilla extract
1½ cups cake flour
1 teaspoon baking powder
½ teaspoon baking soda
¼ teaspoon table salt

Preheat oven to 350 degrees. Spray a 9-inch round cake pan with butter-flavored cooking spray. In a small bowl, combine half & half and vinegar. Set aside. Lock food processor bowl in position. Insert the steel knife blade. Drop pecans into the food processor bowl. Attach food chute cover and lock in place. Turn on processor and pulse 3 or 4 times or until pecans are finely chopped. Transfer chopped pecans to a small bowl. Place banana pieces, margarine, and Splenda into the food processor bowl. Re-cover and pulse 10 or 12 times or until mixture is well blended. Remove food pusher and with processor still running, drop eggs, half & half mixture, and vanilla extract through chute. Continue processing for 5 seconds. Turn off processor and remove cover. Add cake flour, half of pecans, baking powder, baking soda, and salt. Re-cover and pulse 5 or 6 times or just until combined. Evenly spread batter into prepared cake pan. Evenly sprinkle remaining pecans over top. Bake for 30 minutes. Place cake pan on a wire rack and let set for at least 15 minutes. Divide into 8 servings.

Each serving equals:

HE: 1 Bread • 1 Fat • ½ Fruit • ¼ Protein • 16 Optional Calories

169 Calories • 5 gm Fat • 5 gm Protein • 26 gm Carbohydrate •
302 mg Sodium • 66 mg Calcium • 1 gm Fiber

DIABETIC EXCHANGES: 1 Starch • 1 Fat • ½ Fruit

CARB CHOICES: 1½

A Homemade
Taste of This
and That

Here's where I love to share all those recipes that don't fit into any other chapter but make life—and eating—so much livelier and satisfying. You may not *need* any of these dishes to make it through a day, a week, or a holiday season, but when you've got these in your culinary arsenal, you're ready for anything—especially guests, parties, and lots of hungry folks!

Send out the invitations and tidy the living room—then stand back and enjoy your guests' reactions to such party favorites as *Guacamole with Tomatoes* and my *Terrific Taco Dip*. You'll want to give your Christmas buffet some extra sparkle by offering tangy *Onion Tuna Spread* and *Holiday Cranberry Relish*. And why not offer Santa some *Carrot Walnut Muffins* with his midnight glass of milk? But you won't need any special occasions to serve your family *Fresh Applesauce*, *Corn Relish Supreme*, or *Garden-Fresh Zucchini-Walnut Bread*. They're all in here, just waiting for you!

Blueberry Syrup

Wouldn't it be fun to make your very own homemade pancake and French toast topping? You *can!* What's great about this recipe is that it tastes great whether you use fresh or frozen berries.

☺ Serves 4 (scant ½ cup)

> 1½ cups fresh or frozen blueberries, thawed
> 1 cup Diet Mountain Dew
> ¾ cup Splenda Granular
> 1 tablespoon cornstarch

Lock food processor bowl in position. Insert the steel knife blade. Add blueberries, Diet Mountain Dew, Splenda, and cornstarch to food processor bowl. Attach food chute cover and lock in place. Position food pusher in chute to prevent mixture from splashing out of bowl. Turn on processor and pulse 4 or 5 times or until well blended. Transfer mixture to a medium saucepan and cook over medium heat for 10 to 12 minutes or until mixture thickens, stirring often.

HINT: Good warm or cold.

Each serving equals:

HE: ½ Fruit • ¼ Slider • 5 Optional Calories

56 Calories • 0 gm Fat • 0 gm Protein • 14 gm Carbohydrate • 6 mg Sodium • 3 mg Calcium • 1 gm Fiber

DIABETIC EXCHANGES: ½ Fruit • ½ Other Carbohydrate

CARB CHOICES: 1

Fresh Applesauce

If you've got young children at home, you can use your food processor to prepare wonderfully fresh applesauce for them! They'll love being involved in the preparation from start to finish, from apple-picking to spooning up each bite.

◐ Serves 4 (¼ cup)

> 3 medium cooking apples, cored, peeled, and each cut into
>   quarters
> 1 tablespoon lemon juice
> 1 tablespoon water
> 2 tablespoons Splenda Granular
> ½ teaspoon ground cinnamon

Lock food processor bowl in position. Insert the shredder disc. Attach food chute cover and lock in place. Drop apples into the food chute. Position food pusher over apples. Turn on processor and use light pressure to push apples through. Transfer shredded apples to a medium bowl. Remove shredder disc from food processor and insert the steel knife blade. Return apples to food processor bowl. Add lemon juice, water, Splenda, and cinnamon. Attach food chute cover and lock in place. Turn on processor and pulse 10 or 15 times or until mixture is smooth. Spoon mixture into a medium bowl. Cover and refrigerate for at least 15 minutes. Gently stir again just before serving.

Each serving equals:

HE: 1 Fruit • 3 Optional Calories

---

64 Calories • 0 gm Fat • 0 gm Protein • 16 gm Carbohydrate •
0 mg Sodium • 3 mg Calcium • 4 gm Fiber

DIABETIC EXCHANGES: 1 Fruit

CARB CHOICES: 1

Pecan Cream Cheese Spread

Here's where your motorized kitchen helper can be such a blessing—preparing spreads and dips for entertaining guests! This tangy, nutty blend is terrific on crudités and also a savory topper for chips. ● Serves 6 (¼ cup)

1 (8-ounce) package Philadelphia fat-free cream cheese
¼ cup Kraft fat-free mayonnaise
1 teaspoon prepared yellow mustard
6 tablespoons pecans

Lock food processor bowl in position. Insert the steel knife blade. Place cream cheese, mayonnaise, and mustard in food processor bowl. Attach food chute cover and lock in place. Turn on processor and pulse 4 times or just until mixture is blended. Drop pecans through food chute and pulse 10 times or just until pecans are chopped. Transfer mixture to a serving bowl. Cover and refrigerate for at least 15 minutes. Gently stir again just before serving.

Each serving equals:

HE: 1 Fat • ⅔ Protein • 7 Optional Calories

89 Calories • 5 gm Fat • 6 gm Protein • 5 gm Carbohydrate •
276 mg Sodium • 108 mg Calcium • 1 gm Fiber

DIABETIC EXCHANGES: 1 Fat • 1 Meat

CARB CHOICES: 0

Veggie Salad Spread

Party food, party food, ready in no time at all! This is an amazingly colorful combo that is a perfect invitation to partake in tasty, healthy food and enjoy each other's company. ☻ Serves 8 (⅓ cup)

1 dill pickle spear
1 small red bell pepper, stem and seeds removed and cut into
*   6 strips*
1 small unpeeled cucumber, cut in half lengthwise and
*   crosswise*
1 medium stalk celery, trimmed and cut into 2-inch pieces
1 small onion, peeled and cut into 4 wedges
1 medium tomato, peeled and cut into 6 wedges
1 (8-ounce) package Philadelphia fat-free cream cheese
½ cup Kraft fat-free mayonnaise
2 sprigs fresh parsley, stems removed

Lock food processor bowl in position. Insert the steel knife blade. Drop pickle spear into the food processor bowl. Attach food chute cover and lock in place. Turn on processor and pulse 3 or 4 times or until finely chopped. Transfer pickle to a medium bowl. Repeat process with red pepper, cucumber, celery, onion, and tomato. Transfer chopped vegetables to bowl with pickle. Place cream cheese in food processor bowl in chunks. Add mayonnaise and parsley. Attach food chute cover and lock in place. Turn on processor and pulse 6 to 8 times or just until blended. Remove cover. Evenly spoon chopped vegetables over cream cheese mixture. Re-cover and pulse 10 or 12 times or just until mixture is blended. Do not overprocess.

HINT: Can be used as a sandwich spread or spread over wheat or
    rye crackers as an appetizer.

Each serving equals:

HE: ½ Protein • ½ Vegetable • 10 Optional Calories

40 Calories • 0 gm Fat • 4 gm Protein • 6 gm Carbohydrate •
313 mg Sodium • 88 mg Calcium • 1 gm Fiber

DIABETIC EXCHANGES: ½ Meat • ½ Vegetable

CARB CHOICES: ½

Cheesy Olive Spread

For anyone who loves olives, this is a luscious treat to be enjoyed at parties and at home in front of the TV. You don't need a special occasion to bring this dish out, but it's special enough to feature on a festive buffet.   ☻   Serves 4 (¼ cup)

>   5 pimiento-stuffed green olives
>   ⅓ cup Land O Lakes no-fat sour cream
>   1 teaspoon olive oil
>   1 cup shredded Kraft reduced-fat Cheddar cheese

Lock food processor bowl in position. Insert the steel knife blade. Drop olives into the food processor bowl. Attach food chute cover and lock in place. Turn on processor and pulse 3 or 4 times or until olives are finely chopped. Remove food chute cover. Add sour cream, olive oil, and Cheddar cheese to processor bowl. Attach food chute cover and lock in place. Turn on processor and pulse 5 or 6 times or until mixture is well blended. Spoon into a small bowl. Cover and refrigerate for at least 1 hour. Gently stir again just before serving.

HINT: Good with crackers or vegetables.

Each serving equals:

HE: 1 Protein • ½ Fat • 15 Optional Calories

123 Calories • 7 gm Fat • 9 gm Protein • 6 gm Carbohydrate • 489 mg Sodium • 249 mg Calcium • 0 gm Fiber

DIABETIC EXCHANGES: 1 Meat • ½ Fat

CARB CHOICES: ½

Onion Tuna Spread

You can mix and mix with a fork and a little elbow grease, but you can't make a tuna spread as smooth and silken as your food processor can! It does such a great job of mixing and churning whatever you ask it to do.　❂　Serves 4 (½ cup)

> 1 small onion, peeled and cut into 4 wedges
> 1 (6-ounce) can white tuna, packed in water, drained and
>   flaked
> ½ cup (4 ounces) Philadelphia fat-free cream cheese
> 2 tablespoons Kraft fat-free mayonnaise
> 2 tablespoons sweet pickle relish
> ⅛ teaspoon black pepper

Lock food processor bowl in position. Insert the steel knife blade. Drop onion wedges into the food processor bowl. Attach food chute cover and lock in place. Turn on processor and pulse 3 or 4 times or until onion is finely chopped. Remove food chute cover. Add tuna, cream cheese, mayonnaise, pickle relish, and black pepper to processor bowl. Attach food chute cover and lock in place. Turn on processor and pulse 25 or 30 times or until ingredients are well mixed, stopping as necessary to scrape down bowl using a rubber spatula. Transfer mixture to a medium bowl. Cover and refrigerate for at least 10 minutes. Gently stir again just before serving.

HINT: Great with crackers, celery sticks, or as a sandwich filling.

Each serving equals:

HE: 1½ Protein • ¼ Vegetable • 15 Optional Calories

93 Calories • 1 gm Fat • 13 gm Protein • 8 gm Carbohydrate •
396 mg Sodium • 90 mg Calcium • 0 gm Fiber

DIABETIC EXCHANGES: 1½ Meat • 1½ Other Carbohydrate

CARB CHOICES: ½

Chicken Salad Spread

Even if you don't love munching radishes from a platter of raw veggies, give this recipe a chance. You may find that when this sharp-flavored vegetable is chopped up and blended into the mix, it adds just the right touch of sparkle! ☻   Serves 6 (½ cup)

2 full cups chopped cooked chicken breast
1 medium stalk celery, trimmed and cut into 2-inch pieces
1 small onion, peeled and cut into 4 wedges
4 red radishes, trimmed and each cut in half
2 sprigs parsley, stems removed
½ cup Kraft fat-free mayonnaise
⅛ teaspoon black pepper

Lock food processor bowl in position. Insert the steel knife blade. Drop chicken pieces into the food processor bowl. Attach food chute cover and lock in place. Turn on processor and pulse 3 or 4 times or until chicken is chopped. Transfer chopped chicken to a large bowl. Drop celery, onion, radishes, and parsley into the food processor bowl. Attach food chute cover and lock in place. Turn on processor and pulse 4 or 6 times or until vegetables are finely chopped. Add finely chopped vegetables to chicken. Mix well to combine. Stir in mayonnaise and black pepper. Cover and refrigerate for at least 15 minutes. Gently stir again just before serving.

HINT: Good as a sandwich spread or served with crackers.

Each serving equals:

HE: 2 Protein • ½ Vegetable • 15 Optional Calories

106 Calories • 2 gm Fat • 18 gm Protein • 4 gm Carbohydrate •
208 mg Sodium • 15 mg Calcium • 1 gm Fiber

DIABETIC EXCHANGES: 2 Meat

CARB CHOICES: 0

Guacamole with Tomatoes

How ripe should a ripe avocado be? So soft you don't even need a knife to pull it apart (as long as you don't mind a bit of a mess!). Some people worry about the natural fat in avocado, but in reasonable quantities, it's very good for you—and great for your skin, too!

○ Serves 6 (⅓ cup)

1 clove garlic, peeled
1 small onion, peeled and cut into 4 wedges
1 tablespoon lemon juice
¼ teaspoon Worcestershire sauce
1 teaspoon chili seasoning
¼ cup Land O Lakes no-fat sour cream
2 very ripe avocadoes, peeled, halved, pitted, and each cut into 1-inch pieces
2 medium tomatoes, peeled and each cut into 4 wedges

Lock food processor bowl in position. Insert the steel knife blade. Drop garlic into the food processor bowl. Attach food chute cover and lock in place. Turn on processor and pulse 3 or 4 times or until finely chopped. Drop onion wedges through food chute and pulse 3 or 4 times or until finely chopped. Remove cover. Add lemon juice, Worcestershire sauce, chili seasoning, and sour cream. Re-cover and pulse 5 times or until mixture is finely blended. Drop avocado pieces and tomato wedges through food chute. Pulse 20 or 30 times or until mixture is smooth. Transfer to a medium bowl. Cover and refrigerate for at least 1 hour. Gently stir again just before serving.

Each serving equals:

HE: 2 Fat • ½ Vegetable • 10 Optional Calories

116 Calories • 8 gm Fat • 2 gm Protein • 9 gm Carbohydrate • 25 mg Sodium • 16 mg Calcium • 5 gm Fiber

DIABETIC EXCHANGES: 2 Fat • ½ Vegetable

CARB CHOICES: ½

Guacamole Dip

This is a fluffier version of the Mexican classic, one that stirs up lighter but with no less flavor! I tried them both on my husband, Cliff, and he was hard-pressed to decide which he liked better.

◐ Serves 4 (¼ cup)

> 1 small onion, peeled and cut into 4 wedges
> 1 very ripe avocado, peeled, halved, pitted, and cut into 1-
>   inch pieces
> ¼ cup Kraft fat-free mayonnaise
> ¼ cup Land O Lakes no-fat sour cream
> 1 tablespoon lemon juice
> ½ teaspoon lemon pepper
> ½ teaspoon chili seasoning

Lock food processor bowl in position. Insert the steel knife blade. Drop onion into the food processor bowl. Attach food chute cover and lock in place. Turn on processor and pulse 3 or 4 times or until onion is finely chopped. Remove food chute cover. Add avocado, mayonnaise, sour cream, lemon juice, lemon pepper, and chili seasoning. Attach food chute cover and lock in place. Turn on processor and hold pulse button down for 1 minute or until mixture is smooth, stopping as necessary to scrape down bowl using a rubber spatula. Spoon into a serving dish. Cover and refrigerate for at least 15 minutes. Gently stir again just before serving.

Each serving equals:

HE: 1½ Fat • ¼ Vegetable • ¼ Slider • 6 Optional Calories

115 Calories • 7 gm Fat • 2 gm Protein • 11 gm Carbohydrate • 195 mg Sodium • 31 mg Calcium • 3 gm Fiber

DIABETIC EXCHANGES: 1½ Fat • ½ Starchs/Carbohydrate

CARB CHOICES: 1

Fresh Sweet Salsa

You don't need your own giant vegetable patch to start making your own salsa, but it helps! There's really no comparison between homemade salsa and the kind you buy in a jar. The freshness of the ingredients makes it truly special.   ○   Serves 6 (⅓ cup)

3 medium tomatoes, peeled and
    each cut into 6 wedges
1 small red onion, peeled and
    cut into 4 wedges
1 small red bell pepper, stem
    and seeds removed and
    cut into 4 strips

1 small green bell pepper, stem
    and seeds removed and
    cut into 4 strips
½ cup Splenda Granular
3 fresh basil leaves
⅛ teaspoon black pepper

Lock food processor bowl in position. Insert the steel knife blade. Drop tomato wedges into the food processor bowl. Attach food chute cover and lock in place. Turn on processor and pulse 3 or 4 times or until tomatoes are chopped medium-fine. Transfer chopped tomatoes to a large bowl when full level is reached. Repeat process as necessary. Transfer ¼ cup chopped tomatoes to a small bowl. Set aside. Repeat process with onion. Pulse 3 or 4 times or until finely chopped. Transfer onion to large bowl with chopped tomatoes. Repeat process with red and green pepper. Remove food chute. Place reserved ¼ cup chopped tomatoes into food processor bowl. Add Splenda, basil leaves, and black pepper. Attach food chute cover and lock in place. Turn on processor and pulse 2 or 3 seconds or until mixture is smooth. Add blended mixture to tomato mixture. Mix well to combine. Cover and refrigerate for at least 15 minutes. Gently stir again just before serving.

HINT: Hot salsa variation: Add 1 or 2 seeded jalapeno peppers, omit Splenda, and replace basil leaves with cilantro.

Each serving equals:

HE: 1 Vegetable • 8 Optional Calories

32 Calories • 0 gm Fat • 1 gm Protein • 7 gm Carbohydrate •
5 mg Sodium • 20 mg Calcium • 2 gm Fiber

DIABETIC EXCHANGES: 1 Vegetable

CARB CHOICES: ½

Terrific Taco Dip

If you've got teenagers at home—or you still feel like one yourself—this is a party favorite you'll probably make again and again. With this and a bag of baked chips, you're set for an entire football game, or maybe back-to-back episodes of *America's Next Top Model!* ● Serves 8 (¼ cup)

1 medium onion, peeled and cut into 6 wedges
8 ounces extra-lean ground sirloin beef or turkey breast
1 medium green bell pepper, stem and seeds removed and cut into 4 strips

1 (15-ounce) can Bush's red kidney beans, rinsed and drained
¼ cup water
¼ cup reduced-sodium ketchup
1½ teaspoons taco seasoning
⅛ teaspoon black pepper

Lock food processor bowl in position. Insert the steel knife blade. Drop onion wedges into the food processor bowl. Attach food chute cover and lock in place. Turn on processor and pulse 3 or 4 times or until onion is finely chopped. Transfer chopped onion to a large skillet sprayed with butter-flavored cooking spray. Brown onion and meat. Meanwhile, drop green pepper into the food processor bowl. Attach food chute cover and lock in place. Pulse until coarsely chopped. Stir chopped green pepper into meat mixture and continue cooking. Place kidney beans and water in food processor bowl. Cover and process for 5 seconds or until beans are smooth. Stir beans into meat mixture. Add ketchup, taco seasoning, and black pepper. Mix well to combine. Lower heat and simmer for 10 minutes, stirring occasionally. Serve warm.

HINT: Good with corn chips or as a topping for baked potatoes.

Each serving equals:

HE: 1 Protein • ½ Vegetable • ¼ Bread • 8 Optional Calories

81 Calories • 1 gm Fat • 8 gm Protein • 10 gm Carbohydrate • 174 mg Sodium • 14 mg Calcium • 3 gm Fiber

DIABETIC EXCHANGES: 1 Meat • ½ Vegetable • ½ Starch

CARB CHOICES: ½

Homemade Barbecue Sauce

Regular barbecue sauce is notoriously high in sugar and sometimes in fat as well. But a tangy good barbecue sauce is important to a lot of us, so I took on the challenge to create a healthy version that also tasted out of this world. ☻ Serves 4 (¼ cup)

1 small onion, peeled and cut into 4 wedges
1 small green bell pepper, stem and seeds removed and cut
*   into 6 strips*
1 (8-ounce) can Hunt's Tomato Sauce
2 tablespoons Splenda Granular
1 teaspoon Worcestershire sauce
⅛ teaspoon black pepper

Lock food processor bowl in position. Insert the steel knife blade. Drop onion wedges and green pepper strips into the food processor bowl. Attach food chute cover and lock in place. Turn on processor and pulse 4 or 5 times or until vegetables are finely chopped. Add tomato sauce, Splenda, Worcestershire sauce, and black pepper to processor bowl. Attach food chute cover and lock in place. Position food pusher in chute to prevent mixture from splashing out of bowl. Turn on processor and pulse 25 or 30 times or until mixture is smooth. Transfer mixture to a medium saucepan and simmer for 30 minutes, stirring occasionally.

Each serving equals:

HE: 1½ Vegetable • 3 Optional Calories

36 Calories • 0 gm Fat • 1 gm Protein • 8 gm Carbohydrate • 335 mg Sodium • 15 mg Calcium • 1 gm Fiber

DIABETIC EXCHANGES: 1½ Vegetable

CARB CHOICES: ½

Creole Sauce

A blend of cultures as much as it is a blend of ingredients, this sauce draws from the flavors enjoyed by Spanish and French visitors to Louisiana, with some native American spice mixed in. It's a melting pot all on its own.　　○　Serves 6 (½ cup)

> 1 large onion, peeled and cut into 8 wedges
> 2 medium stalks celery, trimmed and each cut into 2-inch pieces
> 1 medium green bell pepper, stem and seeds removed and cut into 8 strips
> 2 cloves garlic, peeled
> 2 tablespoons I Can't Believe It's Not Butter! Light Margarine
> 2 medium tomatoes, peeled and each cut into 6 wedges
> ¼ cup reduced-sodium ketchup
> ¼ cup water
> 1 teaspoon chili seasoning

Lock food processor bowl in position. Insert the steel knife blade. Drop onion wedges into the food processor bowl. Attach food chute cover and lock in place. Turn on processor and pulse 4 or 5 times or until onion is finely chopped. Transfer onion to a large bowl. Repeat process with celery, green pepper, and garlic. Melt margarine in a medium saucepan sprayed with butter-flavored cooking spray. Stir in chopped vegetables. Sauté for 5 minutes. Meanwhile, drop tomato wedges through food chute. Pulse 3 or 4 times to chop. Add chopped tomatoes to sautéed vegetables. Stir in ketchup, water, and chili seasoning. Lower heat and simmer for 30 minutes, stirring occasionally.

Each serving equals:

HE: 1 Vegetable • ½ Fat • 10 Optional Calories

54 Calories • 2 gm Fat • 1 gm Protein • 8 gm Carbohydrate • 79 mg Sodium • 21 mg Calcium • 1 gm Fiber

DIABETIC EXCHANGES: 1 Vegetable • ½ Fat

CARB CHOICES: ½

Cool Cucumber Sauce

This lovely, pale green dressing can be poured over seafood for an elegant lunch with friends, and its creamy fresh flavor can transform something ordinary into something sensational.

❍ Serves 6 (2 full tablespoons)

> ½ small unpeeled cucumber, cut in half lengthwise and
>   seeded
> ¾ cup Land O Lakes no-fat sour cream
> 1 teaspoon dried dill weed
> 1 teaspoon dried onion flakes
> ⅛ teaspoon black pepper

Lock food processor bowl in position. Insert the shredder disc. Attach food chute cover and lock in place. Drop cucumber into the food chute. Position food pusher over cucumber. Turn on processor and use light pressure to push cucumber through. Transfer shredded cucumber to a small bowl. Add sour cream, dill weed, onion flakes, and black pepper. Mix well to combine. Cover and refrigerate for at least 30 minutes. Gently stir again just before serving.

HINT: Great with tuna, salmon, and seafood.

Each serving equals:

HE: ¼ Slider • 10 Optional Calories

28 Calories • 0 gm Fat • 1 gm Protein • 6 gm Carbohydrate • 40 mg Sodium • 45 mg Calcium • 0 gm Fiber

DIABETIC EXCHANGES: ½ Other Carbohydrate

CARB CHOICES: ½

Creamy Mushroom Sauce

How do I use a sauce like this hearty-rich one? You could ladle it over mashed potatoes or cooked carrots; you could top a minute steak with it and delight your husband; or you could create a fancy-looking chicken entrée using leftovers!

☕ Serves 4 (½ cup)

1 cup fresh whole mushrooms, each cut in half
1 tablespoon + 1 teaspoon I Can't Believe It's Not Butter!
*   Light Margarine ☆*
3 tablespoons all-purpose flour
1 sprig parsley, stem removed
1 (12-fluid-ounce) can Carnation Evaporated Fat Free Milk
½ cup water
⅛ teaspoon black pepper

Lock food processor bowl in position. Insert the slicer disc. Attach food chute cover and lock in place. Drop mushrooms into the food chute. Position food pusher over mushrooms. Turn on processor and use light pressure to push mushrooms through. In a large skillet sprayed with butter-flavored cooking spray, melt 2 teaspoons margarine. Stir in sliced mushrooms. Sauté for 5 minutes. Meanwhile, remove slicer disc from food processor and insert the steel knife blade. Add flour, remaining 2 teaspoons margarine, parsley sprig, evaporated milk, water, and black pepper to processor bowl. Attach food chute cover and lock in place. Position food pusher in chute to prevent milk from splashing out of bowl. Turn on processor and pulse 8 or 10 times or until mixture is smooth. Transfer milk mixture to skillet with mushrooms. Continue cooking for 4 to 5 minutes or until mixture thickens, stirring constantly.

Each serving equals:

HE: ¾ Fat Free Milk • ½ Fat • ¼ Bread • ¼ Vegetable

114 Calories • 2 gm Fat • 7 gm Protein • 17 gm Carbohydrate • 166 mg Sodium • 243 mg Calcium • 1 gm Fiber

DIABETIC EXCHANGES: 1 Fat Free Milk • ½ Fat

CARB CHOICES: 1

Cranberry Fruit Relish

Perk up a boring plate of meat and potatoes with this colorful and tart-sweet fruit combo—it's a great palate cleaner, and also tastes great piled on top of leftover turkey on an after-the-holiday sandwich! ☻ Serves 6 (½ cup)

> 1 medium unpeeled orange, quartered and seeded
> 2 medium cooking apples, cored, peeled, and each cut into
>   quarters
> 1½ cups fresh or frozen whole cranberries, thawed
> ¾ cup Splenda Granular

Lock food processor bowl in position. Insert the shredder disc. Attach food chute cover and lock in place. Drop orange and apples into the food chute. Position food pusher over fruit. Turn on processor and use light pressure to push fruit through. Transfer shredded fruit to a large bowl. Remove shredder disc from food processor and insert the steel knife blade. Drop cranberries and Splenda into the food processor bowl. Attach food chute cover and lock in place. Turn on processor and pulse 5 or 6 times or until cranberries are finely chopped. Transfer cranberry mixture to bowl with orange mixture. Mix well to combine. Cover and refrigerate for at least 1 hour. Gently stir again just before serving.

Each serving equals:

HE: ¾ Fruit • 12 Optional Calories

56 Calories • 0 gm Fat • 0 gm Protein • 14 gm Carbohydrate •
1 mg Sodium • 7 mg Calcium • 3 gm Fiber

DIABETIC EXCHANGES: 1 Fruit

CARB CHOICES: 1

Holiday Cranberry Relish

You can't really make a dish like this one without your food processor—it's just too much work, and even a great chopper can't quite get the pieces small enough. So celebrate the season with this ruby gem of a "trimming." (As in, "Deck the Halls!")

○ Serves 8 (⅓ cup)

> 3 cups whole fresh or frozen cranberries
> 1 medium unpeeled orange, seeds removed and cut into 6 wedges
> 1½ cups Splenda Granular
> 6 tablespoons apricot spreadable fruit
> 1 tablespoon Diet Mountain Dew

Lock food processor bowl in position. Insert the steel knife blade. Drop cranberries into the food processor bowl. Attach food chute cover and lock in place. Turn on processor and pulse 4 or 5 times or until cranberries are finely chopped. Transfer cranberries to a medium bowl. Repeat process with orange wedges. Add cranberries, Splenda, spreadable fruit, and Diet Mountain Dew to the food processor bowl. Attach food chute cover and lock in place. Turn on processor and pulse 10 or 15 times or until well mixed. Transfer mixture back to medium bowl. Cover and refrigerate for at least 2 hours. Gently stir again just before serving.

Each serving equals:

HE: 1 Fruit • 18 Optional Calories

76 Calories • 0 gm Fat • 0 gm Protein • 19 gm Carbohydrate • 1 mg Sodium • 12 mg Calcium • 2 gm Fiber

DIABETIC EXCHANGES: 1 Fruit

CARB CHOICES: 1

Corn Relish Supreme

I just love finding a scoop of a savory veggie blend under a slice of meat—it's like getting a present when you least expect it! That's how many restaurant chefs use a vegetable relish, but it's only one option among many.   ○   Serves 8 (¼ cup)

1 small red bell pepper, stem and seeds removed and cut into 6 strips
1 small green bell pepper, stem and seed removed and cut into 6 strips
1 medium onion, peeled and cut into 4 wedges

3 cups frozen whole-kernel corn, thawed
½ cup chili sauce
¼ cup Splenda Granular
¼ cup apple cider vinegar
¼ teaspoon table salt
½ teaspoon celery seed

Lock food processor bowl in position. Insert the steel knife blade. Drop red and green pepper pieces into the food processor bowl. Attach food chute cover and lock in place. Turn on processor and pulse 3 or 4 times or until vegetables are finely chopped. Transfer chopped vegetables to a medium saucepan. Repeat chopping process with onion wedges. Add chopped onion, corn, chili sauce, Splenda, vinegar, salt, and celery seed to vegetables in saucepan. Mix well to combine. Cook over medium heat until mixture starts to boil, stirring often. Lower heat and simmer for 15 to 20 minutes, stirring often. Transfer mixture to a medium bowl. Cover and refrigerate for at least 2 hours. Mix well before serving.

HINT: Thaw corn by rinsing in a colander under hot water for 1 minute.

Each serving equals:

HE: ¾ Bread • ½ Vegetable • ¼ Slider • 3 Optional Calories

88 Calories • 0 gm Fat • 2 gm Protein • 20 gm Carbohydrate • 506 mg Sodium • 11 mg Calcium • 2 gm Fiber

DIABETIC EXCHANGES: 1 Starch • ½ Vegetable

CARB CHOICES: 1

Grande Veggie Relish

Let's clean out the vegetable drawer and make this one! I'm half kidding, but it's not a bad idea to take those orphan veggies and transform them into a dish that proves that "many heads are better than one." ☯ Serves 6 (⅓ cup)

> 1 medium unpeeled zucchini, cut in half lengthwise and
>   crosswise
> 2 medium carrots, scraped and cut into 2-inch pieces
> 1 small red bell pepper, stem and seeds removed and cut into
>   4 strips
> 1 small onion, peeled and cut into 4 wedges
> ⅓ cup Kraft Fat Free Catalina Dressing
> 1 teaspoon chili seasoning

Lock food processor bowl in position. Insert the shredder disc. Attach food chute cover and lock in place. Drop zucchini pieces into the food chute. Position food pusher over zucchini. Turn on processor and use medium pressure to push zucchini through. Transfer shredded zucchini to a medium bowl. Repeat process with carrots, red pepper, and onion. Add Catalina dressing and chili seasoning to shredded vegetables. Mix well to combine. Cover and refrigerate for at least 30 minutes. Gently stir again just before serving.

Each serving equals:

HE: 1 Vegetable • 15 Optional Calories

32 Calories • 0 gm Fat • 1 gm Protein • 7 gm Carbohydrate •
154 mg Sodium • 9 mg Calcium • 2 gm Fiber

DIABETIC EXCHANGES: 1 Vegetable

CARB CHOICES: ½

Sweet Pickle Relish

I've tasted many excellent varieties of pickle relish in the jar, but it just made me curious about whether what I could stir up was just as good or even better! (I'm ambitious that way. . . .) We had fun testing this on family and friends, and I think we succeeded in creating a winner.

> 3 large unpeeled cucumbers, cut lengthwise and crosswise
>   and seeds removed
> 2 medium stalks celery, trimmed and each cut into 2-inch
>   pieces
> 1 medium onion, peeled and cut into 6 wedges
> 1 large green bell pepper, stem and seeds removed and cut
>   into 6 strips
> 1 large red bell pepper, stem and seeds removed and cut into
>   6 strips
> 3 tablespoons canning salt
> 1 cup water
> 1¼ cups apple cider vinegar
> 1½ cups Splenda Granular
> 1 teaspoon mustard seed

Lock food processor bowl in position. Insert the shredder disc. Attach food chute cover and lock in place. Drop cucumbers into the food chute. Position food pusher over cucumbers. Turn on processor and use medium pressure to push cucumbers through. Transfer shredded cucumbers to a very large bowl when full level is reached. Repeat process as necessary. Remove shredder disc from food processor and insert the steel knife blade. Drop celery and onion into the food processor bowl. Attach food chute cover and lock in place. Turn on processor and pulse 3 or 4 times or until vegetables are finely chopped. Transfer chopped vegetables to bowl with cucumbers. Repeat process with green and red peppers. Gently mix vegetables together. Evenly sprinkle salt over vegetables. Pour water evenly over top. Mix gently to combine. Cover and let set for 1 hour. Drain well. In a large saucepan, combine vinegar, Splenda, and mustard seed. Bring mixture to a boil. Add drained vegetables. Mix well to combine. Lower heat and simmer for 15 minutes, stirring occasionally. Carefully ladle hot mixture into hot sterilized pint jars, leaving a ½-inch headspace. Seal and process in a boiling-water canner for 10 minutes. Makes about 3 pints or 6 half-pints.

Each 1 tablespoon serving equals:

HE: 4 Optional Calories

4 Calories • 0 gm Fat • 0 gm Protein • 1 gm Carbohydrate • 219 mg Sodium • 2 mg Calcium • 0 gm Fiber

DIABETIC EXCHANGES: Free Food

CARB CHOICES: 0

Cheddar Cheese Pennies

You can get great value out of your food processor when it comes to making hors d'oeuvres, those party appetizers that everyone loves to nibble. These are bright and lively in color and flavor.

◐ Serves 8 (3 each)

> 1 cup shredded Kraft reduced-fat Cheddar cheese
> 1 cup + 2 tablespoons Bisquick Heart Smart Baking Mix
> ¼ cup I Can't Believe It's Not Butter! Light Margarine
> ¼ cup Land O Lakes no-fat sour cream
> 1 teaspoon prepared yellow mustard
> 2 sprigs parsley, stems removed

Preheat oven to 400 degrees. Lock food processor bowl in position. Insert the steel knife blade. Place Cheddar cheese, baking mix, margarine, sour cream, mustard, and parsley in food processor bowl. Attach food chute cover and lock in place. Turn on processor and pulse 15 or 20 times or until mixture forms a ball. Remove steel knife blade from food processor. Roll dough into 1-inch balls. Place balls on ungreased baking sheet. Bake for 12 to 14 minutes. Serve warm.

Each serving equals:

HE: ¾ Bread • ¾ Fat • ½ Protein • 12 Optional Calories

134 Calories • 6 gm Fat • 6 gm Protein • 14 gm Carbohydrate •
411 mg Sodium • 131 mg Calcium • 1 gm Fiber

DIABETIC EXCHANGES: 1 Starch • 1 Fat • ½ Meat

CARB CHOICES: 1

Carrot-Walnut Muffins

These are oh-so-moist and crunchy, too. They freeze and reheat beautifully, so you can take them for lunch or a snack at work (and avoid the dangerous coffee cart!). ○ Serves 12

3 medium carrots, scraped and
    each cut into 2-inch pieces
¼ cup walnuts
6 tablespoons + 2 teaspoons I
    Can't Believe It's Not
    Butter! Light Margarine
⅓ cup Land O Lakes no-fat
    sour cream

½ cup Splenda Granular
2 eggs, or equivalent in egg
    substitute
1¼ cups Bisquick Heart Smart
    Baking Mix
1 teaspoon baking powder
¼ teaspoon ground cinnamon

Preheat oven to 350 degrees. Spray 12 muffin wells with butter-flavored cooking spray or line with paper or foil liners. Lock food processor bowl in position. Insert the steel knife blade. Drop carrot pieces and walnuts into the food processor bowl. Attach food chute cover and lock in place. Turn on processor and pulse 4 or 5 times or until finely chopped. Remove food chute cover. Add margarine, sour cream, Splenda, and eggs. Attach food chute cover and lock in place. Turn on processor and hold pulse button down for 40 to 45 seconds or until mixture is well blended. Uncover and add baking mix, baking powder, and cinnamon. Re-cover and pulse 3 or 4 times or just until combined, scraping sides of bowl with a rubber spatula as needed. Evenly spoon batter into prepared muffin wells. Bake for 25 to 30 minutes or until a toothpick inserted in center comes out clean. Place muffin pan on a wire rack and let set for 10 minutes. Remove muffins and continue cooling on wire rack.

Each serving equals:

HE: 1 Fat • ½ Bread • ¼ Protein • ¼ Vegetable • 11 Optional Calories

118 Calories • 6 gm Fat • 3 gm Protein • 13 gm Carbohydrate • 285 mg Sodium • 55 mg Calcium • 1 gm Fiber

DIABETIC EXCHANGES: 1 Starch/Carbohydrate • 1 Fat

CARB CHOICES: 1

Banana Chocolate Chip Muffins

These are so luscious and rich, they're really more of a dessert than a breakfast food, but you're an adult and you get to decide when and where to eat them! Use really ripe bananas for the very best flavor. ☉ Serves 12

½ cup fat-free milk
½ cup Land O Lakes Fat Free Half & Half
1½ teaspoons vanilla extract
½ cup I Can't Believe It's Not Butter! Light Margarine
2 eggs, or equivalent in egg substitute
1 cup Splenda Granular
2 very ripe medium bananas, each cut into 2-inch pieces
2¼ cups all-purpose flour
1 teaspoon baking powder
1 teaspoon baking soda
¼ cup mini chocolate chips

Preheat oven to 375 degrees. Spray 12 muffin wells with butter-flavored cooking spray or line with paper or foil liners. In a small bowl, combine milk, half & half, and vanilla extract. Set aside. Lock food processor bowl in position. Insert the steel knife blade. Place margarine, eggs, and Splenda in food processor bowl. Attach food chute cover and lock in place. Turn on processor and hold pulse button down for 2 minutes, scraping sides of bowl with a rubber spatula as needed. Drop banana pieces through the food chute. Turn on processor and pulse 3 or 4 times or until bananas are chopped. Pour milk mixture through food chute and pulse 5 times. Remove lid and add flour, baking powder, and baking soda. Re-cover and pulse 3 or 4 times or just until flour is incorporated. Remove cover and stir chocolate chips into batter using a rubber spatula. Evenly spoon batter into prepared muffin wells. Bake for 30 to 35 minutes or until a toothpick inserted in center comes out clean. Place muffin pan on a wire rack and let set for 10 minutes. Remove muffins from pan and continue cooling on wire rack.

Each serving equals:

HE: 1 Bread • 1 Fat • ⅓ Fruit • ¼ Slider • 17 Optional Calories

174 Calories • 6 gm Fat • 4 gm Protein • 26 gm Carbohydrate •
260 mg Sodium • 53 mg Calcium • 2 gm Fiber

DIABETIC EXCHANGES: 1½ Starch/Carbohydrate • 1 Fat

CARB CHOICES: 1½

Garden-Fresh
Zucchini-Walnut Bread

Here's a great summer bread that takes wonderful advantage of your garden's abundance! It makes a terrific hostess gift when wrapped in colorful plastic wrap and a pretty ribbon.

● Serves 8

½ cup walnuts
*1 medium unpeeled zucchini, cut in half lengthwise and
    crosswise*
¼ cup I Can't Believe It's Not Butter! Light Margarine
¼ cup unsweetened applesauce
1 cup Splenda Granular
2 eggs, or equivalent in egg substitute
2 teaspoons vanilla extract
1 teaspoon baking powder
½ teaspoon baking soda
½ teaspoon ground cinnamon
1½ cups all-purpose flour
½ cup seedless raisins

Preheat oven to 350 degrees. Spray a 9-by-5-inch loaf pan with butter-flavored cooking spray. Lock food processor bowl in position. Insert the slicer disc. Attach food chute cover and lock in place. Drop walnuts into the food chute. Position food pusher over walnuts. Turn on processor and use medium pressure to push walnuts through. Transfer sliced walnuts to a large bowl. Remove the slicer disc from food processor and insert the shredder disc. Attach food chute cover and lock in place. Drop zucchini pieces into the food chute. Position food pusher over zucchini. Turn on processor and use medium pressure to push zucchini through. Transfer shredded zucchini to large bowl with walnuts. Remove shredder disc from food processor and insert the steel knife blade. Add margarine, applesauce, Splenda, eggs, vanilla extract, baking powder, baking soda, and cinnamon to processor bowl. Attach food chute cover and lock in place. Turn on processor and pulse 15 times or until mixture is smooth. Add flour to bowl and pulse 2 or 3 times to mix. Stop and scrape down sides of bowl. Pulse 10 or 12 times more or until well blended. Add batter to zucchini mixture. Stir in raisins. Spread batter into prepared loaf pan. Bake for 55 to 65 minutes or until a toothpick inserted in center comes out clean. Place pan on a wire rack and let set for 10 minutes. Remove loaf from pan and continue cooling on wire rack. Cut into 8 slices.

Each serving equals:

HE: 1 Bread • 1 Fat • ½ Protein • ½ Fruit • ¼ Vegetable •
15 Optional Calories

221 Calories • 9 gm Fat • 5 gm Protein • 30 gm Carbohydrate •
216 mg Sodium • 55 mg Calcium • 2 gm Fiber

DIABETIC EXCHANGES: 1½ Starch • 1½ Fat • ½ Fruit

CARB CHOICES: 2

Basic Banana Bread

Every home cook needs a great banana bread, and this is a very good one. If you don't care for nuts (or you have someone at home who doesn't eat them), you can substitute raisins or even mini M & Ms! ☻ Serves 8

> *2 very ripe medium bananas, each cut into 2-inch pieces*
> *¼ cup I Can't Believe It's Not Butter! Light Margarine*
> *¼ cup walnuts*
> *1½ cups Bisquick Heart Smart Baking Mix*
> *¾ cup Splenda Granular*
> *1 egg, or equivalent in egg substitute*
> *1 teaspoon baking powder*
> *¾ teaspoon ground cinnamon*

Preheat oven to 350 degrees. Spray a 9-by-5-inch loaf pan with butter-flavored cooking spray. Lock food processor bowl in position. Insert the steel knife blade. Place banana pieces, margarine, and walnuts in food processor bowl. Attach food chute cover and lock in place. Turn on processor and pulse 2 or 3 times or until bananas and walnuts are finely chopped. Remove cover and add baking mix, Splenda, egg, baking powder, and cinnamon. Re-cover and pulse 10 or 15 times or until mixture is blended. Evenly spread batter into prepared pan. Bake for 55 to 65 minutes or until a toothpick inserted in center comes out clean. Place loaf pan on a wire rack and let set for 10 minutes. Remove bread from pan and continue cooling on wire rack. Cut into 8 servings.

HINT: Do not overprocess, as it will make for a coarse bread.

Each serving equals:

HE: 1 Bread • 1 Fat • ½ Fruit • ¼ Protein • 9 Optional Calories

---

179 Calories • 7 gm Fat • 3 gm Protein • 26 gm Carbohydrate •
388 mg Sodium • 63 mg Calcium • 2 gm Fiber

DIABETIC EXCHANGES: 1 Starch • 1 Fat • ½ Fruit

CARB CHOICES: 1½

Menus for a Marvelous Machine

Now that you've got your "kitchen assistant" trained, it's time to start creating meals that put your helper to work for you! Here are some fun occasion menus to get you going, just a few ideas of ways to mix and match recipes from this collection.

"Winterfest" Sunday Supper

Three-Cheese Veggie Soup
Classic Chicken Cacciatore
Sunday Best Asparagus Bake
Apple-Walnut Cinnamon Crisp

"Keepin' Cozy" Card Party Lunch

Midwest Chicken Gumbo
California Vegetable Bake
Cheesy Zucchini-Tomato Quiche
Open-Faced Pear Pie

"June Grad" Celebration Dinner

Baked Chicken Breast with Vegetables
Rice Pilaf
Tangy Copper Pennies Salad
Cheyanne's Peach Crumb Pie

"Dog Days of Summer" Family Picnic

Layered Summer Salad
Rainbow Pasta Salad
Dilled Chicken Salad Sandwiches
Blueberry Buckle

"Falling Leaves and Football" Buffet

Cheesy Olive Spread
Grande Baked Sloppy Joes
Bountiful Carrot and Apple Sauté
Autumn Harvest Pie

"Phew!" Post-Christmas Brunch

Cranberry Fruit Relish
Turkey Hash
Maple Sweet Potato–Apple Bake
Aloha Carrot Cake

Making Healthy Exchanges Work for You

You're ready now to begin a wonderful journey to better health. In the preceding pages, you've discovered the remarkable variety of good food available to you when you begin eating the Healthy Exchanges way. You've stocked your pantry and learned many of my food preparation "secrets" that will point you on the way to delicious success.

But before I let you go, I'd like to share a few tips that I've learned while traveling toward healthier eating habits. It took me a long time to learn how to eat *smarter*. In fact, I'm still working on it. But I am getting better. For years, I could *inhale* a five-course meal in five minutes flat—and still make room for a second helping of dessert!

Now I follow certain signposts on the road that help me stay on the right path. I hope these ideas will help point you in the right direction as well.

1. **Eat slowly** so your brain has time to catch up with your tummy. Cut and chew each bite slowly. Try putting your fork down between bites. Stop eating as soon as you feel full. Crumple your napkin and throw it on top of your plate so you don't continue to eat when you are no longer hungry.

2. **Smaller plates** may help you feel more satisfied by your food portions *and* limit the amount you can put on the plate.

3. **Watch portion size.** If you are *truly* hungry, you can always add more food to your plate once you've finished your initial serving. But remember to count the additional food accordingly.

4. **Always eat at your dining-room or kitchen table.** You deserve better than nibbling from an open refrigerator or over the sink. Make an attractive place setting, even if you're eating alone. Feed your eyes as well as your stomach. By always eating at a table, you will become much more aware of your true food intake. For some reason, many of us conveniently "forget" the food we swallow while standing over the stove or munching in the car or on the run.

5. **Avoid doing anything else while you are eating.** If you read the paper or watch television while you eat, it's easy to consume too much food without realizing it, because you are concentrating on something else besides what you're eating. Then, when you look down at your plate and see that it's empty, you wonder where all the food went and why you still feel hungry.

Day by day, as you travel the path to good health, it will become easier to make the right choices, to eat *smarter*. But don't ever fool yourself into thinking that you'll be able to put your eating habits on cruise control and forget about them. Making a commitment to eat good healthy food and sticking to it takes some effort. But with all the good-tasting recipes in this Healthy Exchanges cookbook, just think how well you're going to eat—and enjoy it—from now on!

Healthy Lean Bon Appétit!

Index

341

food, belief ruts, 4
Food Processor II software, 27–28
food processors, cooking healthy with, 13–19
    beliefs about, 1–3
    blade use guidelines, 14–15
    bowl, filling level, 14
    bowls, extra, 16
    cheese and, 14
    Chopping Chart, 17–19
    chopping nuts, 14
    cleaning, 15
    directions (machine), reading, 13
    disc storage holder, 15–16
    filling food tube, 14, 15
    filling level of bowl, 14
    food remaining on top of disc, 14
    foods to avoid, 13, 14
    food tube, filling, 14, 15
    Fruits Chopping Chart, 18
    hard foods, pressure for, 13
    Healthy Exchanges and, 7, 9
    hot liquids or food, avoiding, 14
    invention of, 1
    juicers vs., 14
    juicy foods and, 15
    KitchenAid, 2, 11–12, 13
    lid, keeping clean, 15
    meat (cooked) and, 14
    meat (frozen) and, 13
    menus, 337–38
    nuts, chopping, 14
    packing food tube, 14, 15
    positioning items in food tube, 15
    preparation ease from, 2, 3, 6–7
    pressure for shredding and slicing, 13
    resting guidelines, 15
    S-Blade use guidelines, 15
    sharpening vs. replacement of blades, 15
    Shredder disc use guidelines, 15
    Slicer disc use guidelines, 15
    soft foods, pressure for, 13
    staining of plastic parts, 14
    unwanted parts of food, trimming, 14
    Vegetables Chopping Chart, 17, 18–19
    whipping cream, hand mixer for, 14
    See also commandments of successful
        cooking; cooking tips; desserts; Healthy
        Exchanges; main dishes; salads; sides;
        soups; substitutions; this and that;
        vegetables
food remaining on top of disc, 14
foods to avoid for food processors, 13, 14
food tube, filling, 14, 15
"Football and Falling Leaves" Buffet (menu),
    338
Franks and Cabbage Dinner, Creamed, 261–62
Freezes Well (Snowflake), 28

French Onion Soup, Easy, 49
Fresh Applesauce, 300
Fresh Pineapple Pie, 289–90
Fresh Stewed Tomatoes with Rosemary, 129–30
Fresh Sweet Salsa, 317
frozen meat and food processors, 13
fruit
    Bountiful Blessings Fruit Salad, 94
    Cranberry Fruit Relish, 323
    Fruited Lemon Salad, 92
Fruits Chopping Chart, 18

Garden-Fresh Zucchini-Walnut Bread, 333–34
Garden Patch Meat Loaf, 215–16
Garden Scalloped Corn, Bountiful, 171–72
Garden Spicy Salad, 85
Garlic Sautéed Mushrooms, 106
gazpacho
    Chunky Gazpacho Soup, 31
    Grande Gazpacho Pasta Salad, 99
German Potatoes, Baked, 151–52
Golden Gate Veggie Sauté, 123–24
Golden Nugget Meat Loaf, 213
Goulash, Hungarian Hamburger, 225
"Grad, June" Celebration Dinner (menu), 337
Grande Baked Sloppy Joes, 231
Grande Gazpacho Pasta Salad, 99
Grande Veggie Relish, 326
Grandma's Salmon Casserole, 191–92
Great Mushroom Meat Loaf, 217
green beans
    Chilled Cauliflower and Green Bean Salad,
        77
    Far-East Green Bean Bake, 113–14
    Green Beans Oriental, 116
    thawing tips, 113, 116, 123, 237
green peppers
    Kielbasa Sausage with Peppers and Onion,
        263–64
    Sautéed Peppers and Mushrooms, 122
guacamole
    Guacamole Dip, 316
    Guacamole with Tomatoes, 315
Gumbo, Midwest Chicken, 61–62

halving recipes, 22–23
ham
    Ham and Swiss Sandwich Bake, 259
    Octoberfest Ham Skillet, 260
hamburger
    Hamburger Stroganoff, 226
    Hungarian Hamburger Goulash, 225
    Speedy Hamburger Soup, 71
hard foods, pressure for, 13
Harvest Autumn Pie, 287–88
Hash, Turkey, 209–10
Hawaiian Chicken Salad, 101–2

I Want to Hear from You . . .

Besides my family, the love of my life is creating "common folk" healthy recipes and solving everyday cooking questions in The Healthy Exchanges Way. Everyone who uses my recipes is considered part of the Healthy Exchanges Family, so please write to me if you have any questions, comments, or suggestions. I will do my best to answer. With your support, I'll continue to stir up even more recipes and cooking tips for the family in the years to come.

Write to: JoAnna M. Lund
            c/o Healthy Exchanges, Inc.
            P.O. Box 80
            DeWitt, IA 52742-0080

If you prefer, you can fax me at 1-563-659-2126 or contact me via e-mail by writing to HealthyJo@aol.com. Or visit my Healthy Exchanges website at www.healthyexchanges.com.

Now That You've Seen *Cooking Healthy with a Food Processor*, Why Not Order *The Healthy Exchanges Food Newsletter?*

If you enjoyed the recipes in this cookbook and would like to cook up even more of my "common folk" healthy dishes, you may want to subscribe to *The Healthy Exchanges Food Newsletter.*

This monthly 12-page newsletter contains 30-plus new recipes *every month* in such columns as:

- Reader Exchange
- Reader Requests
- Recipe Makeover
- Micro Corner
- Dinner for Two

- Crock Pot Luck
- Meatless Main Dishes
- Rise & Shine
- Our Small World

- Brown Bagging It
- Snack Attack
- Side Dishes
- Main Dishes
- Desserts

In addition to all the recipes, other regular features include:

- The Editor's Motivational Corner
- Dining Out Question & Answer
- Cooking Question & Answer
- New Product Alert
- Success Profiles of Winners in the Losing Game
- Exercise Advice from a Cardiac Rehab Specialist
- Nutrition Advice from a Registered Dietitian
- Positive Thought for the Month

The cost for a one-year (12-issue) subscription is $25. To order, call our toll-free number and pay with any major credit card—or send a check to the address on page 353 of this book.

1-800-766-8961 for Customer Orders
1-563-659-8234 for Customer Service

Thank you for your order, and for choosing to become a part of the Healthy Exchanges Family!

JoAnna Lund gives a whole new meaning to "processed" food!

Today's food processing machines are more versatile, affordable, and easier to us than ever before. And now is the time to discover—or rediscover—the health goodness and time-saving convenience of your food processor.

With more than 200 easy-to-prepare recipes, you'll save time and effort—and lot of fat and calories as well.

In just minutes, you can make a dazzling array of healthy, yummy dishes. Even th cook who's all thumbs can easily whip up soups (like Easy French Onio Soup or Anytime Vegetable Soup), vegetables (such as Zucchini–Sou Cream Sauté or Dilled Potato Vegetable Bake), main dishes (Pork Tenders an Potato Bake or Chicken-Zucchini Casserole)—even desserts (Aloha Carrot Cake c Cheyanne's Peach Crumb Pie).

Cooking Healthy with a Food Processor features:
Easy-to-follow, step-by-step instructions for any kind of food processor
Easy-to-find ingredients
Complete nutritional ....ic exchanges for every recipe
JoAnna's Top Ten tips for getting the most out of your food processor
Lots of advice for stocking the pantry and making mealtime a healthy pleasure

JoAnna M. Lund is the author of the bestselling Healthy Exchanges® series She has been profiled in national and local publications including *People*, th *New York Times*, and *Forbes*, and has been featured on hundreds of radio an television shows. A popular speaker with weight-loss, cardiac, and diabeti support groups, JoAnna lives in DeWitt, Iowa, where she publishes the Health Exchanges® newsletter and creates healthful, delicious recipes. Visit her wek site at www.healthyexchanges.com.

JoAnna Lund's Healthy Exchanges® cookbooks are featured on www.penguin.cor

ISBN 0-399-53281-1

$17.95 U.S.
$22.50 CAN

9 780399 532818   51795

COOKBOOK/HEALTH
www.penguin.com